RESEGREGATION AS CURRICULUM

Resegregation as Curriculum offers a compelling look at the formation and implementation of school resegregation as contemporary education policy, as well as its impact on the meaning of schooling for students subject to such policies. Working from a ten-year study of a school district undergoing a process of resegregation, Rosiek and Kinslow examine the ways this "new racial segregation" is rationalized and the psychological and sociological effects it has on the children of all races in that community. Drawing on critical race theory, agential realism, and contemporary pragmatist semiotics, the authors expose how these events functioned as a hidden curriculum that has profound influence on the students' identity formation, self-worth, conceptions of citizenship, and social hope. This important account of racial stratification of educational opportunity expands our understanding of the negative consequences of racial segregation in schools and serves as a critical resource for academics, educators, and experts who are concerned about the effects of resegregation nationwide.

Jerry Rosiek is an Associate Professor of Education Studies at the University of Oregon.

Kathy Kinslow graduated with a Ph.D. in the Social Foundations of Education from the University of Alabama in 2009 and currently works as an independent scholar in Syracuse, New York.

The Critical Educator

Edited by Richard Delgado and Jean Stefancic

RESEGREGATION AS CURRICULUM

The Meaning of the New Segregation in U.S. Public Schools

Jerry Rosiek and Kathy Kinslow

Routledge
Taylor & Francis Group

NEW YORK AND LONDON

First published 2016
by Routledge
711 Third Avenue, New York, NY 10017

and by Routledge
2 Park Square, Milton Park, Abingdon, Oxon, OX14 4RN

Routledge is an imprint of the Taylor & Francis Group, an informa business

© 2016 Taylor & Francis

Library of Congress Cataloging-in-Publication Data
Names: Rosiek, Jerry, author. | Kinslow, Kathy, author.
Title: Resegregation as curriculum : the meaning of the new segregation in U.S. public schools / Jerry Rosiek and Kathy Kinslow.
Description: New York, NY : Routledge is an imprint of the Taylor & Francis Group, an Informa business, [2016] | Includes bibliographical references and index.
Identifiers: LCCN 2015025888| ISBN 9781138812802 (hardback) | ISBN 9781138812819 (pbk.) | ISBN 9781315748566 (ebook)
Subjects: LCSH: Segregation in education—United States. | Discrimination in education—United States. | Educational equalization—United States.
Classification: LCC LC212.52 .R67 2016 | DDC 379.2/63—dc23
LC record available at http://lccn.loc.gov/2015025888

ISBN: 978-1-138-81280-2 (hbk)
ISBN: 978-1-138-81281-9 (pbk)
ISBN: 978-1-315-74856-6 (ebk)

Typeset in Bembo
by Keystroke, Station Road, Codsall, Wolverhampton

... despite the Supreme Court's early emphasis on the more institutional and associational effects of school desegregation on the life chances and "hearts and minds" of African American students, the bulk of social science research designed to measure the effects of school desegregation has focused on standardized test scores. . . . This research manages to miss the larger sociological point related to black students' access to and association with higher status educational institutions and the potential long-term effects of that access and association. It also misses some of the extremely important contextual issues related to the process of desegregation—namely, how desegregation was experienced at the school and community level. . . . I argue that one of the many reasons why we, as a society, have given up on school desegregation as a solution to racial inequality is that we put too much emphasis on the wrong set of "consequences."

Amy Stuart Wells, 2000, "The Consequences of School Desegregation: The Mismatch Between the Research and the Rationale," p. 774

As I told you at the outset, Geneva, it's something about being a lawyer and having the feeling that you can convince reasonable people that your point of view is correct. And, of course, I truly believe that analysis of legal developments through fiction, personal experience, and the stories of people at the bottom illustrates how race and racism continue to dominate our society. The techniques also help in assessing sexism, classism, homophobia, and other forms of oppression.

Derrick Bell, 1993, *Faces at the Bottom of the Well*, p. 144

We begin our inquiry assured that there is no way black subjects have not lost something. Our work is imbued with an epistemology of mourning: How do subjects understand their own loss? In what ways might they still be grasping to articulate it? How do we as researchers, know this loss in our bodies and express it in our words? Following from this, it becomes important for us to create research designs that allow space for participants to reflect on and reveal their own suffering, in ways that are safe, and in ways that allow them to remain the protagonists of their own narratives, survivors rather than damaged victims.

Michael Dumas, 2015, "'Losing an Arm': Schooling as a Site of Black Suffering," p. 26

CONTENTS

SERIES EDITORS' INTRODUCTION

The Critical Educator series publishes books that examine problems of education through a critical lens. The fifth in the series, *Resegregation as Curriculum* analyzes the consequences for black schoolchildren of the new wave of resegregation that has arrived in the wake of rulings by conservative judges lifting desegregation decrees.

Some of this resegregation took place earlier when white families, faced with judicial orders dismantling segregation in city schools, moved to the suburbs. At other times, as with "Riverton," it arrived when school authorities built a new school and reconfigured attendance zones so that mainly white students attended the new one and large numbers of black students ended up in one of the older, dilapidated buildings.

Derrick Bell, one of the founding figures of critical race theory, argued that separate schools for black children were not necessarily bad—particularly if the alternative was a long bus ride to a hostile environment presided over by unreceptive white teachers and administrators. Even more so—Bell wrote—if desegregation meant that the formerly black schools closed entirely, spelling the loss of a community nerve center, as well as many jobs for black teachers and principals. This issue, in fact, caused enough friction between Bell, then a young attorney with the NAACP Legal Defense and Education Fund, and his superiors that he was forced to leave his position with the organization, which was ideologically committed to the pursuit of desegregation.

Jerry Rosiek and Kathy Kinslow's fine book suggests that Bell's supervisors may have been right all along. Through interviews and archival research, they show how separate schools in one city seriously harmed the black children forced to suffer the indignity of assignment to a racially segregated school whether they wanted to be there or not. *Brown v. Board of Education* rejected regimes like this ("separate but equal") for precisely this reason: It risked scarring the hearts and minds of black schoolchildren in a way unlikely to be undone.

Of course, *Brown*'s mandate did not always take hold. White parents resisted in countless ways, and school boards found ways to accommodate their wishes. *Resegregation as Curriculum* tells how this happened in one community, recounting in painful detail how resegregation and white resistance stigmatized and demoralized one community and its children. Some of the interviews describing how black children experienced their own relegation to a newly all-black school are almost too painful to bear.

The advent of the scientific concept of stereotype threat adds force to Rosiek and Kinslow's findings. Developed by Stanford psychologist Claude Steele and his co-author Joshua Aronson, stereotype threat explains that non-Asian minorities are apt to perform much worse on tests of cognitive ability if the tester is white or the test instructions remind them of their race, for example by asking for demographic information at the beginning of the test. Because members of these groups know they are invested with a stigma or stereotype that they are deemed inferior intellectually to whites and Asians, they perform in line with the stereotype, that is, badly.

Black students crammed into all-black schools suffer a double such reminder. First, they suffer the damage that the Supreme Court warned of in *Brown*, internalizing the message that they are not good enough to go to school with white kids. But they suffer a second reminder when, as is often the case in the newly resegregated schools, a majority of the teachers and administrators are white. From those teachers, black students internalize a second time the salience of race. The teacher, white and an authority figure, is in charge. The students must measure up or else suffer the ignominy of failure as racial persons, as society tacitly expects.

Educational psychologists have discovered simple measures that a teacher or tester can deploy to mitigate stereotype threat for students who are black or brown. But, as Rosiek and Kinslow show, many of the teachers at schools like Riverton are apt to be poorly trained or so demoralized by their assignment that they do not take the trouble to do so.

Schools like those in Riverton, then, are apt to serve as little but producers of failure for brown and black students enrolled there. What about their effects for society in general and for white students individually?

We know less about these other consequences, but they are apt to be just as pernicious as the ones *Resegregation as Curriculum* demonstrates for black kids. The Supreme Court told us recently, in the affirmative action decision *Grutter v. Bollinger*, that society needs future leaders who are at ease in an increasingly multiracial world. For this reason, the Court permitted universities to carry out affirmative action programs that include race as one factor of many in assembling an entering class. The Supreme Court's judgment is in line with a large body of social science research showing the value of social contact in decreasing intergroup friction and alienation. Society at large, then, benefits when schools provide early and frequent contact on equal terms to children of different races and backgrounds.

At the same time, another body of experience is confirming this benefit for individual whites. Fearful white parents who manipulate the system or move to the suburbs thus often end up doing their children little favor. The schools may have a few more extracurricular activities or AP courses. But the classroom will lack the electricity and broad range of perspectives that the Supreme Court valued in the *Grutter* case. Children raised in all-white neighborhoods and sent to all-white schools often realize that they missed something along the way and try hard to make up for it in college or early adult life.

At the same time, they often end up exposed to an environment that is stressful and outright dangerous. Consider for example the events that took place in the Denver, Colorado area beginning in the late 1960s when a coalition of black and brown parents brought an action against the Denver school district for intentional, de jure discrimination.

For the first time, school desegregation was targeting a city outside the South. The atmosphere was charged, the battles contentious. When the minority plaintiffs won a number of early rulings and it looked as though they might prevail, the white community rose up in fear: Desegregation seemed likely to arrive. Angry parents marched in protest. Nearly fifty school buses were fire bombed. A bomb went off outside the home of the federal judge hearing the case.

The case bounced up and down to the federal appeals court a few times, but the writing was on the wall. The plaintiffs would prove their case and win. By the mid-1970s a large exodus took place of parents leaving for surrounding cities and towns. Suburban communities like Aurora, Littleton, and Boulder grew rapidly as white middle-class parents sought safety for their children from the feared assault on the sanctity of their schools.

The surrounding towns, which had formerly been blue collar, sleepy, and somewhat integrated, both racially and economically, became much more affluent as well as whiter. The atmosphere in the schools changed as well. They became much more competitive, with students vying for the highest grades and SAT scores, best clothes and car, places on the cheerleading squad and debate team, and student government. It was in this pressure-cooker atmosphere that two students on the fringe, hounded and ridiculed by their classmates, exploded in deadly rage a few years later, killing two teachers and several of their classmates.

It turns out that the safest and healthiest school for a child negotiating the struggles and stresses of adolescence is a diverse, multiracial one. There, every student is apt to be able to find a peer group. Athletes can hang out with athletes. Intellectuals with the intellectual set. Theater groupies with other theater groupies. Rappers with each other, and so on. Adolescents fear nothing so much as social exclusion, ostracism, and ridicule. This danger is much greater in a solidly white, upper class school like Columbine, the white flight school. At integrated, mixed-race schools one sees shouting matches and the occasional fist fight. But the type of brooding that can lead to murderous rage occurs mainly in all-white suburban schools. All of the serial school shootings carried out by students occurred in settings like these. In an ironic twist, the fearful parents who sought safety in the suburbs for their children in the wake of desegregation instead subjected them to a deadly menace.

Segregation, then, including the kind that arrives as a result of resegregation, is bad for black students. But it is bad for society and white students as well. Mildly eccentric loners lose the opportunity to take refuge with kindred souls when the world is too much for them right then. And all students lose the opportunity during a formative period to learn how to talk, socialize, and interact across racial lines. *Resegregation as Curriculum* shows the folly of this course from the perspective of the black students. But it is also poor policy for society as a whole and for white parents and children.

Richard Delgado
The University of Alabama School of Law

Jean Stefancic
The University of Alabama School of Law

CRITICAL RACE THEORY, AGENTIAL REALISM, AND THE EVIDENCE OF EXPERIENCE

A Methodological and Theoretical Preface

Jerry Rosiek

I begin with a confession. I had read many Derrick Bell essays before this project commenced. I read a great deal more critical race theory (CRT) during the roughly ten years we collected data for this project. Somehow, however, I had not read Dr. Bell's (1992) fictional short story *Space Traders* until the writing of this book was well underway. If you have not read it, it tells of the arrival of space aliens on U.S. soil whose technology is far in advance of our own. The aliens offer to provide the U.S. with technology that will clean the environment and provide a limitless supply of energy, as well as wealth that will stabilize our economy and ensure a decent standard of living for all its citizens. In exchange they ask that the U.S. hand over all of its Black citizens, who will be taken off the planet to an unknown fate. The story recounts the brief national debate that ensues, after which the leaders of the nation, with support from its citizenry, ultimately accept the deal.

My first response to this essay was disappointment with the author. I have spent most of my adult life studying racial politics and racial inequities in our school system. I am familiar with and persuaded by scholarship that argues that racism is a structural feature of our economy. I am persuaded that the discursive production and maintenance of racial binaries are a foundational feature of the U.S. national identity and of conceptions of liberal progress that never seem to deliver on promises of racial justice. Racism is more than an aggregate of personal moral mistakes that people keep making over and over. It is a highly adaptive social system that shapes our desires and practices in ways that have produced racialized hierarchies of wealth and status repeatedly throughout our national and global history. I considered, at some level, that the discourses of whiteness might even be influencing my feelings about the short story. Still, the idea that the white majority of citizens would simply march their Black

acknowledgement

neighbors, friends, colleagues, fellow citizens, cousins, partners, brothers and sisters, onto an alien ship to an indeterminate fate seemed ludicrous to me. Pessimism about institutionalized racism was one thing, I thought as I placed the book on the nightstand, but this felt like jumping the shark. It cheapened the more thoughtful arguments I had read Dr. Bell make in other essays.

The next morning I went to my office to continue work on this book. I was midway through Chapter 2, which recounts the way the Riverton community rationalized creating an all-Black high school where there had not been one before, zoning the schools in such a way that the school would have higher concentrations of low-income students, less boosterism, lower test scores, and lower enrollment. The community did this in the vague hope that creating two other high schools with higher percentages of white students would stem the exodus of white students from the public schools, thus preserving the district's financial solvency. As I wrote that morning, it slowly became apparent to me that I was writing a story that was very similar to *Space Traders*. In fact it was worse than the *Space Traders* story. The Riverton community had been willing to march half of the Black students in the district into a situation they *knew* would be harmful for a *relatively small and uncertain payoff*.

I had always been scandalized by the resegregation we witnessed in the Riverton schools. In that moment, however, the stark callousness of this policy presented itself to me in a way it had not before. The almost casual sacrifice of the well-being of the students attending the all-Black school felt suddenly more predatory and raw. This sacrifice required an erasure of the significance of their lived experience that manifested not just in the machinations of school board members, but also in the lethargic and confused political reaction of erstwhile progressive citizens of the area—white and Black. As I read the voices of students repeatedly objecting to what was happening to them, I wondered at the fact so few of us there at the time were registering the full moral and political implications of their complaints.

The experience was vertiginous. It was not just the flood of moral implications and empathy for students indignant in their isolation, which was considerable. Equally, if not more disconcerting was that, despite having studied the resegregation of Riverton schools for so long, I had not yet appreciated the scope of the dehumanization it had involved. Why had I not? I had been appalled enough to commit a significant part of my career to bearing witness to what was happening and to recruit others into this project. But this was something new. I had remained desensitized to the scope of the human drama unfolding before me, which raised questions about what else I was missing—about whether I could trust my own thoughts and feelings to do justice to the topic. My attempt to tell the story of Riverton, as a consequence, felt at once more urgent and dangerous.

Derrick Bell's story had done some part of what I suppose it was intended to do. It had precipitated a change in my understanding of the real scope of racism, not just at a conceptual level, but also at an affective level. The story brought me into a relation with the reality of racism that I was probably reluctant to face or dwell upon. As critical race theorist Richard Delgado (1989) explains in his essay "Storytelling for Oppositionists," this is the reason the development of well-crafted stories need to be encouraged and accepted as a form of scholarship.

> Most oppression, as was mentioned earlier, does not seem like oppression to those perpetrating it. It is rationalized, causing few pangs of conscience. The dominant group justifies its privileged position by means of stories, stock explanations that construct reality in ways favorable to it. . . . Artfully designed parables, chronicles, allegories, and pungent tales . . . can jar the comfortable dominant complacency that is the principal anchor dragging down any incentive for reform. . . . Because this is a white-dominated society in which the majority race controls the reins of power, racial reform must include them. Their complacency—born of comforting stories—is a major stumbling block to racial progress. Counterstories can attack that complacency.
>
> *(p. 2438)*

This, then, is part of what *Resegregation as Curriculum* sets out to do. We tell the story of the resegregation of Riverton public schools largely from the perspective of the students attending the schools 1) to contribute to the considerable body of empirical research that demonstrates the resegregation of our schools is doing real harm, *and* 2) to affectively jar some of us out of our complacency about this policy dynamic that is happening all across the nation, so that we might engage together in ameliorative resistance to this systemic social violence.

Critical race theory, which originated in the field of legal studies, has been increasingly applied to social science research practices over the last two decades (Obasogie, 2015; Paul-Emile, 2015; Ladson-Billings, 2005), though not without complications (Carbado & Roithmayr, 2014; Gómez 2012). There are risks that the emphasis on grounding arguments in objective empirical evidence in the social sciences will "undermine CRT's . . . critique of neutrality and objectivity" (Carbado & Roithmayr, 2014, p. 155) or that CRT might become domesticated and stripped of its politically provocative force (Ladson-Billings, 2005). There are also post-structuralist critiques of methodological over-reliance on the authority of personal accounts of experience, not because those accounts lack objectivity, but because they uncritically adopt categories of thought that reproduce the hegemonies critical scholars seek to disrupt (Mazzei & Jackson, 2009; Lather, 2007; Scott, 1981; St. Pierre, 2015). In what remains of this preface, I will address some of these methodological and theoretical considerations, which have informed the writing of this book.

Evidence, Education Policy, and CRT

Contemporary educational policy discourse in the U.S. tends to focus almost exclusively on "evidence-based practices" and "data-driven" decision making (No Child Left Behind [NCLB], 2003). In these discourses, "data" and "evidence" are most often defined as quantifiable measures of educational outcomes—be it standardized test scores, high school graduation rates, or transitions to college. Additionally, it is expected that sound policy will be based on research that uses experimental or quasi-experimental designs. The No Child Left Behind Act of 2001 (NCLB, 2003) included provisions that restricted federal funding to only those educational reforms that could demonstrate effectiveness using these narrow definitions of evidence and inference. These restrictions have been reauthorized with minor revisions repeatedly through 2015.

At one level, this seems imminently reasonable. It is difficult to fault policy makers for preferring to support programs that can show clearly measurable positive effects on student learning. However, there are two logical problems with the current state of "evidence-based" policy making, logical problems that have significant practical implications. First, the evidence-based requirement for policy and practice is applied as a criterion of *exclusion* as opposed to a criterion of *inclusion*. The law prohibits the funding of research that cannot provide rigorous evidence of their positive benefits. However, it does not require policy makers to implement all reforms that can show such evidence. This leaves the door open for ideological exclusions of viable evidence-based reforms under the cover of allegedly science-based policy mandates.

Nowhere are the ideological limitations of the current "data-driven" ethos more clearly visible than when we consider the reception that research on the racial resegregation of public schools has been given by contemporary policy makers. Thirty years of rigorously designed and disciplined social science research by scholars such as Gary Orfield and his colleagues at the UCLA Civil Rights Project (Orfield, 1983; Orfield, Kim, & Sunderman, 2006; Orfield, Kucsera, & Siegel-Hawley, 2012; Orfield & Yun, 1999), Sean Reardon and his colleagues at the Stanford Policy Institute (Reardon, Grewal, Kalogrides, & Greenburg, 2012; Reardon & Yun, 2003), James Coleman formerly at the University of Chicago (Coleman et al., 1966; Coleman, 1990), Amy Stuart Wells at Teachers College (Petrovich & Wells, 2005; Wells, 2000; Wells, 2009), Charles Clotfelter (2004) at Duke University, Byron Lutz (2005) at the Federal Reserve, and many others have documented school resegregation along race and class lines and that such segregation has a variety of negative effects on students of color in racially isolated schools—effects such as lower test scores, higher drop-out rates, lower levels of college attendance, lower health outcomes, and lower levels of lifetime wealth accumulation, just to name a few. This abundance of evidence that racial integration of schools brings significant measurable educational benefits, however, has not resulted in significant policy changes.

Where the racial segregation of schools is concerned, policy makers are either selectively attending to data whose implications they like, or to data that support policies they think their constituents will tolerate. Either way, it is ideology, not evidence, driving the policy.

The second logical problem with exclusive reliance on "evidence-based practices" is that it presumes that all desirable or undesirable educational outcomes can be measured and indexed using the prescribed standards of evidence. This premise is clearly false, as has been argued by many others at length (e.g. Beghetto, 2005; Ravitch, 2011; Rosiek & Clandinin, in press; St. Pierre, 2002; Zhao, 2014), so I will not rehearse those arguments here. Where the issue of racial resegregation in public schools is concerned, these narrow standards of evidence exclude from consideration the less easily measured consequences of being in a racially isolated, underfunded, socially scorned school, such as its impact on students' identity, emotions, sense of personal possibility, and social hope. In response to such exclusion, this book offers that experiences of institutional neglect and hostility are a *real and significant* consequence of segregated schooling conditions and that any conception of valid educational research whose epistemic standards exclude the possibility of acknowledging such experiences is by definition *unrealistic*.

Critical race theory emerged in response to similar epistemic constraints in the field of law. Narrow definitions of what counted as evidence in legal scholarship, as well as conceptions of legal truth as universal, transcendent, and independent of identity or context, made it difficult to argue for a redress of racial injustices that were historically contingent, particular to specific local formations of racial identity and exclusion, and often recounted in personal and emotional terms (Ladson-Billings & Tate, 1995). Critical race theory called these epistemic premises into question, as Richard Delgado (1989) explains:

> Traditional legal writing purports to be neutral and dispassionately analytical, but too often it is not. In part, this is so because legal writers rarely focus on their own mindsets, the received wisdoms that serve as their starting points, themselves no more than stories, that lie behind their quasi-scientific string of deductions. The supposedly objective point of view often mischaracterizes, minimizes, dismisses, or derides without fully understanding opposing viewpoints. Implying that objective, correct answers can be given to legal questions also obscures the moral and political value judgments that lie at the heart of any legal inquiry.
>
> *(pp. 2440–2441)*

It is not surprising therefore, that a critical mass of educational researchers became interested in CRT around the same time that Procrustean epistemic limitations were being imposed on the kind of research that could influence educational policy. Gloria Ladson-Billings and William Tate (1995) introduced

CRT to the mainstream educational research community in a 1994 presentation at the American Education Research Association meeting. Since then there has been an exponential rise in the application of CRT to educational scholarship (e.g. Brayboy, 2005; Dixson & Rousseau, 2005, 2006; Huber, 2009; Parker, Deyhle, & Villenas, 1999; Ladson-Billings, 2005; Leonardo, 2013; Lynn & Dixson, 2013; Taylor, Gillborn, & Ladson-Billings, 2009; Zamudio, 2011).[1]

This preface is concerned primarily with the methodological implications of CRT. One of these implications is that the content of scholarship is often closely connected to its form and that some insights about race, racism, and racial politics are better communicated through stories, parables, and accounts of personal experience than by statistical analyses of large databases. *Resegregation as Curriculum* is organized around this idea that there is power in listening to the experiences of others and in the telling of stories about experiences that are not easily assimilated into an existing hegemonic order.

The question is what is the nature of that power? Does it lie in the qualities of the experience itself (this would suggest some sort of underlying ontological realism)? Does it lie in the telling (this would suggest some underlying ontological constructivism)? Or does responsibly listening to stories of others' experience require a rethinking of the conceptual vocabulary some of us have inherited from Western (settler society) enlightenment for thinking about the relationship between knowledge and being?

Experience, Epistemologies, and CRT Research Methodologies

Educational researchers operating under the influence of a variety of theoretical frameworks—from CRT, to autoethnography, to standpoint theory—frequently present stories about personal experiences of oppression as a uniquely authoritative form of *knowledge*. Deluded or not, misinterpreted or not, the experience itself is real and therefore morally significant. The self-evident nature of people's experience in such cases is treated as a possible source of emancipatory truth. Knowledge derived from such experience is out of the reach of the invalidation of hegemonic discourses because it is brought into being by that hegemony, but through refusing silence has not been entirely defined by it and therefore is useful as a lever against oppression. At one level, *Resegregation as Curriculum* could look like a study that rests its validity on such authoritative accounts of experience.

Over the course of the last decade, in collaboration with more than a dozen graduate students (including most prominently my co-author Kathy Kinslow), I designed, directed, and conducted a study of a school district in the U.S. Southeast that was undergoing a process of restructuring that led to an increased level of racial segregation in its schools. Interviews with over 200 public school students are the primary data used for this book.[2] Students' accounts of what the new school arrangement meant to them were, in a way, authoritative. Whether students correctly or incorrectly interpreted the motivations behind the policies affecting them, whether or not their interpretations were shaped by the discourses in which they were immersed (which they certainly were), the fact remains that they lived the interpretations, many of which were alienating to them and outrageous to those of us paying attention. The study offers some rather straightforward descriptions of how students experienced a racially segregated school, experiences that may have gone unnoticed or ignored by policy makers and educators. I believe there are things that can be learned from this monograph when it is regarded in this way.

This, however, would not be an adequate nor accurate description of the conceptual approach we took with *Resegregation as Curriculum*. I have read too much post-structural and post-colonial theory to be comfortable with the idea that amelioration of oppressive social conditions will inevitably emerge from an emancipatory research project that seeks to "reveal" the reality of oppression by documenting the voices of those who are being oppressed. From Joan Scott's (1981) and Gayatri Spivak's (1999) critiques of the limitations of the claims of authenticity upon which such projects often rely, to the deconstructions of the politics of voice in qualitative research by folk like Lisa Mazzei and Alecia Youngblood Jackson (2009), to Lauren Berlant's (2011) cautions about the cruel, self-defeating, optimism of many foundationalist political projects, I am convinced that simply describing experiences to communities who haven't heard them is not an adequate conception of what scholarship can contribute to social change. I don't believe that whiteness and white supremacist discourses are sustained by epistemic practices—that all we are lacking is good information.

Neither, however, do I believe that it is only the discursive categories of race that hold us in their thrall, and that all we need is to deconstruct the categories of race or performatively displace them from our community discourses and this will transform the material facts of racial hierarchy in our communities. The psychic wounds and material bruises of racial segregation in the school district we studied were substantive. Memories of those hurts were obdurate. The grinding logic of property values and racially stratified wealth disparities had a momentum that carried discourse in its wake.

This theoretical and methodological tension between the need for specific epistemic foundations that can leverage calls for action and an aversion to endorsing any particular version of those foundations for fear of getting caught in the trap of naturalized identities and overly narrow horizons of possibility is not new. In fact it is by now a well-rehearsed debate, one with which scholars in a variety of fields have been growing increasingly weary (Barad, 2007; Lather, 2007; Latour, 2004; Rosiek, 2013a, 2013b). Jared Sexton (2012), for example, identifies the conceptual tensions between the need to historicize racial identity formation and the need for a conception of racial identity that is more onto-logically substantive than discursive performance as a defining feature of the field of anti-Blackness theory. He takes as central the following question: "Can anti-racist politics be approached in ways that denaturalize the color line, retain the specificities of discrepant histories of racialization, and think through their relational formation?"

The best CRT has been characterized by an informed impatience with these apparent contradictions. Tracing its roots to the more general field of critical legal studies (CLS), which grew out of applications of post-structuralist deconstructions to the field of law, CRT scholars both embraced and moved beyond the post-modern politics of aporia and ironic suspension. Cornel West (1993) describes this ambivalence with CLS felt by many CRT scholars:

> Critical legal theorists fundamentally question the dominant liberal para-digms prevalent and pervasive in American culture and society. This thor-ough questioning is not primarily a constructive attempt to put forward a conception of a new legal and social order. Rather, it is a pronounced disclosure of inconsistencies, incoherences, silences, and blindness of legal formalists, legal positivists, and legal realists in the liberal tradition. Critical legal studies is more a concerted attack and assault on the legitimacy and authority of pedagogical strategies in law school than a comprehensive announcement of what a credible and realizable new society and legal system would look like.
>
> *(p. 196)*

CRT scholars were not satisfied with CLS's politics, a praxis based primarily on problematizing the foundational justifications of legal decisions. CRT scho-lars used the opening provided by CLS's foundational critiques to assert an alternative approach to legal scholarship focused on the project of addressing the pervasive reality of racism in contemporary society. They highlighted the way racist ideologies distorted standards of evidence and the choice of relevant precedent in U.S. jurisprudence. They called for different standards of evidence and styles of argumentation in legal proceedings, policy making, and scholarship that would make an effective response to endemic racism possible.

One of the primary rhetorical and methodological means CRT scholars adopted for exposing the realism of racism was the practice of telling stories about the experience of racism in U.S. societies. Reflecting a disregard for methodological purity, multiple—often contradictory—rationales for storytelling have been forwarded in the CRT literature. For example, in his widely cited essay "Storytelling for Oppositionists," Richard Delgado (1989) offers no less than five distinct uses for storytelling in legal scholarship. According to this essay, narrative accounts of the experience of oppression can:

- Document the realities of oppression obscured by dominant ideologies (p. 2414).

- Serve as a means of psychic self-preservation for the targets of oppression by refuting the messages that they are to blame for their own oppression (p. 2437).
- Breakdown isolation and promote solidarity among members of an oppressed group (p. 2437).
- Subvert or destroy prevailing mindsets that organize legal and political discourse (p. 2438).
- Transform the mindsets of members of the oppressor group by humanizing excluded others, thus making possible new forms of political collectivity (p. 2438).

Each of these rationales is compelling and together they serve a shared purpose of contributing to the transformation of oppressive social conditions. However, these are five very different ways for thinking about the utility of documenting and circulating stories about the experience of oppression. They each have different ontological premises which in turn yield different methodological implications. Documenting realities obscured by entrenched ideologies, for example, is closely related to the CRT premise that racism is a permanent structural feature of American society.[3] Overcoming widespread denial of this condition would require a careful empirical documentation of this reality. "Thus, the [methodological] strategy becomes one of unmasking and exposing racism in its various permutations," (Ladson-Billings, 1998, p. 12). The therapeutic goal of sharing stories that help heal the psychological wounds of oppression, however, attends to the reality of racism as it is subjectively and emotionally experienced by the oppressed. The purpose of sharing stories in this case is not so much to coerce belief, as it is to assuage feelings of isolation and self-blame. This would require attending to the emotionally salient features of the story and attempting to evoke them in a way that was recognizable to survivors of oppression. Similarly, stories intended to subvert oppressive mindsets among privileged groups attend to a subjective reality as well, however their purpose would retain a coercive intent. This would involve developing stories— actual or fictional—that serve a deconstructive function. Such stories would rely less on fidelity to empirical detail, and more on careful crafting that lays bare the contradictory premises upon which a social order rests or the way an erstwhile progressive social view actually serves to reproduce oppressive conditions. Finally, going beyond the purpose of producing the effects of aporia or heteroglossia to positively transforming the mindset of members of oppressive groups in such a way that a new effective collective solidarity might be made possible, presumes a certain malleability to those mindsets. Methodologically, the validity of stories developed to serve this transformative purpose would rely simultaneously on their fidelity to antecedent empirical reality (to earn credibility) and to the desirability of the futurity toward which they are directed (to motivate embrace of the change). Clearly, more could be said about these distinctions. For now, the point is to highlight the divergent methodological implications harbored within the CRT call for the use of experience-based stories in social analysis.

As educational researchers have embraced CRT, it is the first use of stories listed above that has most often been taken up. Researchers have been drawn to documenting experiences of racial oppression as a means of exposing the real consequences of racism that are obscured by white supremacist ideologies (e.g. Chapman, 2007; Duncan, 2005; Solorzano, 1998; Solorzano & Yosso, 2002). This emancipatory realism often methodologically resembles critical ethnography (Fine, 1991; Madison, 2012; Willis, 1981) in that it relies on claims of accurate description of the lives of those being studied to leverage its calls for change. Alternatively, it takes the form of what might be called a critical grounded theory (Gibson, 2007) providing thematic analyses of interviews of students of color as a means of substantiating the corrosive effects of racism in our educational institutions. The work of Daniel Solorzano and his colleagues using the concept of racial microaggressions as a way of empirically operationalizing CRT research could be considered an example of this (Solorzano, 1998; Solorzano, Ceja, & Yosso, 2000; Yosso, Smith, Ceja, & Solorzano, 2009). *Resegregation as Curriculum* could be read in this way as well, though not only in this way.

There is a risk involved, however, in relying on the familiar rhetoric of descriptive realism, one that sees description of "the truth" of racial oppression as a necessary precursor to transformative action. Such reliance can retain the radical structural critiques of CRT, but lose track of CRT's radical epistemological and methodological implications. "The 'gift' of CRT," according to Ladson-Billings, (2000). "is that it unapologetically challenges the scholarship that would dehumanize and depersonalize us" (p. 272). The power of the work of Paul Willis and Daniel Solorzano, for example, does not lie (in my opinion) exclusively in the empirical accuracy of their accounts of student experience. It lies also in the way their accounts of students' lives evoke a sense of empathic identification, the way they make it possible for the reader to bear witness to the suffering of students without pathologizing them. Instead, the craft of their accounts of students' experiences invites the reader to appreciate the dignity and intelligence of students' struggles and precipitates feelings of outrage at the pathology of the institutions in which they are required to live and learn. This evocation of connection is as much a part of the methodological value of CRT as is its relentless critique of the structural nature of racial oppression.

Education scholars have explored many ways of theorizing the relation between the evocative and realist methodological implications of CRT (Atwood & Lopez, 2014; Duncan, 2005; Lynn & Dixson, 2013; Parker & Lynn, 2002). Adrienne Dixson and Celia Rousseau (2006) have written fictional stories as part of their CRT scholarship and Dixson (2006) has written about CRT as a jazz methodology characterized by epistemic improvisation. Thandeka Chapman

(2007) has used portraiture methodologies to bring the expressive and descriptive elements of CRT together in her research. Lindsay Huber (2009) has drawn upon the testimonio literature for similar purposes. Minerva Chávez (2012) appropriates autoethnography for use in her CRT scholarship in education. Bryan Brayboy (2005) has explored the way Indigenous practices of knowing and theorizing can complement and extend CRT in his research on the experiences of Indigenous students.

This proliferation of methodological adaptations of CRT might be interpreted as a form of confusion—a lack of clarity about the epistemological status of experience as a form of evidence or a lack of a defined object of study within the field. However, given the inadequacy of any particular philosophical framework—such as post-positivism, critical theory, or post-structuralism—to provide a comprehensively satisfactory engagement with the racial stratification of educational opportunity world-wide, the methodological opportunism of CRT seems justified, wise even. In his book *Race Frameworks*, Zeus Leonardo (2013) offers that this conceptual and methodological diversity is not a weakness, but is a strength of CRT and one of the reasons it has become so influential in educational research.

> As resourceful as it is trenchant in its critique, CRT leaves no intellectual stone unturned. Because racism in education and society is multifaceted, so must its analysis attest to the complexity of the problem, and CRT recruits allies from across the aisle as well as across university departments.
>
> *(p. 12)*

Leonardo's observation here is itself trenchant. CRT's willful refusal to be bound by narrow epistemological and methodological constraints is justified, he offers, by the protean ontology of racism. Twenty years after Ladson-Billings and Tate's 1994 AERA address (Ladson-Billings & Tate, 1995) introducing CRT to the field of educational research, we can see an influence that goes beyond inspiring innovation in methodological technique. The epistemic questions raised by trying to put CRT to work in the social sciences over the last two decades haven't generated a consensus about new methodological practices that can serve the cause of racial justice as much as they are provoking even more fundamental ontological questions about the relationship between research and social change. As Atwood and Lopez (2014) observe:

> CRT not only ask[s] us to shift our understanding of "what" we know, but also ask us to re-think "how we know what we know, how we come to believe such knowledge, and how we use it in our daily lives" (Pillow, 2003, p. 183) . . . Such a shift asks us to question the very nature of reality itself.
>
> *(p. 1147)*

Other scholars focused on the study of racial oppression, such as Stefano Harney and Fred Moten (2013), Alexander Weheliye (2014), and Sylvia Wynter and Katherine McKittrick (2015), have come to similar conclusions. It is not that a new form of knowledge is needed, but that enlightenment settler societal conceptions of the relationship between knowledge, being, and action is itself a part of the operation of racial oppression, or is at least frequently co-opted by it. The response by these authors and others has been to shift their attention from epistemological considerations to a search for alternate ontologies to inform their intellectual, cultural, and political engagements.

This provocation to ontological reorientation will not be surprising to some communities[4] and should not be surprising at all. The persistence of institutionalized racism despite the sheer scope of the suffering it causes—its resilience in the face of multigenerational organized resistance, the way it adapts to and subverts every political and intellectual intervention—suggests that we are dealing with more than a mere conceptual mistake. It suggests that empirical research on the phenomenon of racism, white supremacy, whiteness, anti-Blackness—whatever our theoretical suppositions lead us to call it—will ask more of scholars than adopting alternative epistemologies and practices of description. It will require changes in our practices of being and our ontological relation to the process of inquiry. The question is what form will those changes take?

Agential Realism in Social Research Methodologies

A preface to a book, of course, is not the place to attempt to answer such a profound question, or even to adequately perform a non-answer. However, some reflections on the implications of the question about the relation between ontology and methodological practice for the present study is needed in order to locate this book's analysis and findings in the currents of thought that actually influenced it.

It turns out similar questions about the ontological implications of our ways of knowing have long been a part of some traditions of scholarship such as indigenous studies or classic and contemporary pragmatist philosophy (e.g. Deloria, 1999, 2012; Doerfler, Sinclair, & Stark, 2013; Eastman, 2003; Kohn, 2013; Peirce, 1992; Pratt, 2011; Short, 2007; Watts, 2013). Additionally, they have recently become the focus of vigorous attention in other areas of study, most notably in science studies and what is being called new materialism, feminist materialism, post-humanism, and/or the ontological turn (e.g. Alaimo & Heckman, 2008; Bennett, 2010; Braidotti, 2013; Coole & Frost, 2010).[5] These literatures take up many provocative and promising philosophical themes.[6] For my purposes here, I would like to focus on a concept all of these traditions of thought take up in one way or another: the concept of agential realism (Barad, 2007), also referred to as agent ontology.

Agential realism refers to the idea that it is neither adequate to think of our research being conducted on passive objects awaiting accurate representation, nor as if those objects are "social constructions" whose boundaries are determined entirely by human activity. Instead, it is preferable and more accurate to think of the objects of our studies as active non-human agents that by their nature cannot be adequately captured in a single representation. *Agential realism* is part of a constellation of ideas that treats inquiry not as the clarification of an epistemic representation but instead as the establishment of provisional onto-ethical relations between different agents, often between human and non-human agents. To those unfamiliar with this literature, the concept of non-human agents may sound far-fetched and impractical. However, there are compelling reasons why many social science methodologists are drawn to these ideas.

Physicist, philosopher, and one of the originators of the new materialist movement, Karen Barad (2007), speaks of the relation established between different agents in an inquiry as an "intra-action." Intra-actions are determined in part by the making of ontological "cuts" that define the boundaries between one agent and another agent, but that could always be made otherwise.[7] "Cuts" are made through certain conceptualizations that lead to creating an "apparatus" for an inquiry—an experimental instrument or a methodological practice. The world exerts its agency by responding to the apparatus in ways that can't entirely be predicted. Once certain cuts are made, and an inquiry is conducted, ontological agents become "entangled" in specific ways. One value of this conceptualization is that it provides an account of how inquiries can be staged and lead to surprising outcomes—discoveries—about real things. However, it also highlights how inquiries can always be staged differently—involve different ontological cuts—which establish very different, sometimes contradictory, relational discoveries that are no less real. The world—including the world of matter—is framed as agential precisely because it is not reducible to any single representation, nor triangulation of multiple representations. According to this philosophical view, the substance of existence is different—it responds differently—and shapes us differently—depending on how we enter into relation with it.

Barad uses the diffraction grating experiments in the field of physics that led to the development of quantum mechanics to illustrate this counter-intuitive metaphysical idea. Depending on how a diffraction grating experiment is set up, a person is able to intra-act with light as a particle, or as a wave, but not both. This is not a failure of triangulation. It is not as if there is a more integrated phenomena of light out there awaiting a better experiment or description. Light is really a wave. Light is really a particle. It cannot be both at the same time. And we cannot encounter light as both in the same experiment. It is as if the nature of the light changes in response to the way we measure it. Experiments of increasing sophistication have tested and confirmed this principle of ontological exclusion (e.g. Jacques et al., 2007; Manning, Khakimov, Dall, &

Truscott, 2015). Methodologically careful efforts to document one of these qualities causes the other not to manifest. The implication, according to Barad (2007), is that we live in an ontologically active and pluralist world. Our representations of the world can be accurate, can describe real things, without exhausting that reality. "Agency" is one of the few ontological concepts we have that fits within this logic. We regularly describe real qualities in other persons—to whom we attribute agency—but recognize that those qualities may change as a result of their agency. The phenomenon of light passing through a diffraction grating, Barad offers, can be thought of as a non-conscious agent, the reality of which shifts in response to the way we interact with it.

Barad and others who take up this line of analysis do not limit their attribution of agency to subatomic particles. It gets applied to a host of topics such as political processes (Bennett, 2010), gender (Braidotti, 2013; Coole & Frost, 2010; Jackson & Mazzei, 2012), ecology and environmentalism (Braidotti, 2013; Kohn, 2013), medicine (Johnson, 2008; Michael & Rosengarten, 2012; Roberts, 2014), education (Childers, 2013; de Freitas & Sinclair, 2014; Jackson & Mazzei, 2012; Lenz-Taguchi, 2010), and colonialism (Lea, 2015; Nxumalo, Pacini-Ketchabaw, & Rowan, 2011). According to this agential realist view, our responsibility when conducting inquiries is not exhausted by the confirmation of any one representation of a phenomena. There is also a performative aspect to our inquiries—a way in which the design of our inquiries—conceptually and materially—constitute the phenomena we study and they in return constitute us as subjects.[8] These mutually constituting processes—entanglements—have ethical implications because they have consequences and could always be otherwise. In this way, every inquiry is organized not just by a conception of present conditions, but also by a conception of futurity—how things might and should be (Kelley, 2002; Muñoz, 2009; West, 1989; Peirce, 1992; Rosiek, 2013b; Tuck & McKenzie, 2015; Weheliye, 2014).

Although I find Barad's language and examples particularly helpful, it is important to acknowledge that the new materialists are not the first to explore this kind of ontological theorizing. Indigenous studies scholars such as Vine Deloria (1999), Eva Garroute and Kathleen Westcott (2013), Bill Neidjie (2002), Angayuqaq Oscar Kawagley (2006), Ralph Bunge (1984), Charles Eastman (2003), Gregory Cajete (1994, 2000), Thomas Peacock (2011), Makere Stewart-Harawira (2005), George Tinker (2004, 2008), Eduardo Duran and Bonnie Duran (1995), and many, many others have written about the agency of matter, objects, land, animals, collectives, stories, and other non-human entities.[9] Similarly, American pragmatist philosophers have explored these themes as well. Writing over a century ago, Charles Sanders Peirce critiqued linguistic nominalism that located all meaning within the human activity of representation. He argued for a more substantive relational ontology, posited that agency and inquiry were characteristics of all things of this world, and spoke of inquiry as making "cuts" in an ontologically infinite "sheet of assertion" (Peirce, 1974,

p. 332). There are striking similarities between these three broad philosophical traditions and the way they are being taken up by contemporary social science research methodologists. There are also salient differences, one of which is pivotal to the inquiry reported in this book.

Indigenous studies and contemporary pragmatism conceptualize non-human agency somewhat differently than Barad and other new materialists. The former include "purpose" as a salient feature of non-human agency, whereas the latter have largely resisted associating "purpose" with non-human agency. The new materialist hesitance to include purpose as a feature of non-human agency appears to be motivated by a concern that the attribution of purpose would constitute an anthropomorphizing of non-human agents, and would be a move back in the direction of centering the human subject.[10]

Some new materialists have drawn upon Deleuze's and Guattari's (2004) "desiring-machine" language to describe non-human agency (MacLure, 2013; Mazzei, 2010). The machine-metaphor permits acknowledging the self-reproducing systemic nature of material and cultural "assemblages" without conveying human-like consciousness onto those systems. The machine-metaphor, however, seems to move back in the direction of treating the object of inquiry as an object, albeit a dynamic object. The concept of desire loses its agential quality and takes on the character of a natural force. For example, in *Vibrant Matter* Jane Bennet (2010) uses the term "trajectory" (p. 32) to describe the movement of political assemblages, a term that suggests inertial motion, motion that doesn't change until acted upon from without—the opposite of agency. This sounds very much like the agent-structure dichotomy of familiar emancipatory theories of social change. There is a danger here that the radical ontological departure encoded into the concept of agential realism could be lost. Research focused on documenting the activity of material-cultural assemblages could become another form of phenomenological description of the obduracy of non-human things.

Having acknowledged the concerns that attributing purpose to non-human agents constitutes an anthropomorphizing regression into a narrow humanism, it seems equally valid to claim that retaining the attribute of purpose exclusively for human agents sets up a dualism that is itself an expression of a narrow humanism. This view is supported by the way several indigenous thinkers (Alfred, 2005; Bunge, 1984; Deloria, 1999, 2012; Eastman, 2003; Peacock & Wisuri, 2011) as well as several pragmatist scholars (Halton, 1995; Kohn, 2013; Peirce, 1992; Pratt, 2011; Short, 2007) have theorized non-human agency. T.L. Short (2007), a well-known commentator on Charles Sanders Peirce's philosophy, argues that an agent ontology requires or implies a conception of purpose associated with agents, to avoid devolving into just another descriptive realism using different words. Purpose, according to Short, drawing on Peirce, is a form of ordering activity that seeks not a specific prescribed form of order—but instead a general form. For example, a chalkboard can order the people in a room into a certain general formation, so they are all looking at it. Part of the board's purpose in this case is to organize ordered attention. A seed organizes environmental materials into the general order of an oak tree. Its purpose is to produce not a specific tree, but something in the general form of an oak tree. Its intra-actions with the environment will determine the specific shape and size of the tree. A well-crafted story can take on an agency of its own. It can organize the emotions and thoughts of large numbers of readers in a general way, though its reception will always depend on the combination of its content and contextual factors. Agency need not be conscious or organic, but this ordering activity is what distinguishes a constellation of phenomena as an agent, according to Short. The precise philosophical argument for this conception of agency is long and technical and there is not time for it here.[11] But in what follows I believe I can illustrate its utility for the study of things like the racial resegregation of public schools.

Whiteness as an Agent

It is through the above concept of purpose that agential realism becomes especially promising for the analysis of racial oppression in general, and for informing the application of CRT to social science research specifically. Consider the contemporary conversations about institutionalized racism that often feel the opposing pull of different ontological framings, such as the need to affirm individual experiences of racial oppression as real and the possible basis of an ethics and politics, the need to highlight the real material structural features of racism that transcend the experiences of individuals, and the need to historicize racism as a discursive process and to avoid reifying the categories of racial difference that are ultimately responsible for the individual and structural manifestations of racial oppression. Each of these framings of racist oppression is compelling and each seems to exclude the possibility of granting a robust salience and realism to the other framings.

This is not to say that one of these theories is the right one and the others are wrong, no more than the diffraction grating experiment that measures light as a particle or as a wave is wrong. Light does have properties of a particle. It really is of a particle nature—when we intra-act with it in a certain way, these particle effects are real and consequential. And light really is of a wave nature. But we have learned we cannot expect to study these features of light simultaneously. Similarly we can say racism is a real personal experience, it is really a structural and material feature of our society, and it is really a discursive phenomenon. There are things that can be learned by studying these different, sometimes contradictory, but nonetheless real manifestations of racism. But over a century of studying racism seems to be suggesting that we cannot expect to describe the reality of racism all at once in a unified frame. It is an inheritance of enlightenment settler society foundationalist epistemologies, and the emancipatory theories of social change with which they are associated, that compels us to attempt to synthesize our understanding of racism into a single narrative. Perhaps these mutually exclusive conceptions of the reality of racism should be permitted to remain unsynthesized in our analyses.

The agent ontology literature provides a way of thinking about refusing the limitations of foundationalist conceptions of social change without forsaking a commitment to the realism of racism. It opens the possibility of understanding racism not simply as a single phenomenological or social object in need of description, but as an agent whose activity exceeds any single theory's ability to adequately frame a relation with it. Racism, understood in this way, is an agent whose activity includes both material formations and discursive formations.[12]

So what is the activity of racism as an agent? Here is where the relevance of the concept of purpose in agent-ontology is useful, I think. Racism is a highly adaptable distributed material-semiotic phenomenon whose organizing purpose is producing racialized social hierarchies.[13] Racism operates in our cultural practices, our institutional arrangements, in microaggressive personal interactions, in the standards for what we call knowledge, in our legal code, etc. It is in not one of those places, but in all of them. Expose and oppose it in one area, and its racially stratifying purposes are expressed in other registers.

In order to speak more specifically about the purposes of this agent in this current historical moment and in the context in which this book is set, it will be better to speak of the specific racial formation of *whiteness*.[14] "Racism" is a general term. *Whiteness* is an ontological agent that produces a specific form of racializing assemblage—power-laden social orders that concentrate wealth and privilege with lighter skinned members of a European diaspora through material-discursive formations that dehumanize those with darker skin and naturalize Eurocentric settler society cultural norms.

Anti-racist scholars do not escape the organizing activity of such agents. The discursive manifestations of agential whiteness include even the social theories we often deploy as a means of resisting racism. For example, positivist research on race can reveal important patterns of inequity, but when public policy is limited solely to discussions of matters that can be documented in the narrowest of empirical terms, many real features of racism are occluded from policy discourse and therefore are rendered effectively invisible. Critical theoretic analysis of race provides illumination of the way economic and racial inequity are structurally co-constituted, but critical theory has also been used to justify minimizing race as an epiphenomena of class oppression. Post-structuralist theory enables valuable critiques of racial essentialism, but has also been deployed to invalidate as discursively naïve any argument grounded in the personal experiences of racism, thus becoming an instrument of racist silencing.

Like the diffraction grating experiments, all of these theories and others capture some portion of the reality of whiteness as an agent. And the more closely we examine racism through one of the theoretical apparatuses, the more the other real forms of racism fade from view. In this way fetishizing any single theory or method for analyzing racism makes us vulnerable to becoming instruments of the social ordering activity of whiteness. This activity manifests both through the production of racialized subjects and the materially inequitable conditions of living. Most importantly for our methodological considerations, agential whiteness has a pattern of co-opting the subjects of researchers themselves, bending every theoretical framework that is brought to bear against it to its own racializing activity.

Methodological Implications of Agential Realism for the Study of Racism

The methodological implications of agential realism are being discussed in many quarters (de Freitas & Sinclair, 2014; Garroutte & Westcott, 2013; Jackson & Mazzei, 2012; Rosiek, 2013b; Watts, 2013). This conversation is still too divergent to summarize in any easy way. What I will offer here is my own, relatively preliminary version of those implications for the study of institutionalized racism. It will be useful, as a way of beginning, to point out what I think the implications are *not*.

The project of a social inquiry practice informed by agential realism cannot be to describe the agent itself in some final fashion. In the case of research on whiteness as an agent, the project cannot be to describe in some authoritative and comprehensive fashion the operation of racism in contemporary society. To make this the project would be to deny the basic premise of agential realism, that any particular form of inquiry is itself a specific form of entanglement with another agent—one in which both subject and object are constituted in specific provisional ways. For example, presenting descriptive statistics of patterns of resegregation provides a picture of the scope of the consequences of racism and positions us as a spectator subject viewing those patterns at a considerable distance. Ethnographies and grounded theory studies of the way race is interpreted in a community provide a view of the mechanisms and consequences of racism at a microsocial level and can also position the reader as a spectator to those effects. Critical theory scholarship on race renders racial hierarchies as a feature of economic structural processes and positions the reader as a potential conspirator in resistance to these structural processes. Post-structuralist deconstructions of the categories of race render the boundaries and substance of race unstable and invite the reader-subject into a state of ironic suspension. Arts-based narrative studies can provide evocative accounts of the affective and personal experience of racism that position researchers and readers as subjects in sympathy and solidarity with persons portrayed in a study. These different forms of inquiry all seek to generate different and arguably incommensurable forms of relational engagement with whiteness as an agent. Regarded in this way, there can be no final epistemic arrival point for the study of the activity of whiteness as an agent.

Instead, there are only choices between different possibilities for ontological entanglement with the real agent of whiteness. The project of agential realist inquiry is to engage in particular ways while keeping track that each inquiry generates one entanglement among many possible entanglements with an agent. In this way, agential realism avoids becoming what Patti Lather (2006) has called just another "successor regime" (p. 36) that seeks to displace all other analytics. Instead agential realism serves as a metaphysically minimalist frame for entering into and out of more specific ontological relations through the use of various methodological apparatuses. It also provides a frame for critical conversations about the consequences of these entanglements in specific settings and the futurities they make possible. Research on whiteness as an agent is not, then, ultimately a process of documentation as a prelude to action. It is, instead, a form of action itself—an ontological intervention or a series of varied interventions in the service of the necessarily mutable project of anti-racist struggle.

Alecia Jackson and Lisa Mazzei (2012), in their methodological treatise *Thinking with Theory,* deploy a Deleuzian phrase, "plugging in," to describe this methodological practice of moving in and out of different onto-epistemological entanglements. This means "being deliberate and transparent in what analytical questions are made possible by a specific theoretical concept ... and how the questions that are used to think with emerged in the middle of plugging in." (Jackson & Mazzei, 2012, p. 5). It also involves working and reworking data in various ways to both learn specific things from the data and to become aware that no one learning is essential or foundational.[15] Although Jackson and Mazzei recommend a practice of theoretically plugging in in multiple ways within the same study, their development of this concept could be equally applied across many separate studies of the same topic within a field of study. In that case, every kind of study—even mono-theoretic ones—could constitute a form of ontological plugging in, provided the researcher had a conception of his or her theoretical approach as contingent. This would change a researcher's relation with his or her object of study as well as with other researchers working with other theoretical and methodological apparatuses. Agential realism and the practice of methodological "plugging in" encourages eschewing agonistic cross-disciplinary debates about who has racism "right," while still retaining a place for the value of precision within separate disciplines. If we are going to become entangled in antiracist struggle, we should use all the analytic tools at our disposal to become well entangled. And our conversations about which entanglements are best suited to which situations should be less imperial struggles over who occupies a final truth of the matter, and more situated comparisons of the values guiding our inquiries and the amelioration they make possible.

The similarities between the way CRT has been used in the field of education and the methodological implications of agential realism are, hopefully, apparent. CRT scholarship in education has taken up a multifaceted and opportunistic methodological approach (Leonardo, 2013). It maintains that the personal and political realities in which we live are socially constructed, but is nonetheless unwilling to give up the claim that racism and the suffering it causes is real. It developed practices of documenting the experience of racism that serve as relational interventions within these ontological tensions well before agential realism began to exert influence on the social sciences. It is, in a sense, already self-consciously fully "entangled" in a struggle with whiteness as an agent. Given this prior status, and a cultural transformation project fully underway, it may legitimately be asked why CRT scholars should bother with agential realism and its attendant concepts?

The initial, honest, response, has to be that in many circumstances agential realism may be of little benefit to CRT scholarship. CRT needs no exogenous philosophical justification to support its ongoing work. The conversations taking place under its theoretical umbrella are sovereign and self-justifying. However, for those of us who think the philosophical questions underlying social science methodology are important and who espouse an ethic of leaving no stone unturned, there may be things to be gained by exploring the affinities between these two theoretical literatures. If there is, it will be because agential realism is of some practical use to the broader political and cultural project of CRT. Based on my understanding of these literatures, I see two such practical utilities:

First, as CRT continues to move into the social sciences, there is a persistent risk of it being assimilated into the foundationalist philosophical assumptions underlying practices of empirical inquiry in the those fields—even the so-called emancipatory social sciences. As CRT and critical policy analysis scholars Atwood and Lopez (2014) observe "Academic tradition requires that we build an argument and present appropriate evidence before making any kind of substantive claims" (p. 1148). Without an alternative philosophically defensible claim to realism and rigor, these demands will work a toll on CRT scholarship seeking a broader audience or will keep it on the margins of policy debate. Agential realism as outlined above underwrites both a critique of the limits of imperial foundationalist social science and a claim that CRT's disciplinary and methodological eclecticism reflects a more robust realism.

Second, agential realism can help refine conversation within CRT scholarship by emphasizing the need for comparing and contrasting different methodological approaches to CRT scholarship. It provides a vocabulary for such comparisons that does not devolve into competing totalizing claims of capturing "the truth." Instead it draws attention to the need for comparing the scope and viability of the transformed futurity to which research seeks to contribute. Ladson-Billings (2005) speaks of the need for critical conversations about the purpose of CRT counterstories:

> I sometimes worry that scholars who are attracted to CRT focus on storytelling to the exclusion of the central ideas such stories purport to

illustrate. Thus I clamour for richer, more detailed stories that place our stories in more robust and powerful contexts. . . . The point . . . is not the titillation of the story, but rather . . . They are a part of larger social contexts that can be used to exploit one person or group while simultaneously advantaging another.

(p. 117)

This, then, is the theoretical context out of which *Resegregation as Curriculum* emerges. It locates itself in the critical race theory tradition of counter story-telling. It reports on the experiences of students living through the racial resegregation of their schools. It places those experiences in a broader policy and ideological context, one characterized by a deliberate creation of racially stratified educational opportunity and status. It recounts the distress, disappointment, and anger this caused students, especially, but not exclusively, Black students. It reports on their efforts at rebuttal and resistance. These stories are not told as a form of titillation or pitiable spectacle, but are instead intended to 1) add to the body of already overwhelming evidence that resegregation of public schools is happening in the U.S. and that it has detrimental effects on students in racially isolated schools, 2) evoke feelings of respectful empathy with the students in this study and outrage that they have to endure such neglect and malfeasance, feelings that can motivate acts of solidarity with students and their families.

This project is also informed by the agential realist literature reviewed above. As such we regard the use of CRT framework as a way of plugging in (Jackson & Mazzei, 2012) to the phenomena of racial stratification in school. It treats developing accounts of students' experience of the resegregation, not as a singularly privileged unmediated way of accessing the reality of racism, but instead as one form of ontological entanglement with whiteness as an agent as it currently operates in our public schools—one among many possible forms of productive entanglement. Our purpose in choosing this form of onto-epistemic engagement is to provide some cognitive insight into how resegregation impacts children and to sensitize the reader to the broader affective consequences of racial resegregation in schools. The combination of these, we hope, can help us to re-imagine our own involvement as teachers, citizens, and scholars in the social violence of resegregation.

Agential realism also requires us to acknowledge that we are not the only agents involved in an entanglement. It is not just us acting on the world, but the world acting on us—not just physically, but in our thoughts and our very constitution as subjects. Where *Resegregation as Curriculum* is concerned, my coauthor and I are aware that our research may be subverted into the service of reproducing racialized hierarchies in some way. The ideology of whiteness can deform our motivations or it can cause us to miss some essential aspect of events in Riverton, as my account of reading the Derek Bell story, *Space Traders*, illustrated at the beginning of this essay.

There are some, for example, who would argue that attempting to evoke empathy for the students in this story is not boundary pushing at all, but is a reversion to a white neo-liberal displacement of macrosocial politics with individual morality or bourgeois sentimentality. In the end, we cannot rule out this possibility. As it stands at this moment, however, I believe this view falsely presumes empathy is merely personal sentiment and that is not a constitutive part of the structure, history, and conceptual architecture of race relations. A comprehensive response to such objections is not possible here, but suffice it to say that the historical record makes clear that the rhetorical dehumanization of persons of color—framing race as the limit case of empathy for human subjects— has always been a necessary, if not sufficient, condition for state-sponsored racial oppression (Patterson, 1996; Sexton, 2012). It follows, then, that any effective transformation of this particular form of racial oppression will include a simultaneous reconfiguration of conceptual frameworks *and* habits of feeling.

Here then is the contribution this study seeks to make in some small way— to sensitize readers to the deprivation, disappointment, and dignified intelligent outrage that students experience in the face of resegregating schools, a sensitization that does not try to step outside of discourse to know the oppressive brutalizing processes before we act, but a cultivation of felt appreciation that starts in the middle of always already mediated social processes. Empathic solidarity alone will not be a sufficient basis for a renewed political struggle against racially stratified educational opportunity, but without felt connection, any struggle for change will lack animating force and cohesion. At the most immediate level, the struggle against the damage being done by the new segregation may or may not take the form of a second desegregation movement. If it does, it can't be a replay of the civil rights era segregation.[16] It will have to be informed by a greater level of respect and commitment to the well-being of students of color in these schools. This will require scholarship and discourse that makes apparent the cognitive and affective terrain of racial politics in our schools. This study seeks to contribute to such a project.

At the broadest level, this study seeks to contribute to a general ongoing struggle with the real (violent) transubstantial agent of whiteness, an agent that can simultaneously move school buildings, influence property values, erase the humanity of children, and reach into our most rigorous thoughts, turning them to its purpose. In this struggle our academic ideals of epistemic clarity and methodological rigor provide little shelter. Worse they can actually become the instruments of racist oppression. Instead, the protean nature of racism calls us to an ethical practice of inquiry that is antecedent to our ideals of descriptive and conceptual clarity. Perhaps it points to the need for a form of interdisciplinary mixed methods scholarship, not organized by the idea that triangulating methods gives us a more objective picture of resegregation, but by the onto-ethical goal of tracking and hampering the material semiotic beast of whiteness by any methodological means necessary.

~~~

Some Methodological Specifics

The book is based on ten years of data collection that consisted of interviews with over 260 persons—parents, teachers, administrators, journalists, and students. The persons we interviewed were opportunistically recruited. Parents were most often recruited based on the referral of teachers and administrators.[17] We recruited teachers for interviews at faculty meetings or by approaching them individually based on referrals from students or other teachers. Students were recruited through brief requests for volunteers made in home room meetings at their schools. Occasionally students approached us asking to be interviewed or teachers volunteered to host a focus group in their room during the lunch break or after school.[18] Data for the study also included hundreds of hours of on-site school and classroom observation, as well as observation of school board meetings and at least one public protest. It also included extensive archival and media research including examining district committee reports, court records, school board minutes, as well as reading newspaper reports and listening to local talk radio shows where call-in commentary about the school restructuring in Riverton was often quite lively.

No effort was made to collect a random sample of students across the district. We spent most of our time on the campus of the district's all-Black high school,[19] consequently approximately 70% (~140) of the students interviewed were students from this school.[20] Within the students interviewed at that high school, the sample was diverse, including students of various grade levels, academic tracks, and neighborhoods. Because of the large and varied sample size of students within the all-Black high school whose enrollment was never much more than 800, because of the consistency of student responses and comments, because of the intricacy of those responses, and because of the corroboration of contextual data, this study makes claims about pervasive qualities of the experiences at this high school.[21]

The study is organized into seven chapters. The first two chapters provide the context in which the student experience of the resegregation takes place. Chapter 1 outlines the history of racial desegregation and resegregation in U.S. public schools. Riverton school district is presented as a microcosm of the national macrocosm of segregation politics in schools. Chapter 2 provides archival and interview evidence that the racial resegregation of Riverton schools was undertaken deliberately with clear knowledge that this would result in the creation of an all-Black school in a way that would not be in the interests of the students attending that school. It then provides evidence that, once the schools restructured, the all-Black school was stigmatized, under-resourced, and its students pathologized.

The next four chapters document the ways students interpreted the social text of the resegregation of Riverton schools. Chapter 3 reports on the ways students interpreted the demographic differences between the schools.

Chapter 4 inventories a variety of ways, other than its racial identity, that the all-Black high school was marked as a lower status school and how students interpreted the signifiers of that lower status. Chapter 5 examines the way students interpreted the complex interactions of their material deprivation and symbolic stigmatization. Most notably they tracked the way their being under-enrolled led to reductions in advanced curriculum, which was in turn interpreted in the community as evidence students at the school did not desire the advanced curriculum. Students regarded this ever tightening material-semiotic net of resegregation as a set-up for failure. Chapter 6 examines the various ways students' self-concept, sense of belonging in their community, and expectations of racial justice in general were affected by the constant barrage of negative and pathologizing messages that resulted from the resegregation of their school. It observes that although there is some evidence that students internalized the negative messages about themselves, the more prevalent response was one of indignation and disappointment in the adults in the community. Some acts of organized student resistance are recounted and their significance interpreted. The final chapter, Chapter 7, examines some implications of the study for teacher education curriculum, desegregation policy, and jurisprudence. It concludes with a discussion of the need to sensitize educators, policy makers, and citizens to the broad human consequences of the new segregation in U.S. public schools.

Some Notational Conventions

In writing this book, some textual conventions have been used that merit explanation. These primarily concern the way we describe the race, gender, and professions of our respondents in the study. All persons quoted have been identified with an alphanumeric that indicates their profession, primary school affiliation, race, gender, and a number signaling the order in which they appear in the text.

- P=Parent, E=Educator, S=Student, I=Interviewer
- Number indicates the order in which the person appears within his or her category.
- N=Northbrook High, G=Garner High, U=Union High (these are pseudonyms for the schools)
- B=Black, W=White, A=Asian (no one outside these categories was interviewed to our knowledge)
- M=Male, F=Female (no one outside these categories was interviewed to our knowledge)

So for example a quote by P5NWM would be a quote by the fifth parent to be quoted, whose children go to Northbrook, and who is a white man. As some of these categorizations are ethically and politically complicated, our choice to use them merits some explanation.

Race

We have used the basic racial categories in circulation in the community: Black, white, and Asian.[22] Although these categories are contingent social constructions and the use of them risks reifying them in essentializing ways we would consider pernicious, the racial identity of the speakers seemed an important component of the meaning of their remarks. Providing that information to the reader therefore was deemed necessary.[23]

We chose to use the term "Black" as opposed to "African-American" for three primary reasons. First, the term "Black" is used more frequently in the CRT literature in which this study is located and in the literature on race and schooling that seeks to contribute to structural social change. Second, it conveys a connotation of resistance to assimilation that African-American does not. We are in solidarity with that resistance and do not think assimilation of Black distinctiveness is a legitimate end of schooling. Third, recent research has shown that white citizens in the U.S. react more sympathetically to characters in stories described as African-American as opposed to those described as Black (Hall, Phillips, & Townsend, 2015). It therefore might have served the interest of fostering solidarity with Riverton students among our white readers if we had used the phrase African-American in our study. This, however, seemed like it would be a capitulation to agential whiteness, in that it would not be asking that much of readers or ourselves. Integrity and ambition, in our opinion, lie with trying to craft a text that fosters an empathy robust enough to sustain solidarity with an identity less accommodating of whiteness.

We chose to capitalize "Black" in this text because, again, doing so is a convention in much of the literature in which we wish to locate the study. Uncapitalized, this term signifies simply a demographic category. Capitalized, it signifies a conscious project of resisting institutionalized racism. We chose not to capitalize "white" because at this point in our history there is no collective "White" identity organized around the project of resistance to institutionalized racism. Liberal individualism that advocates for color-blind civil rights is not that project in our opinion.

Gender

The question of whether to designate gender was more difficult. At first pass, the gender of the respondents would not seem to matter to this study. Additionally, we are aware of the damage that can be done by reifying an over-simplified male/female binary. It erases the existence of genderqueer, transgender, and gender non-conforming students and adults. Such violence could have been avoided simply by not indicating the gender of our respondents at all. However, when we read the study without gender designations we realized this made it more difficult to identify with the experience of the students. Gender is a real part of human experience and identity, and removing it from the account rendered the students somewhat abstract and less sympathetic. We chose therefore to include gender designations in our descriptions of student respondents.[24] We highlight this choice here in the methodological preface to signal that it was a choice, that we are aware of the contingency and limitations of binary gender categories, and do not wish to naturalize such procrustean categories.

Professions

We used the term "teacher" or "educator" to refer to all teachers, counselors, and administrators. We did this to protect the anonymity of the professionals in unique positions, like principals.

Citation of news articles

We omitted citations from any publications, such as news articles and court records that would identify the location of the town. Readers who wish to access those sources are encouraged to contact one of the authors and request the citations.

Notes

1   Narrow epistemologies constraining policy debates are not the only reason CRT has gained currency among educational researchers. There are many themes in the CRT literature that make it relevant to the study of institutionalized racial inequality in public schools, such as the following foundational observations (Ladson-Billings & Tate, 1995): racism is an endemic and structural feature of U.S. society, as opposed to an individual character flaw; civil rights laws based on an ideal of color-blind justice have not effectively produced more just and equitable communities; racism is tied to property rights and entitlement to white identity and white spaces functions as a form of property. Educational scholarship, including *Resegregation as Curriculum* has been informed by and corroborates all three of these insights.
2   We also conducted interviews with parents, teachers, and administrators, observed school board and faculty meetings, and examined archival data, all of which provided a backdrop for our analysis of the way students made sense of the material facts and adult discourse about the resegregation of their schools.
3   This premise is forwarded in CRT as an alternative to the liberal assumption that pervasive racism is an epiphenomenal historical aberration that can be remedied through piecemeal and temporary policy fixes like affirmative action programs and court-ordered school desegregation. The assumption that these policies would be temporary has permitted them to be dismantled and subverted in recent years.

4   As will be reviewed later in the essay, indigenous thinkers and scholars have been writing about relational ontologies and ways of knowing that presume ontological consequences since time immemorial. Also, there have been Western traditions of thought throughout the twentieth and twenty-first centuries that have resisted the Western academy's privileging of epistemic foundationalism (e.g. McKenna & Pratt, 2014).

5   At a recent conference entitled "Beyond Advocacy and Reflexivity: The Ontological Turn in Educational Research Methodology" held at the University of Oregon, scholars from some of these communities of inquiry—including indigenous studies, material feminism, revisionist pragmatism, philosophically reflexive positivism, arts-based research, and politicized action research—were brought together to discuss social inquiry as an ontologically generative practice. The methodological musing in what remains of this preface was inspired and informed by the conversations at that conference.

    The conference was made possible by a generous grant from the American Education Research Foundation. Invited participants included Becky Atkinson, Cathy Coulter, Elizabeth De Freitas, Ezekiel Dixon-Roman, Eva Garroutte, Michael Hames-Garcia, Te Kawehau Hoskins, Alecia Youngblood Jackson, Patti Lather, Maggie MacLure, Lisa Mazzei, Roland Mitchell, Leigh Patel, Scott Pratt, Jerry Rosiek, Stephanie Springgay, Eve Tuck, Linda Tuhiwai Smith, and Elvin Wylie. Readings, artifacts, video interviews with invited participants, transcripts of panel discussions, and a syllabus for a course of study based on the conference can be found at https://coe.uoregon.edu/ontology

6   For example, conversations at the Beyond Advocacy and Reflexivity conference (see fn. 5) focused on topics such as agential realism, the materiality of language, the relationship of land and place to inquiry, the need to articulate the theory of change that underlies our research as opposed to taking for granted that epistemic revelation leads to action, and the way that the object- and subject-constituting effects of inquiry might be considered, not simply as excesses that destabilize the goal of description, but as an opportunity for a new defining purpose for social science research.

7   In human inquiry, cuts can be made in a carefully premeditated way as in a scientific experiment or a carefully organized sociological study that decides what its object of inquiry is and how attention will be focused. However, sometimes such cuts are forced upon us by other agents, such as when the tire on a vehicle is flat, and commandeers our attention against our will, or something we desire enters our field of experience and becomes the focus of our thought and attention. In such cases intra-actions may or may not be formalized forms of inquiry, but involve some form of experiential exploration or problem-solving.

8   This philosophical frame builds on Judith Butler's notion of performativity, but reaches beyond its limited linguistic semiotics for a more ontologically substantive understanding of performance (Barad, 2011).

9   Some indigenous scholars such as Eve Tuck (2015) and Valerie Watts (2013), have been concerned in recent years to point out that New Materialists often fail to acknowledge and engage this indigenous thought, and by so doing partake in a long-standing practice of settler society erasure of indigenous culture and significance.

10 This impression is based on several panel discussions at annual meetings of the American Educational Research Association and the International Congress of Qualitative Inquiry as well as conversations at the 2014 Beyond Reflexivity and Advocacy conference at the University of Oregon (transcripts of those conversations available at https://coe.uoregon.edu/ontology).

11   Thomas Short's entire book, *Peirce's Theory of Signs,* deals with the concept of purpose as it relates to Charles Sanders Peirce's ontologically substantive semiotic theory and the theory of non-human agency therein. However, of particular note for this argument are pp. 108–112 and 144–150.)

12   In his excellent book *Habeas Viscus,* Alexander Weheliye (2014) suggests something similar. Drawing on the writings of Deleuze and Guattari, he uses terminology such as "racializing assemblages" to describe the material semiotic fluidity and object+subject producing aspects of racism. This has appeal in that it puts the ontology of white supremacy into motion and frames the discursive and material aspects of racializing assemblages as continuous—which is what we found in our study. For reasons mentioned earlier, however, the language of "assemblage" does not have all of the advantages of agential ontologies for the purposes of this study.

13   Note that this was not phrased as "Racism can be thought of as . . ." To use such phrasing would suggest a kind of constructivist nominalism that located the reality of racializing agents in humans conceiving of them as such. Agential realism is a form of realism, and so the phrase "Racism is . . ." has been used. (There is a form of recursive logic lurking behind this rhetorical decision. Since the appeal of agential realism is that it alludes to real agents that exceed any single discursive representation of it, one might legitimately argue that even agential realism is but one more discursive representation. This conundrum must be granted. But it has more of the quality of a challenge than a contradiction. It will take the development of a protean tradition of anti-racist scholarly practice and activism, rather than a logical argument, to satisfactorily address the concern that agential realism can be co-opted just as easily as any other theory. CRT may be such a theoretical tradition, as long as in its continuing migration to the social sciences it retains what Leonardo (2013) called its multifaceted nature and avoids becoming identified with any single ontological frame or methodological practice.)

14   I considered making a different ontological cut here by using the even more specific term "anti-Blackness," having recently encountered the rapidly growing anti-Blackness theory literature (e.g. Hartman, 2007; Sexton, 2010; Wilderson, 2010). Anti-Blackness theory draws attention to the unique history and formations of different types of racial exclusion, as well as the historically central role the dehumanization of Black persons has played in the development of Western settler society culture. There is much to recommend engaging the events in Riverton as an entanglement with anti-Blackness as an agent. The discourse about schooling in Riverton was saturated with aversion to the presence of Black bodies and Black subjects. Blackness, specifically, was the focus of recoil, not persons-of-color, non-whiteness, or poverty. Also, anti-Blackness theory emphasizes the way Blackness is not simply framed as inferior, but is framed as not human, as the limiting case against which "the human" has been defined in Western settler society. In our study of Riverton, we saw both. Black students were at times marked as inferior. However, the resegregation of the schools was made possible by an erasure of the humanity of Black students as a significant moral consideration, especially the students assigned to the all-Black high school. The consequences of the restructuring for them was never an overriding concern for Riverton's educational policy makers.

The term "whiteness" however, draws attention to the treatment of whiteness as a form of property, which is a central feature of CRT and was present in the Riverton resegregation process (Harris, 1993). It also rhetorically draws attention to the complicity of white citizens in this dynamic. Being at this moment more familiar with CRT and critiques of whiteness, I have chosen to engage agential whiteness. I experience this as a form of analytical trade-off more than an assertion of a particular truth about racism. Ultimately, in the struggle with agential racializing assemblages as realities that exceed our ability to represent them in any singular fashion, I assume it will be necessary to shift my theoretical treatment of this topic over time—perhaps attending to agential anti-Blackness in future analyses.

15 Note, this is not a call for a new form of triangulation, which presumes multiple forms of data or multiple methods of analysis will help us arrive at a more comprehensive single picture of reality. Plugging in implies that the substantive reality of a phenomena changes depending on how we methodologically plug in with it.

16 There is a great deal of scholarship that documents the limitations of the civil rights era desegregation jurisprudence. The brief period in which some, mostly southern, schools were desegregated never achieved desegregation at the classroom level. It resulted in the elimination of whole segments of Black professional educators, few of whom were hired to work in the newly segregated schools. It provided Black students access to better resourced schools, at the cost of subjecting Black students to immersion in institutional contexts in which they were pathologized, expected to fail, and even despised. See, for example: Bell, 1976, 1979; Fultz, 2004; Haney, 1978; Hudson & Holmes, 1994; Ladson-Billings, 2004; Walker, 1996.

17 This meant parents interviewed for the study included a higher than average number of active parents.

18 All students had to have permission slips, so this created a practical attrition of volunteers. More students volunteered to be interviewed than got back with signed permissions slips.

19 We had an office on the school site for two years.

20 Roughly 66% of these were collected in the first three years after the restructuring.

21 Even if the experiences we identified were unique to the sample we recruited, which is unlikely in the extreme, the experiences of such a large number of students would be morally and politically significant in themselves.

22 There were few Latinos, indigenous students, or students of other racial or cultural groups in Riverton schools and of those, none volunteered for interviews with us.

23 In most cases respondents were asked to self-identify. On the few occasions that did not occur, the interviewer assigned identity based on school records or their best judgment.

24 No students in our interviews identified as transgender or gender non-conforming, though this is not surprising given the acute heteronomativity of the locale in which the study was conducted.

Bibliography

Alaimo, S., & Hekman, S. J. (Eds.). (2008). *Material feminisms*. Bloomington, IN: Indiana University Press.

Alfred, G. R. (2005). *Wasa'se: indigenous pathways of action and freedom*. Peterborough, Ont.; Orchard Park, NY: Broadview Press.

Anyon, J. (1979). Ideology and United States history textbooks. *Harvard Educational Review*, *49*(3), 361–386.

Apple, M. W. (1990). *Ideology and curriculum* (2nd ed.). New York: Routledge.

Atwood, E., & López, G. R. (2014). Let's be critically honest: towards a messier counterstory in critical race theory. *International Journal of Qualitative Studies in Education*, *27*(9), 1134–1154.

Barad, K. M. (2007). *Meeting the universe halfway: quantum physics and the entanglement of matter and meaning.* Durham, NC: Duke University Press.

Barad, K. M. (2011). Nature's queer performativity. *Qui Parle: Critical Humanities and Social Sciences, 18*(2), 121–168.

Beghetto, R. A. (2005). Does assessment kill student creativity? *The Educational Forum, 69*(3), 254–263.

Bell, D. A. (1976). Serving two masters: integration ideals and client interests in school desegregation litigation. *Yale Law Journal, 85*(4), 470–516.

Bell Jr., D. A. (1979). *Brown v. Board of Education* and the interest-convergence dilemma. *Harvard Law Review, 93*, 518.

Bell, D. A. (1992). *Faces at the bottom of the well: the permanence of racism.* New York, NY: Basic Books.

Bennett, J. (2010). *Vibrant matter: a political ecology of things.* Durham, NC: Duke University Press.

Berlant, L. G. (2011). *Cruel optimism.* Durham, NC: Duke University Press.

Braidotti, R. (2013). *The posthuman.* Cambridge, UK ; Malden, MA, USA: Polity Press.

Brayboy, B. M. J. (2005). Toward a tribal critical race theory in education. *The Urban Review, 37*(5), 425–446.

Bunge, R. (1984). *An American urphilosophie: an American philosophy, BP (before pragmatism).* Lanham, MD: University Press of America.

Cajete, G. (1994). *Look to the mountain: an ecology of indigenous education.* Durango, CO: Kivakí Press.

Cajete, G. (2000). *Native science: natural laws of interdependence.* Santa Fe, NM: Clear Light Publishers.

Carbado, D. W., & Roithmayr, D. (2014). Critical race theory meets social science. *Annual Review of Law and Social Science, 10*(1), 149–167.

Chapman, T. K. (2007). Interrogating classroom relationships and events: using portraiture and critical race theory in education research. *Educational Researcher, 36*(3), 156–162.

Chávez, M. S. (2012). Autoethnography, a Chicana's methodological research tool: the role of storytelling for those who have no choice but to do critical race theory. *Equity & Excellence in Education, 45*(2), 334–348.

Childers, S. M. (2013). The materiality of fieldwork: an ontology of feminist becoming. *International Journal of Qualitative Studies in Education, 26*(5), 599–609.

Clotfelter, C. T. (2004). *After Brown the rise and retreat of school desegregation.* Princeton, NJ: Princeton University Press.

Coleman, J. S. (1990). *Equality and achievement in education.* Boulder: Westview Press.

Coleman, J. S., United States Office of Education, & National Center for Education Statistics. (1966). *Equality of educational opportunity.* Washington, DC: U.S. Dept. of Health, Education, and Welfare, Office of Education [for sale by the Superintendent of Documents, U.S. Govt. Print. Off.].

Coole, D. H., & Frost, S. (Eds.). (2010). *New materialisms: ontology, agency, and politics.* Durham, NC; London: Duke University Press.

Coraboeuf, E., Deroubaix, E., & Hoerter, J. (1976). Control of ionic permeabilities in normal and ischemic heart. *Circulation Research, 38*(5 Suppl 1), I92–98.

de Freitas, E., & Sinclair, N. (2014). *Mathematics and the body: material entanglements in the classroom.* New York: Cambridge University Press.

Deleuze, G., & Guattari, F. (2004). *Anti-Oedipus: capitalism and schizophrenia.* London: Continuum.

Delgado, R. (1989). Storytelling for oppositionists and others: a plea for narrative. *Michigan Law Review, 87*(8), 2411. http://doi.org/10.2307/1289308

De Lissovoy, N. (2012). Education and violation: conceptualizing power, domination, and agency in the hidden curriculum. *Race Ethnicity and Education, 15*(4), 463–484. http://doi.org/10.1080/13613324.2011.618831

Deloria, V. (1999). *Spirit and reason: the Vine Deloria, Jr., reader.* Golden, CO: Fulcrum.

Deloria, V. (2012). *The metaphysics of modern existence.* Golden, CO: Fulcrum.

Dewey, J. (1997). *Democracy and education: an introduction to the philosophy of education.* New York: Free Press.

Dixson, A. D. (2006). The fire this time: jazz, research and critical race theory. In A. D. Dixson, & C. K. Rousseau (Eds.), *Critical race theory in education: all God's children got a song.* New York: Routledge.

Dixson, A. D., & Rousseau, C. K. (2005). And we are still not saved: critical race theory in education ten years later. *Race Ethnicity and Education, 8*(1), 7–27. http://doi.org/10.1080/1361332052000340971

Dixson, A. D., & Rousseau, C. K. (Eds.). (2006). *Critical race theory in education: all God's children got a song* (pp. 213–231). New York: Routledge.

Doerfler, J., Sinclair, N. J., & Stark, H. K. (Eds.). (2013). *Centering Anishinaabeg studies: understanding the world through stories.* East Lansing: Michigan State University Press; Winnipeg: University of Manitoba Press.

Dumas, M. J. (2014). "Losing an arm": schooling as a site of black suffering. *Race Ethnicity and Education, 17*(1), 1–29. http://doi.org/10.1080/13613324.2013.850412

Dumas, M. J., & Anderson, G. (2014). Qualitative research as policy knowledge: framing policy problems and transforming education from the ground up. *Education Policy Analysis Archives, 22*(11).

Duncan, G. A. (2005). Critical race ethnography in education: narrative, inequality and the problem of epistemology. *Race Ethnicity and Education, 8*(1), 93–114. http://doi.org/10.1080/1361332052000341015

Duran, E., & Duran, B. (1995). *Native American postcolonial psychology.* Albany: State University of New York Press.

Durkheim, E. (2002). *Moral education.* Mineola, NY: Dover Publications.

Eastman, C. A. (2003). *The soul of the Indian.* New York: Dover Publications.

Ehman, L. H. (1980). The American school in the political socialization process. *Review of Educational Research, 50*(1), 99–119. http://doi.org/10.3102/00346543050001099

Fine, M. (1991). *Framing dropouts: notes on the politics of an urban public high school.* Albany: State University of New York Press.

Fultz, M. (2004). The displacement of Black educators post-*Brown*: an overview and analysis. *History of Education Quarterly, 44*(1), 11–45.

Garroutte, E., & Westcott, K. (2013). The story is a living being: companionship with stories in Anishinaabe Studies. In J. Doerfler, N. J. Sinclair, & H. K. Stark (Eds.), *Centering Anishinaabeg studies: understanding the world through stories.* East Lansing: Michigan State University Press; Winnipeg: University of Manitoba Press.

Gibson, B. (2007). Accommodating critical theory. In A. Bryant, & K. Charmaz, (Eds.), *The SAGE Handbook of Grounded Theory.* London: Sage.

Giroux, H. A. (2001). *Theory and resistance in education: towards a pedagogy for the opposition* (Rev. and expanded ed.). Westport, CT: Bergin & Garvey.

Gómez, L. E. (2012). Looking for race in all the wrong places: looking for race. *Law & Society Review, 46*(2), 221–245. http://doi.org/10.1111/j.1540-5893.2012.00486.x

Hall, E., Phillips, K., & Townsend, S. (2015). A rose by any other name? The consequences of subtyping "African-Americans" from "Blacks." *Journal of Experimental Social Psychology*, *56*, 183–190.

Halton, E. (1995). *Bereft of reason: on the decline of social thought and prospects for its renewal*. Chicago: University of Chicago Press.

Haney, J. E. (1978). The effects of the *Brown* decision on black educators. *Journal of Negro Education*, *47*(1), 88–95.

Harney, S., & Moten, F. (2013). *The undercommons: fugitive planning and black study*. Wivenhoe, UK: Minor Compositions.

Harris, C. I. (1993). Whiteness as property. *Harvard Law Review*, *106*(8), 1707–1791.

Hartman, S. V. (2007). *Lose your mother: a journey along the Atlantic slave route*. New York: Farrar, Straus and Giroux.

Huber, L. P. (2009). Disrupting apartheid of knowledge: *testimonio* as methodology in Latina/o critical race research in education. *International Journal of Qualitative Studies in Education*, *22*(6), 639–654.

Hudson, M. J., & Holmes, B. J. (1994). Missing teachers, impaired communities: the unanticipated consequences of *Brown v. Board of Education* on the African American teaching force at the precollegiate level. *Journal of Negro Education*, *63*, 388–393.

Jackson, A. Y., & Mazzei, L. A. (2012). *Thinking with theory in qualitative research: viewing data across multiple perspectives*. Abingdon, UK; New York: Routledge.

Jackson, P. W. (1990). *Life in classrooms*. New York: Teachers College Press.

Jacques, V., Wu, E., Grosshans, F., Treussart, F., Grangier, P., Aspect, A., & Roch, J.-F. (2007). Experimental realization of Wheeler's delayed-choice gedanken experiment. *Science*, *315*(5814), 966–968. http://doi.org/10.1126/science.1136303

Johnson, E. (2008). Simulating medical patients and practices: bodies and the construction of valid medical simulators. *Body & Society*, *14*(3), 105–128. http://doi.org/10.1177/1357034X08093574

Kawagley, A. O. (2006). *A Yupiaq worldview: a pathway to ecology and spirit* (2nd ed.). Long Grove, IL: Waveland Press.

Kelley, R.D.G. (2002). *Freedom dreams: the Black radical imagination*. Boston: Beacon Press.

Kiss, J., Szeger, K., & Hera, G. (2013). Prejudices, social competencies and political orientations in relation to schools' hidden curriculum. *Intercultural Education*, *24*(3), 277–287. http://doi.org/10.1080/14675986.2013.793028

Kohn, E. (2013). *How forests think: toward an anthropology beyond the human*. Berkeley: University of California Press.

Ladson-Billings, G. (1998). Just what is critical race theory and what's it doing in a nice field like education? *International Journal of Qualitative Studies in Education*, *11*(1), 7–24. http://doi.org/10.1080/095183998236863

Ladson-Billings, G. (2000). Racialized discourses and ethnic epistemologies. In N. K. Denzin & Y. S. Lincoln (Eds.), *Handbook of qualitative research*. Thousand Oaks, CA: Sage.

Ladson-Billings, G. (2004). Landing on the wrong note: the price we paid for *Brown*. *Educational Researcher*, *33*(7), 3–13.

Ladson-Billings, G. (2005). The evolving role of critical race theory in educational scholarship. *Race Ethnicity and Education*, *8*(1), 115–119. http://doi.org/10.1080/1361332052000341024

Ladson-Billings, G., & Tate, W. (1995). Toward a critical race theory of education. *Teachers College Record*, *87*(1), 47–67.

Lather, P. (2006). Paradigm proliferation as a good thing to think with: teaching research in education as a wild profusion. *International Journal of Qualitative Studies in Education, 19*(1), 35–57. http://doi.org/10.1080/09518390500450144

Lather, P. (2007). *Getting lost: feminist efforts toward a double(d) science.* Albany: State University of New York Press.

Latour, B. (2004). Why has critique run out of steam? From matters of fact to matters of concern. *Critical Inquiry, 30*(2), 225–248. http://doi.org/10.1086/421123

Lea, T. (2015). What has water got to do with it? Indigenous public housing and Australian settler-colonial relations. *Settler Colonial Studies*, 1–12. http://doi.org/10.1080/22014 73X.2014.1000911

Lenz-Taguchi, H. (2010). *Going beyond the theory/practice divide in early childhood education: introducing an intra-active pedagogy.* London; New York: Routledge.

Leonardo, Z. (2013). *Race frameworks: a multidimensional theory of racism and education.* New York: Teachers College.

Lutz, B. F. (2005). Post *Brown vs. the Board of Education*: the effects of the end of court-ordered desegregation. (No. 2005-64.) Washington, DC: Federal Reserve Board.

Lynn, M., & Dixson, A. D. (Eds.). (2013). *Handbook of critical race theory in education.* New York: Routledge.

MacLure, M. (2013). Researching without representation? Language and materiality in post-qualitative methodology. *International Journal of Qualitative Studies in Education, 26*(6), 658–667. http://doi.org/10.1080/09518398.2013.788755

Madison, D. S. (2012). *Critical ethnography: method, ethics, and performance* (2nd ed.). Thousand Oaks, CA: SAGE.

Manning, A. G., Khakimov, R. I., Dall, R. G., & Truscott, A. G. (2015). Wheeler's delayed-choice gedanken experiment with a single atom. *Nature Physics, 11*, 539–542. http://doi.org/10.1038/nphys3343

Mazzei, L. A. (2010). Thinking data with Deleuze. *International Journal of Qualitative Studies in Education, 23*(5), 511–523. http://doi.org/10.1080/09518398.2010.497176

Mazzei, L. A., & Jackson, A. Y. (Eds.). (2009). *Voice in qualitative inquiry: challenging conventional, interpretive, and critical conceptions in qualitative research.* London; New York: Routledge.

McKenna, E., & Pratt, S. L. (2014). *American philosophy: from Wounded Knee to the present.* New York: Bloomsbury Academic.

McKittrick, K. (Ed.). (2015). *Sylvia Wynter: on being human as praxis.* Durham, NC: Duke University Press.

Michael, M., & Rosengarten, M. (2012). Medicine: experimentation, politics, emergent bodies. *Body & Society, 18*(3–4), 1–17. http://doi.org/10.1177/1357034X12451860

Muñoz, J. E. (2009). *Cruising utopia: the then and there of queer futurity.* New York: New York University Press.

Neidjie, B. (2002). *Gagadju man.* Marlston, Australia: JB Books.

No Child Left Behind (NCLB) Act of 2001, 20 U.S.C.A. § 6301 et seq. (West 2003).

Nxumalo, F., Pacini-Ketchabaw, V., & Rowan, M. (2011). Lunch time at the child care centre: neoliberal assemblages in early childhood education. *Journal of Pedagogy/Pedagogický Časopis, 2*(2), 195–223. http://doi.org/10.2478/v10159-011-0010-4

Obasogie, O. (2015). Foreword: critical race theory and empirical methods. *Irvine Law Review, 3*(2), 183–186.

Orfield, G. (1983). *Public school desegregation in the United States. 1968–1980.* Washington, D.C.: Joint Center of Political Studies.

Orfield, G., & Eaton, S. E. (1996). *Dismantling desegregation: the quiet reversal of* Brown v. Board of Education. New York: The New Press.

Orfield, G., Kim, J., & Sunderman, G. (2006). *NCLB meets realities: lessons from the field.* Thousand Oaks, CA: Corwin Press.

Orfield, G., Kucsera, J., & Siegel-Hawley, G. (2012). *E pluribus . . . separation: deepening double segregation for more students.* UCLA: The Civil Rights Project.

Orfield, G., & Yun, J. T. (1999). *Resegregation in American schools.* Harvard University: The Harvard Civil Rights Project.

Parker, L., Deyhle, D., & Villenas, S. A. (Eds.). (1999). *Race is—race isn't: critical race theory and qualitative studies in education.* Boulder, CO: Westview Press.

Parker, L., & Lynn, M. (2002). What's race got to do with it? Critical race theory's conflicts with and connections to qualitative research methodology and epistemology. *Qualitative Inquiry, 8*(1), 7–22. http://doi.org/10.1177/107780040200800102

Patterson, O. (1996). *Freedom. Vol. 1: Freedom in the making of Western culture.* New York, NY: Basic Books.

Paul-Emile, K. (2015). Foreword: critical race theory and empirical methods conference. *Fordham Law Review, 83*(6), 2953–2960.

Peacock, T. D., & Wisuri, M. (2011). *Ojibwe waasa inaabidaa: we look in all directions.* Saint Paul: Minnesota Historical Society Press.

Peirce, C. S. (1974). The simplest mathematics. In C. Hartshorne & P. Weiss (Eds.), *Collected papers,* Vol. 4. Cambridge, MA: Belknap Press of Harvard Univ. Press.

Peirce, C. S. (1992). *The essential Peirce: selected philosophical writings.* (N. Houser & C.J.W. Kloesel, Eds.). Bloomington: Indiana University Press.

Petrovich, J., & Wells, A. S. (Eds.). (2005). *Bringing equity back: research for a new era in American educational policy.* New York: Teachers College Press.

Pillow, W. (2003). Race-based methodologies: multicultural methods or epistemological shifts? In G. R. Lopez & L. Parker (Eds.), *Interrogating racism in qualitative research methodology.* New York: Peter Lang.

Pratt, S. (2011). American power: Mary Parker Follett and Michel Foucault. *Foucault Studies,* (11), 76–91.

Ravitch, D. (2011). *The death and life of the great American school system: how testing and choice are undermining education* (Rev. and expanded ed.). New York: Basic Books.

Reardon, S. F., Grewal, E., Kalogrides, D., & Greenburg, E. (2012). *Brown* fades: the end of court ordered school desegregation and the resegregation of American public schools. *Journal of Policy Analysis and Management, 31*(4), 876–904.

Reardon, S. F., & Yun, J. T. (2003). Integrating neighborhoods, segregating schools: the retreat from school desegregation in the South, 1990–2000. *North Carolina Law Review, 81*(4), 1563–1596.

Roberts, C. (2014). The entanglement of sexed bodies and pharmaceuticals: a feminist analysis of early onset puberty and puberty-blocking medications. *Subjectivity, 7*(4), 321–341. http://doi.org/10.1057/sub.2014.17

Rosiek, J. L. (2013a). Beyond the autoethnography vs. ironist debates: using Charles Sanders Peirce and Cornel West to envision an alternative inquiry practice. In N. Denzin & M. Giardina (Eds.), *Global dimensions in qualitative inquiry* (pp. 157–180). Walnut Creek, CA: Left Coast Press.

Rosiek, J. L. (2013b). Pragmatism and post-qualitative futures. *International Journal of Qualitative Studies in Education, 26*(6), 692–705. http://doi.org/10.1080/09518398.201 3.788758

Rosiek, J. & Clandinin J. (in press). Teachers as curriculum makers. In D. Wyse, L. Haywood, & J. Pandya (Eds.), *The Sage Handbook of Curriculum, Pedagogy, and Assessment*. Thousand Oaks: Sage Publishing.

Sarat, A. (Ed.). (2004). *The Blackwell companion to law and society*. Malden, MA: Blackwell.

Scott, J. (1981). The evidence of experience. *Critical Inquiry*, *17*(4), 773–797.

Sexton, J. (2010). People-of-color-blindness: notes on the afterlife of slavery. *Social Text*, *28*(2 103), 31–56.

Sexton, J. (2012). Ante-anti-blackness: afterthoughts. *Lateral*, (1), http://lateral.cultural studiesassociation.org/issue1/content/sexton.html

Short, T. L. (2007). *Peirce's theory of signs*. Cambridge, UK; New York: Cambridge University Press.

Solorzano, D. G. (1998). Critical race theory, race and gender microaggressions, and the experience of Chicana and Chicano scholars. *International Journal of Qualitative Studies in Education*, *11*(1), 121–136. http://doi.org/10.1080/095183998236926

Solorzano, D. G., Ceja, M., & Yosso, T. (2000). Critical race theory, racial microaggressions, and campus racial climate: the experiences of African American college students. *Journal of Negro Education*, *69*(1–2), 60–73.

Solorzano, D. G., & Yosso, T. J. (2002). Critical race methodology: counter-storytelling as an analytical framework for education research. *Qualitative Inquiry*, *8*(1), 23–44. http://doi.org/10.1177/107780040200800103

Spivak, G. C. (1999). *A critique of postcolonial reason: toward a history of the vanishing present*. Cambridge, MA: Harvard University Press.

St. Pierre, E. A. (2002). Comment: "science" rejects postmodernism. *Educational Researcher*, *31*(8), 25–27. http://doi.org/10.3102/0013189X031008025

St. Pierre, E. A. (2015). Refusing human being in humanist qualitative inquiry. In N. Denzin & M. Giardina (Eds.), *Qualitative inquiry—past, present, and future: a critical reader* (pp. 103–119). Walnut Creek, CA: Left Coast Press.

Stewart-Harawaira, M. (2005). *The new imperial order: Indigenous responses to globalization*. London: Zed Books.

Taylor, E., Gillborn, D., & Ladson-Billings, G. (Eds.). (2009). *Foundations of critical race theory in education*. New York: Routledge.

Tinker, G. E. (2004). *Spirit and resistance: political theology and American Indian liberation*. Minneapolis: Fortress Press.

Tinker, G. E. (2008). *American Indian liberation: a theology of sovereignty*. Maryknoll, NY: Orbis Books.

Tuck, E. (2015). Re-visioning social, re-visioning context, re-visioning agency. Paper presented at the 2015 Annual Meeting of the American Educational Research Association annual meeting, Chicago, IL.

Tuck, E., & McKenzie, M. (2015). *Place in research: theory, methodology, and methods*. New York; London: Routledge, Taylor & Francis Group.

Walker, V. S. (1996). *Their highest potential: an African American school community in the segregated South*. Chapel Hill: University of North Carolina Press.

Watts, V. (2013). Indigenous place-thought and agency amongst humans and non-humans (First Woman and Sky Woman go on a European world tour!). *Decolonization: Indigeneity, Education & Society*, *2*(1), 20–34.

Weheliye, A. G. (2014). *Habeas viscus: racializing assemblages, biopolitics, and black feminist theories of the human*. Durham, NC: Duke University Press.

Wells, A. S. (2000). The "consequences" of school desegregation: the mismatch between the research and the rationale. *Hastings Constitutional Law Quarterly*, (28), 771–797.

Wells, A. S. (Ed.). (2009). *Both sides now: the story of school desegregation's graduates.* Berkeley: University of California Press.

West, C. (1989). *The American evasion of philosophy: a genealogy of pragmatism.* Madison: University of Wisconsin Press.

West, C. (1992, August 2). Learning to talk of race. *New York Times*, pp. 24, 26.

West, C. (1993). *Keeping faith: philosophy and race in America.* New York: Routledge.

Wilderson, F. B. (2010). *Red, white and black: cinema and the structure of U.S. antagonisms.* Durham, NC: Duke University Press.

Willis, P. E. (1981). *Learning to labor: how working class kids get working class jobs* (Morningside ed.). New York: Columbia University Press.

Yosso, T., Smith, W., Ceja, M., & Solórzano, D. (2009). Critical race theory, racial microaggressions, and campus racial climate for Latina/o undergraduates. *Harvard Educational Review*, 79(4), 659–691. http://doi.org/10.17763/haer.79.4.m6867014157m707l

Zamudio, M. (Ed.). (2011). *Critical race theory matters: education and ideology.* New York: Routledge.

Zhao, Y. (2014). *Who's afraid of the big bad dragon? Why China has the best (and worst) education system in the world.* San Francisco, CA: Jossey-Bass & Pfeiffer Imprints, Wiley.

ACKNOWLEDGEMENTS

The authors would like to thank the following people for advice, comments, and/or timely reviews of chapters along the way that substantively informed the analysis in this text: Becky Atkinson, Nikki Thommen Bingham, Elizabeth de Freitas, Ezekiel Dixon-Román, Michael Dumas, Ingie Givens, Robert Gray, Aoife Macgee, Lisa Mazzei, Kate McCoy, Utz McKnight, Susan Nordstrom, Scott Pratt, Kory Sorrell, Karen Thompson, George Williamson, and Eve Tuck.

We also want to express our gratitude and respect for the students of Riverton school district who participated in this study, understanding that doing so would not benefit them personally in any way, but might contribute to some form of amelioration for those who followed them. Their refusal to fall into silence and their eagerness to speak against the looming edifice of institutionalized racism all around them inspired us throughout the development of this book.

1

INTRODUCTION

Resegregation in Riverton and the Nation

On the morning of Monday March 1, 2004, approximately 200 students walked out of their classrooms in Union High School and began an organized protest march. They were joined outside the school by approximately 100 parents and community members and proceeded to march two and a half miles to the Riverton school board office. They carried signs that read "Union students making history" and "We want our school."

The immediate cause of the protest was concern about the proposed location of a new high school building that the board was three years late in building. The school board was considering building a new Union High campus on the far west boundary of the city limits. The protesters, however, wanted the new school built in the center of town on the site of the former unified high school. There was a widely shared perception that the voting majority on the school board didn't care about what happened to Union students and locating the new school far from town would make it easier to neglect them.

There were many reasons for this concern. But central among them was a fear that the district was returning to an era of racial segregation. Thirty years earlier a federal desegregation order had compelled the district to create a single "mega high school" that served all Riverton[1] high school students. In 1999 the desegregation order had been lifted and the school board had rezoned the district to create three smaller high schools. Two of these schools were demographically balanced. The new Union High was the smallest of the three. It was also 100% Black, had the highest percentage of students on the reduced lunch plan, and the lowest average performance on state standardized tests. District officials maintained that this was an unintended consequence of housing patterns and that they had not intentionally created a racially or economically identifiable school. Many students and parents found this claim dubious at best.

Adding to student and parent concern, the district had built new facilities for the two other schools, while Union High students had been moved to a fifty-year-old building. The two new schools had been provided new equipment, learning technology, sports uniforms, band uniforms, etc. The other school was required to use the aging equipment and uniforms of the former high school whose name and colors it had inherited. The protest, therefore, was not just about building location. It was a part of an ongoing community debate about the way racism and classism appeared to be motivating the rezoning of Riverton's public high schools and the neglect of nearly one third of its students. One student at the protest commented, "Can't they see what is happening? This is segregation, 2000-style."

The Short History of Desegregation and Resegregation in U.S. Public Schools

One of the remarkable things about the political achievements of the U.S. civil rights movement was how quickly they became a normalized part of national identity. Once certain key struggles over voting rights, school attendance, and access to public spaces had been won, racial integration became the new normal in the popular imagination. For a generation born after those struggles took place, the end of things like the racial segregation of schools took on a feeling of remoteness and inevitability similar to the end of Western monarchies or the end of slavery. It seemed inconceivable to many that it could return.

The history of racial desegregation of schools, however, is not that remote, nor were its effects that deep or sustained. At the federal government level, the only period of consistent federal support for the desegregation of schools was in the 1960s, following the hard-won passage of the 1964 Civil Rights Act. Between 1965 and 1969 the federal executive branch and a unanimous Supreme Court pressed aggressively for school desegregation. These five years of proactive federal intervention had an enormous and lasting impact on the practice of public education and on ideas about education in the public imagination. De jure racial segregation in schools was shattered by legislative and court actions. And racial diversity increased in public schools across the nation. Students of color gained access to better resourced schools which had a variety of measurable positive effects on learning and life possibilities (Lutz, 2011; Orfield, 1983).

The reach of these court decisions was limited, however. Classroom level segregation was never effectively addressed. Racial stratification and stigmatization remained a part of students' school experience, albeit in a different form (Ladson-Billings, 2004). And changing political tides began eroding the federal pressure to desegregate shortly after the court orders had become practically effective. Tracing the means used to enforce desegregation policies is instructive here. The 1954 and 1955 *Brown v. Board of Education* decisions are the most widely known and celebrated of the school desegregation court cases.

However, the *Brown* order to desegregate schools "with all deliberate speed" was vague and largely ignored by recalcitrant school districts (Brown, 1954; Brown, 1955). It took another decade of court battles to assemble mechanisms that could effectively enforce the mandate to racially desegregate schools.

Arguably the 1968 *Green v. County School Board* decision was the most important of these subsequent court decisions. This case focused on educational policy in a rural Virginia school district that had delayed implementation of desegregation mandated by the *Brown* decision for a decade. The district had been using a "freedom of choice" approach to enrollment that in practice had left schools almost entirely segregated (Green, 1968). Writing for the majority, Supreme Court Justice William Brennan acknowledged the vagueness of the "all deliberate speed" standard put forth in *Brown*, but made clear that this vagueness was not an invitation to minimalist implementation.

> School Boards . . . operating state-compelled dual systems were nevertheless clearly charged with the affirmative duty to take whatever steps might be necessary to convert to a unitary system in which racial discrimination would be eliminated root and branch . . . The burden on a school board today is to come forward with a plan that promises realistically to work, and promises realistically to work *now*.

After *Green*, Federal courts began engaging in a more direct oversight of the restructuring of schools ordered to racially integrate.

The substance of the *Green* decision turned on the definition of the term "unitary" when describing a school system. In spirit, this meant that before a school district could be returned to local control, it had to convince the courts that the school system had reached a state of unity where discrimination had been eliminated and a return to segregation was not a reasonable possibility. In practice, this standard was operationalized in what came to be known as "the *Green Factors*." According to the practice that emerged from this decision, a district would have to demonstrate the following before control would be returned to the local school board:

- Students are assigned to schools in a non-discriminatory manner. This was generally interpreted to mean that all attendance zones are race neutral, that there are no predominantly one-race schools, and that all schools have been included in the racial desegregation.
- The proportion of majority/minority faculty, staff, and administrators is comparable to the demography of the labor market.
- Extracurricular activities are made available on a nondiscriminatory basis (including cost barriers being addressed).
- Facilities, transportation, and resources are provided without regard to race.
- Per pupil spending is relatively equal across schools.

The impact of the *Green* decision was immediate and profound. It gave federal courts around the country the means to enforce more timely compliance with the *Brown v. Board of Education* decision. School districts that had been delaying or minimizing compliance with that decision were now compelled to substantively desegregate.

Even as enforcement was beginning in earnest, however, the erosion of federal support for school desegregation was beginning. The election of Richard Nixon as president in 1968—the same year as the *Green* decision— marked an inflection point in the struggle. Over the course of his presidency, President Nixon "shut down administrative enforcement of desegregation requirements, shifted the position of the Justice Department from proactive enforcement to passive acceptance, appointed four conservative Justices to the Supreme Court and attacked desegregation rulings." (Orfield, Kucsera, & Siegel-Hawley, 2012, p. 4). The last Supreme Court decision expanding desegregation rights to schools outside the South and to Latinos came in 1973 (Keyes, 1973). By the mid-1970s, the tide had turned on the Supreme Court, and a series of decisions such as *Milliken v. Bradley*[2] and *San Antonio Independent School District v. Rodriguez*,[3] began limiting the reach of court-ordered desegregation.

Separation of powers in the three branches of government and lifetime appointment of judges insulated lower federal courts from the influence of this election for a time. Throughout the 1970s, federal courts kept hearing cases and issuing desegregation orders, though with declining frequency. By the 1980s, the momentum of the desegregation movement had been exhausted and racial segregation in schools began increasing again. The following charts illustrate the trend.

Figure 1.1 illustrates the extent to which the desegregation of U.S. public schools was never fully accomplished. At its highpoint, a third of Black students remained in schools in which 90–100% of the students were racial minorities and over 60% remained in schools in which over half of the students were racial minorities.[4] It also illustrates how much ground has been lost since the initial civil rights era gains. As of 2011 the number of Black students in majority minority schools has risen to 77.1%, higher than it was in 1968. The statistics for Latino students, who were never subject to de jure racial segregation to the same degree that Black students were in the first half of the twentieth century, is even more revealing of the persistent trend towards increased racial segregation. What we see in Figure 1.2 is a steady increase in racial segregation levels over the last four decades.

In addition to these broad demographic patterns, ability tracking in public schools began in earnest during this same time period, providing a mechanism that preserved racial segregation at the classroom level even where districts and schools became more racially diverse (Givens 2009; Meier, Stewart & England, 1989; Mickelson, 2001; Muller, Riegle-Crumb, Schiller, Wilkinson, & Frank,

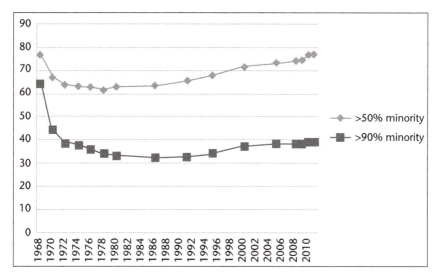

FIGURE 1.1   % Black Students in Majority Minority Schools

Sources: 1968–1980—Orfield, G. (1983). *Public School Desegregation in the United States. 1968–1980*. Washington D.C.: Joint Center of Political Studies, p. 4; 1968–1996—Orfield, G. & Yun, J. T. (1999). *Resegregation in American Schools*. Harvard University: The Harvard Civil Rights Project, p. 14; 1995–2011—National Center for Education Statistics, 2013 tables and figures, Table 216.50, Number and percentage distribution of public elementary and secondary school students, by percentage of minority enrollment in school and student's racial/ethnic group: selected years, fall 1995 through fall 2011.

2010; Rosenbaum, Miller, & Krei, 1996; Welner & Oakes, 1996). Considered together, these facts all point to an inevitable conclusion: although the modest levels of racial desegregation achieved in public schools were materially and culturally important, we have never gotten near full racial desegregation of educational opportunity in this nation.

Against the backdrop of this anemic national effort to achieve equal racial access to educational opportunity, the contemporary backlash against school desegregation looks all the more disturbing. Figures 1.1 and 1.2 illustrate that social forces motivating increased racial segregation in public K-12 schools have never been eradicated and overcame legal defenses against such segregation in the 1980s. Since that time, the limited progress made in creating "a unitary system in which racial discrimination would be eliminated root and branch" has been significantly reversed.[5]

This reversal hasn't been a slow reversion to some natural ethnocentric equilibrium. As with the movement to desegregate schools, the pattern of resegregation has also been an intentional and organized movement. And it has met with organized resistance by parents and students, as with the protests

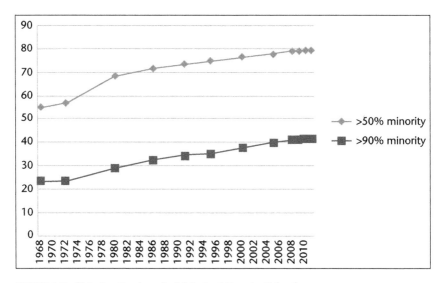

FIGURE 1.2 % Latino Students in Majority Minority Schools

Sources: 1968–1980—Orfield, G. (1983). *Public School Desegregation in the United States. 1968–1980*. Washington D.C.: Joint Center of Political Studies, p. 4; 1968–1996—Orfield, G. & Yun, J. T. (1999). *Resegregation in American Schools*. Harvard University: The Harvard Civil Rights Project, p. 14; 1995–2011—National Center for Education Statistics, 2013 tables and figures, Table 216.50, Number and percentage distribution of public elementary and secondary school students, by percentage of minority enrollment in school and student's racial/ethnic group: selected years, fall 1995 through fall 2011.

recounted at the beginning of this chapter. The resegregation of public schools in the United States has been a process of imposition of the designs of one set of constituencies on other constituencies against their will.

Activists seeking at least partial resegregation of our public schools have employed a carefully crafted court-based strategy in efforts to dismantle the legal infrastructure that supported school desegregation (e.g. San Antonio Independent School District, 1973; Milliken, 1974; Regents of the University of California, 1978; Riddick, 1986; Board of Education of Oklahoma City, 1991; Missouri, 1995; Hopwood, 2000; Parents Involved in Community Schools, 2007). Test cases were chosen carefully. Advocacy for lifting desegregation orders was often framed in the abstract rhetoric of returning governance of schools to local control, but it is almost always followed by school district policy decisions that lead to greater racial segregation in the district (Reardon, Grewal, Kalogrides, & Greenberg, 2012, p. 899). The petitions to lift desegregation orders were not an end in themselves. They were means to another end—increased racial segregation in state-funded schools.

One of the key achievements of this resegregation movement was the 1992 Supreme Court decision in the case of *Freeman v. Pitts*. The *Freeman* decision redefined the standards set in *Green v. County Board of Education* that specified when a district could claim to have achieved "unitary status" and thus have its desegregation order lifted and be returned to local control. Writing for the majority, Justice Anthony Kennedy clarified:

> Although the unitariness concept is helpful in defining the scope of the district court's authority, the term "unitary" does not have a fixed meaning or content, and does not confine the court's discretion in a way that departs from traditional equitable principles. . . . Equitable remedies must be flexible, if these underlying principles are to be enforced with fairness and precision.
>
> *(503 U.S. 467 1992, p. 487)*

Applying this principle of flexibility, the court ruled that "the *Green Factors* need not be a rigid framework" (503 U.S. 467 1992, p. 487). Specifically, the ruling lowered the central *Green* standard from one of eliminating all racially identifiable schools, to demonstrating that racial segregation is not being enforced by school policies and practices.

> Racial balance is not to be achieved for its own sake, but is to be pursued only when there is a causal link between an imbalance and the constitutional violation. Once racial imbalance traceable to the constitutional violation has been remedied, a school district is under no duty to remedy an imbalance that is caused by demographic factors.
>
> *(503 U.S. 467 1992, p. 469)*

This much narrower interpretation of what is required to show a district is desegregated essentially took the teeth out of the *Green* decision. The implication in practice was that school districts could retain or even return to school attendance patterns where there were racially identifiable schools as long as they could reasonably attribute the racial segregation to neighborhood housing patterns not directly created by the district. In the two decades following this ruling, over half of the school districts under court order to desegregate have successfully petitioned to be released from judicial oversight. The result has been a steady trend towards greater racial segregation in schools. A 2012 study by the Stanford Center for Policy Analysis looked at all of these districts and concludes that the effects of federal desegregation orders:

> fade over time, at least in the South, where most of the districts under court order are located. Following the release from court order, white/ black desegregation levels begin to rise within a few years of release and continue to grow steadily for at least 10 years.
>
> *(Reardon, Grewal, Kalogrides, & Greenberg, 2012, p. 899)*

[handwritten margin note: this idea of racism evolves over time/place based on]

The Civil Rights Project at UCLA, directed by Dr. Gary Orfield, has produced hundreds of reports documenting this racial resegregation of schools in the United States over the last twenty years. In a recent report entitled "E Pluribus . . . Separation" Orfield and his colleagues show how contemporary segregation is a double segregation based on both income levels and race. They conclude:

> The time has come to stop celebrating the *Brown* decision and the civil rights movement as if the dream of equal opportunity had been realized. Words on paper are very important, but opponents of the civil rights revolution mobilized against the implementation of those rights, and took over the machinery that interprets and enforces rights. Increasing segregation is a clear sign that we are, in fact, going backwards.
>
> *(Orfield, Kucsera, & Siegel-Hawley, 2012, p. 84)*

Other studies have yielded similar results (e.g. An & Gamoran, 2009; Caldas & Bankston, 2005; Lipman, 2004; Lutz, 2011; Ryan, 2010). An unsentimental review of this recent history leads to an inevitable conclusion: our public schools are being racially resegregated.

A Microcosm of School Segregation History in Riverton

Riverton is a living microcosm of this national history of struggle over racial segregation of public schools. Riverton public schools were initially placed under a federal desegregation order in 1970. This was followed by several years of delay and minimal implementation during which the school district was taken to court again multiple times. It was not until 1979 that a restructuring plan was implemented that guaranteed the high schools would not be racially identifiable. All students of the same grade level were placed in the same school building. This required that the all-Black Oakstreet High School and the all-white Union High School be merged. Because of space constraints, the high school students were distributed across the two buildings with ninth and tenth graders located in the former Oakstreet High building and eleventh and twelfth graders located in the former Union High building. The new unified high school retained the name "Union High."[6] This plan was considered a model of effective racial integration and was adopted in other similar sized districts facing similar orders.

After significant white flight immediately following the restructuring of the schools, the new integrated Union High settled into a roughly fifty/fifty racial demographic. Union High, partially due to its large size, soon boasted many top ranked athletic teams and extracurricular teams in the state. This winning tradition helped build community support for the school. Eventually, the integrated high school became the new normal and a source of local pride.

Comfort with the new arrangement was never, however, total. Over the next twenty years enrollments at local private schools increased and the percentage of white students gradually declined at Union High. By 1991 Union High was 60% Black and 40% white. The district established advanced academic curricular options, including Advanced Placement courses and an International Baccalaureate program, in an effort to lure students back from local private schools. Although some parents reported this as being a strong motivation for keeping their children at Union High, the trend was never reversed. The steady movement of white students to private schools combined with changes in city population shifted the Union High School demographic. By 1999, enrollment was approaching 70% Black and 30% European-American students.

Eventually, members of suburbs north of the city center where property values were highest began to talk about forming their own separate school district, one in which the proportion of white students would be higher. Disincorporation, however, was a lengthy and expensive process and not guaranteed of success. Restructuring the district schools internally was discussed as an alternative means of accomplishing similar demographic ends with less legal and political barriers. Only the federal desegregation order stood in the way.

In the late 1990s, Riverton city council and school district officials began assembling the case to have the desegregation order on the district lifted. In 1999, citing the *Freeman v. Pitts* decision, the district successfully petitioned to have its desegregation order lifted. It took a little over a year for the specific terms of that decision to be formally worked out. Within a week of this finalization, the school board had a fully developed plan to restructure the district schools on its agenda for discussion.

There was a brief period of public debate about whether the district should retain the existing "mega-school" arrangement (one large high school of approximately 2,300 students) or build three smaller "neighborhood schools"[7] (each anticipating enrollments of approximately 800–900 students).[8] Two polls conducted by the local newspaper and an internal district poll revealed that citizens, students, and teachers preferred to retain the mega-school plan. Proponents of restructuring the schools, however, had been organized far longer and their views were more represented on the school board and city council. In public meetings and in public media, these proponents cited multiple potential benefits, including: attending schools closer to their homes, the pedagogical advantages of smaller schools, and reducing white flight from district schools. Supporters of the mega-school arrangement, on the other hand, generally identified with the unified high school and took some pride in the history of successful desegregation it represented. As one Riverton parent explained:

P1UBF: Why fix something that isn't broken? Yes, the court's order has been lifted. But it was the right thing, we all know that. And it gave us a school with a winning tradition. Why break up that winning tradition? . . . and building three schools will be expensive. Very. I just don't see the benefit.

This public debate focused primarily on the relative benefits of school size and school location. It was not until after the restructuring plan was finalized, funds were encumbered, land acquired, and construction was underway that the official new zoning patterns were announced. At that point it became apparent that the new zoning would not create high schools significantly closer to homes. Nor would it create schools with enrollments of 400 or less, generally the size thought necessary to gain the benefits often claimed by proponents of small schools (Bearman & Ahmed, 2012; Bronson, 2013; Cotton, 1996; Fine, 2005; Klonsky & Klonsky, 2008; Meier, 2005; Wasley & Lear, 2001).[9]

It was only when construction was near completion, in the final month of attendance at the unified high school, that the public became generally aware that one of the Riverton schools would be 100% Black in its demography. This news was met with relatively widespread criticism and objection. As one teacher put it:

E1GWF: It's shameful! It's shameful. I don't see how . . . how they think this is ok. Do they think no one will notice? What are we supposed to tell the students?

The sense of scandal was intensified when the district expended all of its funds building the North-Side and East-Side schools, and had to delay the construction of a new school for the western feeder zone, the school at which the enrollment would be 100% Black. In the interim, in a symbolically provocative policy decision, those students were assigned to an older building that was previously the site of the all-Black high school in the pre-civil rights era. Many citizens were caught off-guard by the extremity of these developments. As one parent put it:

P2GWF: What are they [the school board] thinking? Don't they know that was the old segregated high school they are putting Union students in? They have to know, don't they? . . . It's just so brazen. It's awful. They're not even trying to hide what they are doing. It makes you feel [pause] angry, and just [pause] I don't know. Nobody I talk to wants this.

These revelations precipitated objection, public expressions of disappointment, and some organizing, but this would be too little and too late. Mirroring the national pattern, the racial resegregation of public schools in Riverton was already being institutionalized before the public had a chance to debate the implications of this tectonic policy shift.

With two new schools already under construction and the restructuring of the school district already a fait accompli, some organizers turned their focus to the one remaining policy decision that had yet to be resolved—the location of the West-Side high school. The student walkout described at the beginning of this chapter occurred at this political moment. The protests about this issue, however, were divisive. Many believed the location of the school was a distraction. As one Black parent opposed to the restructuring put it:

P3NBM: You don't resort to protest as an initial means of political action. That's the work of a few irresponsible adults manipulating children. Protesting in the street is something to undertake when citizens have been disenfranchised of the ability to participate in democratic processes of governance. No one has been disenfranchised here. We still have the vote. We need to organize and use our right to vote that a previous generation secured for us through protest. Not mindlessly imitate those protests as a means of personal self-promotion.

Others believed that objections to an all-Black school were based on assumptions that amounted to a form of racism, evincing a lack of confidence in the ability of the Black citizens and students on the western side of town to establish a highly functioning school. These advocates argued that West-Side communities were capable of positive self-determination and might even be better off left to their own resources.[10]

P4UBF: We often talk about what was gained after the *Brown* decision. But we don't talk about what—what was lost. Students and teachers had a different kind of relationship in those all-Black schools. Teachers had a different relationship with the community. They were often involved in the churches. People talk about the community they had in the school, even though the building was not up to par, or the supplies. Now we find our children in a school system that lacks that community. People often feel there is a lack of respect for Black parents and Black intelligence. The old Oakstreet High School produced several generations of lawyers, doctors, and community leaders. . . . We lost something when we lost that school. We—some of us—lost belief in ourselves. We—we need to get that back.

A student assigned to the new all-Black Union High School echoed this sentiment.

S1UBF: They just left us over here. Nobody is going to do anything for the West Side unless we do it for ourselves.

Parents of Union High students were the first to actively oppose the resegregation of the district, even if that opposition was often divided on strategy and priorities. Opposition to the resegregation of the schools was not, however, limited to the West-Side feeder zone. Parents from other school zones, including large numbers of white citizens, began meeting to discuss possibilities for action. The Riverton Education Network (REN) formed to bring together concerned citizens across all three school zones to advocate for equality and racial integration in the schools. These groups have had some success forwarding school board candidates, but have yet to achieve a majority capable of reversing the restructuring of the school system.

For citizens on the western side of Riverton, the era of racial desegregation lasted just over twenty years. Barely one generation of students experienced a fully integrated school building. They never experienced full desegregation at the classroom level. A similar pattern has played out across the United States. The racial desegregation of our public schools was never fully achieved. And now, a great deal of what was achieved during the civil rights era is being reversed. Our schools are being deliberately resegregated. Much of this is happening below the radar of broad public debate. It remains to be seen if broad public awareness about this trend can be raised, and if it can, whether that awareness will inspire political and institutional response. As one teacher put it:

E2GWF: When you read the histories of the civil rights era, you look back and think, what would I have done had I been there? Would I have stood up for justice? Would I have been silent? Would I have defended segregation? And now here it is. We don't have to wonder anymore.

The Riverton Study

So what are we doing as a nation in the face of overwhelming evidence that the tide has turned on racial equality in public schools? The answer, unfortunately, is not much.

> A major irony is that we have been abandoning desegregation efforts as the evidence for its value becomes more and more powerful. We have more than a half-century of research about the impacts of diverse schooling and the ways to make integration most successful. Although we decided as a country to desegregate our schools with very little information, we are abandoning the effort now that we have a great deal of knowledge about its benefits.
>
> *(Orfield, Kucsera, & Siegel-Hawley, 2012, p. 6.)*[11]

This trend seems all the more ironic given that we are currently in an era in which public policy makers seem exclusively concerned with the necessity of making large data-based policy decisions. Despite the overwhelming amount of large database studies that show racial segregation is increasing, that it is harmful, and that racial integration of schools has measurable positive effects on things like drop-out rates, academic performance, and lifetime income, politicians and the general public have been unable or unwilling to recommit to desegregating public schools (Orfield, Kucsera, & Siegel-Hawley, 2012). Clearly, data and measurable evidence are not the primary things driving school policy on racial segregation in schools.

It is worth recalling, perhaps, that it was not large database studies that underwrote the *Brown v. Board of Education* decision in 1954. Instead it was Kenneth and Mamie Clark's (1950) doll studies that ultimately persuaded the Supreme Court that de jure racial segregation in schools needed to come to an end.[12] Those studies, based on a mere fourteen brief interviews with young Black children, methodologically amounted to what would now be considered clinical anecdotes. However, it was the humanly and morally compelling way those interviews illustrated the corrosive effects of institutional racism on the inner lives of children that gave the study its persuasive force (Markowitz & Rosner, 1999).

What is missing in large part from the contemporary literature and debate about racial segregation in schools are close-in studies of the effects of this process of resegregation on students. Charts depicting declining test scores can be important rhetorical devices in policy debates. However, such charts do not tell the whole story of the effects of racial segregation on our communities and children. Less easily measurable educational outcomes like the meaning and moral lessons children take from their schooling are often overlooked or, worse, are considered insignificant.

The study of the Riverton school restructuring presented in this book seeks to fill this gap in the literature by documenting the way students make sense of a racial segregation of their schools. Conducted over the span of ten years, this research consisted of interviews with over 200 individuals and groups, attending hundreds of hours of public meetings, analyzing hundreds of policy documents and public media reports. In the remaining chapters of this book we examine this social text of the restructuring of Riverton's schools—the narratives and common understandings of its significance circulated in the community. Then we examine how students interpreted this social text, what messages they took from it, what they learned from it.

We found that students recognized the political and moral significance of what was happening. They experienced it at multiple levels. They had to endure—and continue to endure—its material effects, such as differential allocations of resources, less advanced curriculum, poorer facilities. They also have to endure the psychological effects of resegregation, including feelings of isolation, an eroded sense of faith that adults have their best interests in mind, and an eroded sense of social hope. In other words, the resegregation of Riverton schools was a form of curriculum. It constituted something we as adults were teaching our children.

Curriculum is of course a broad concept, generally referring to *what* is being taught, and is often offered in contrast to the concept of pedagogy, which refers to *how* things are taught. Curriculum has been theorized in many ways. In public discourse it is often used to refer to a mandated curriculum—the curricular content that is mandated by the state, a school board, or some other official governing body. Scholars have contrasted this to the *planned curriculum* (Porter, 2006), which refers to what teachers intend to teach students, and to the *enacted curriculum* (Snyder, Bolin, & Zumwalt, 1992), which refers to what is actually taught in classrooms. Scholars have also written about the *lived curriculum* (Aoki, Pinar, & Irwin 2005), which refers even more broadly to learning that takes place in the many unexpected ways education unfolds in schools. Most salient for this study is the concept of the *hidden curriculum*, which refers to the implicit lessons taught by the organization and symbolic content of school life. Many unspoken assumptions underlie the activities of schooling, such as what knowledge is valuable, whose knowledge is valuable, the need for conformity, punctuality, and deference to authority. Implicit messages about gender, race, and class identity, as well as conceptions of our individual and collective futures, are also often a part of a school's hidden curriculum.

This book can be most succinctly described as a study of the hidden curriculum of racial resegregation in public schools. As such it takes its place in a long tradition of scholarship on the hidden curriculum of schools going as far back as the work of Emile Durkheim (2002) and John Dewey (1997), and continuing into the more recent work of scholars like Michael Apple (1990), Jean Anyon (1979), Paul Willis (1981), Lee Ehman (1980), Phillip Jackson (1990), Henry Giroux (2001), and Noah De Lissovoy (2012). Schools are becoming increasingly racially segregated in the United States. This book examines what segregation meant to students in a single school district, what it taught them about themselves, their community, and the possibility of social hope. To the extent similar dynamics are unfolding in other districts across the country, we intend for this study to raise concerns about the effects of resegregation at those other locales as well.

Notes

1 All personal, place, and school names are pseudonyms.
2 The decision in *Milliken v. Bradley* determined that racial segregation was allowed if it was not considered an explicit policy of the school district.
3 The decision in *San Antonio Independent School District v. Rodriguez* rejected the idea that disparities in per pupil school funding were unconstitutional. This decision was premised on the court's determination that the plaintiff had not sufficiently proven that education was a fundamental right.
4 This is well beyond the national population distribution which in 2012 was 77.9% white and 63.0% white non-Hispanic according to the United States Census Bureau (http://quickfacts.census.gov/qfd/states/00000.html, retrieved November 1, 2013).
5 There is some evidence that the trend towards resegregation is tapering off. And it seems unlikely that the U.S. will ever return to 100% de jure racial segregation in its public schools (Reardon, Grewal, Kalogrides, & Greenberg, 2012). This, however, is cold comfort considering that currently 73% of students of color attend schools

where students of color are significantly over-represented, and over 36% of students of color attend schools that are almost entirely racially segregated.

6 Shortly thereafter, subsequent court decisions extended this desegregation approach to the middle schools, placing all students from the same grade into a single building. It was never fully extended to the elementary schools.

7 For accounts of how the rhetoric of "neighborhood schools" have consistently been used as a cover for racially segregating schools since the 1970s, see: Lowe, 2000; Kaestle, 1983; and Orfield & Eaton, 1996.

8 The restructuring was expected to draw some private school students back into the public school system.

9 The average size of the new schools would be approximately 900 students.

10 For a broader history of the politics and rhetoric of Black self-determination and nationalist movements see: Anderson, 1988; Franklin, 1992; Shabazz, 2004; Gordon, 2006; Manela, 2009; and Reid-Merritt, 2010.

11 Although the measurable benefits of desegregation are well documented, it is important to note here that there is also a significant body of scholarship that highlights the negative consequences of desegregation for Black students and communities. See, for example: Bell, 1980, 1983; Fultz, 2004; Haney, 1978; Hudson & Holmes, 1994; Ladson-Billings, 2004; Patterson, 2002; Siddle-Walker, 1996. The documentation of these negative consequences does not constitute a refutation of the positive outcomes of desegregation, so much as it counsels against an uncritical celebration of civil rights era desegregation jurisprudence and calls for more creative and culturally ambitious responses to racially stratified educational opportunity in the future.

12 In their study, the Clarks (1950) presented young Black children with two dolls, one white and one Black, and asked them a series of questions such as: Which doll would you prefer to play with? Which doll is the good baby? Which doll is more like you? The majority of the children preferred to play with the white doll, considered the white doll to be the "good" one, and several even identified with the white doll. These results were cited as evidence that even young children internalized negative effects from living in a segregated and racist society.

Bibliography

An, B. P., & Gamoran, A. (2009). Trends in school racial composition in the era of unitary status. In C. E. Smrekar & E. B. Goldring (Eds.), *From the courtroom to the classroom: the shifting landscape of school desegregation* (pp. 19–48). Cambridge, MA: Harvard Education Press.

Anderson, J. D. (1988). *The education of Blacks in the South, 1860–1935*. Raleigh, NC: The University of North Carolina Press.

Anyon, J. (1979). Ideology and United States history textbooks. *Harvard Educational Review, 49*(3), 361–386.

Aoki, T., Pinar, W., & Irwin, R. (Eds.). (2005). *Curriculum in a new key: the collected works of Ted T. Aoki.* Mahwah, NJ: L. Erlbaum Associates.

Apple, M. W. (1990). *Ideology and curriculum* (2nd ed.). New York: Routledge.

Bearman, L., & Ahmed, N. (2012). Learning from our students: recovering the purpose of small schools in an era beholden to standardization. In M. Hantzopoulos & A. R. Tyner (Eds.), *Critical small schools: beyond privatization in New York City urban educational reform* (pp. 103–119). Charlotte, NC: Information Age.

Bell, D. (1980). Brown and the interest-convergence dilemma. In D. Bell (Ed.), *Shades of Brown: new perspectives on school desegregation* (pp. 90–106). New York: Teachers College Press.

Bell, D. (1983). Time for the teachers: putting educators back into the Brown remedy. *The Journal of Negro Education, 52*(3), 290–301.

Board of Education of Oklahoma City v. Dowell, No. 498 U.S. 237 (1991).

Bronson, C. E. (2013). Small school reform: the challenges faced by one urban high school. *SAGE Open, 3*(2). http://doi.org/10.1177/2158244013486789

Brown v. Board of Education, No. 347 U.S. 483 (1954).

Brown v. Board of Education, No. 349 U.S. 294 (1955).

Caldas, S. J., & Bankston, C. L. (2005). *Forced to fail: the paradox of school desegregation.* Westport, CT: Praeger.

Card, D., Mas, A., & Rothstein, J. (2008). Tipping and the dynamics of segregation. *Quarterly Journal of Economics, 123*(1), 177–218.

Clark, K. B., & Clark, M. P. (1950). Emotional factors in racial identification and preferences in Negro children. *The Journal of Negro Children, 19*(3), 341–350.

Cotton, K. (1996). *School size, school climate, and student performance* (Close-up No. 20). Portland, OR: Northwest Regional Educational Laboratory.

De Lissovoy, N. (2012). Education and violation: conceptualizing power, domination, and agency in the hidden curriculum. *Race Ethnicity and Education, 15*(4), 463–484.

Dewey, J. (1997). *Democracy and education: an introduction to the philosophy of education.* New York: Free Press.

Dumas, M., & Anderson, G. L. (2014). Qualitative research as policy knowledge: framing policy problems and transforming education from the ground up. *Educational Policy Analysis Archives, 22*(11).

Durkheim, E. (2002). *Moral education.* Mineola, NY: Dover Publications.

Ehman, L. H. (1980). The American school in the political socialization process. *Review of Educational Research, 50*(1), 99–119.

Fine, M. (2005). Not in our name: reclaiming the democratic vision of small school reform. *Rethinking Schools, 19*(4), 11–14.

Franklin, V. P. (1992). *Black self-determination: a cultural history of African-American resistance.* Brooklyn, NY: Lawrence Hill Books.

Freeman v. Pitts, No. 503 U.S. 467 (1992).

Fultz, M. (2004). The displacement of Black educators post-Brown: an overview and analysis. *History of Education Quarterly, 44*(1), 11–45.

Giroux, H. A. (2001). *Theory and resistance in education: towards a pedagogy for the opposition* (Rev. and expanded ed.). Westport, CT: Bergin & Garvey.

Givens, M. (2009). *The evolution of a profession* (Dissertation). University of Alabama, Tuscaloosa, Alabama.

Gordon, D. (2006). *Black identity: rhetoric, ideology, and nineteenth-century black nationalism.* Carbondale: Southern Illinois University Press.

Green v. County School Board, No. 391 U.S. 430 (1968).

Haney, J. (1978). The effects of the Brown decision on Black educators. *The Journal of Negro Education, 47*, 88–95.

Hopwood v. Texas, No. 236 F.3d 256 (2000).

Hudson, M., & Holmes, B. (1994). Missing teachers, impaired communities: the unanticipated consequences of Brown v. Board of Education on the African American teaching force at the precollegiate level. *The Journal of Negro Education, 63*(3), 388–393.

Jackson, P. W. (1990). *Life in classrooms.* New York: Teachers College Press.

Kaestle, C. F. (1983). *Pillars of the Republic: common schools and American society, 1780–1860.* New York: Hill and Wang.

Keyes v. School District No. 1, No. 431 U.S. 189 (1973).

Klonsky, M., & Klonsky, S. (2008). *Small schools: public school reform meets the ownership society.* New York: Routledge.

Ladson-Billings, G. (2004). Landing on the wrong note: the price we paid for Brown. *Educational Researcher,* 3–13.

Lipman, P. (2004). *High stakes education: inequality, globalization, and urban school reform.* New York: Routledge Falmer.

Lowe, R. (2000). Neighborhood schools: déjà vu. *Rethinking Schools, 14,*(3). Retrieved August 29, 2015 from http://www.rethinkingschools.org/archive/14_03/deja143.shtml

Lutz, B. F. (2011). The end of court-ordered desegregation. *American Economic Journal: Economic Policy, 3*(2), 130–168.

Manela, E. (2009). *The Wilsonian moment: self-determination and the international origins of anticolonial nationalism.* New York: Oxford University Press.

Markowitz, G., & Rosner, D. (1999). *Children, race, and power: Kenneth and Mamie Clark's Northside Center.* New York: Routeledge.

Meier, D. (2005). Creating democratic schools. *Rethinking Schools, 19*(4), 28–29.

Meier, K. J., Stewart, J., & England, R. E. (1989). *Race, class, and education: the politics of second-generation discrimination.* Madison, WI: University of Wisconsin Press.

Mickelson, R. A. (2001). Subverting Swann: first- and second-generation segregation in the Charlotte-Mecklenburg schools. *American Educational Research Journal, 38*(2), 215–252.

Milliken v. Bradley, No. 418 U.S. 717 (1974).

Missouri v. Jenkins, No. 515 U.S. 70 (1995).

Muller, C., Riegle-Crumb, C., Schiller, K. S., Wilkinson, L., & Frank, K. A. (2010). Race and academic achievement in racially diverse high schools: opportunity and stratification. *Teachers College Record (1970), 112*(4), 1038–1063.

National Center for Education Statistics. (n.d.). *National Center for Education Statistics, 2013 tables and figures, Table 216.50, Number and percentage distribution of public elementary and secondary school students, by percentage of minority enrollment in school and student's racial/ethnic group.*

Orfield, G. (1983). *Public school desegregation in the United States. 1968–1980.* Washington, DC: Joint Center of Political Studies.

Orfield, G., & Eaton, S. E. (1996). *Dismantling desegregation: the quiet reversal of Brown v. Board of Education.* New York: The New Press.

Orfield, G., Kim, J., & Sunderman, G. (2006). *NCLB meets realities: lessons from the field.* Thousand Oaks, CA: Corwin Press.

Orfield, G., Kucsera, J., & Siegel-Hawley, G. (2012). *E Pluribus . . . separation: deepening double segregation for more students.* UCLA: The Civil Rights Project.

Orfield, G., & Yun, J. T. (1999). *Resegregation in American schools.* Harvard University: The Harvard Civil Rights Project.

Parents Involved in Community Schools v. Seattle Public Schools, No. 551 U.S. 701 (2007).

Patterson, J. T. (2002). *Brown v. Board of Education: a civil rights milestone and its troubled legacy.* Oxford: Oxford University Press.

Porter, A. C. (2006). Curriculum assessment. In J. L. Green, G. Camilli, & P. B. Elmore (Eds.), *Handbook of complementary methods for research in education* (3rd ed.). Washington, DC: American Educational Research Association.

Reardon, S. F., Grewal, E. T., Kalogrides, D., & Greenberg, E. (2012). *Brown* fades: the end of court ordered school desegregation and the resegregation of American public schools. *Journal of Policy Analysis and Management, 31*(4), 876–904.

Reardon, S. F., & Yun, J. T. (2003). Integrating neighborhoods, segregating schools: the retreat from school desegregation in the South, 1990–2000. *North Carolina Law Review, 81*(4), 1563–1596.

Regents of the University of California v. Bakke, No. 438 U.S. 265 (1978).

Reid-Merritt, P. (2010). *Righteous self determination: the Black Social Work Movement in America.* Baltimore: Inprint Editions-Black Classic Press.

Riddick v. School Board of the City of Norfolk, Virginia, No. 784 F.2d 521. (1986).

Rosenbaum, J. E., Miller, S. R., & Krei, M. S. (1996). Gatekeeping in an era of more open gates: high school counselors' views of their influence on students' college plans. *American Journal of Education, 104*(4), 257–279.

Ryan, J. (2010). *Five miles away and a world apart.* New York: Oxford University Press.

San Antonio Independent School District v. Rodriguez, No. 411 U.S. 1 (1973).

Shabazz, A. (2004). *Advancing democracy: African Americans and the struggle for access and equality in higher education in Texas.* Chapel Hill: University of North Carolina Press.

Siddle-Walker, V. (1996). *Their highest potential: an African American school community in the segregated South.* Chapel Hill, NC: University of North Carolina Press.

Snyder, J., Bolin, F. & Zumwalt, K. (1992) Curriculum implementation. In P. Jackson (Ed.), *Handbook of research on curriculum* (pp. 402–435). New York: Macmillan.

Wasley, P. A., & Lear, R. J. (2001). Small schools, real gains. *Educational Leadership, 58*(6), 22–27.

Welner, K. G., & Oakes, J. (1996). (Li)Ability grouping: the new susceptibility of school tracking systems to legal challenges. *Harvard Educational Review, 66*(3), 451–471.

Willis, P. E. (1981). *Learning to labor: how working class kids get working class jobs* (Morningside ed.). New York: Columbia University Press.

2
FORTY ACRES AND A SCHOOL
Community Discourse About Resegregation

In order to understand how students interpreted the resegregation of Riverton public schools, it is necessary to appreciate the variety of ways the new schooling arrangement came to their attention. Students, of course, noticed the demography of their new schools once they were in them. Their understanding of that demography, however, was being shaped well before ground was broken on the new school buildings. From the early stages of the petition to have the desegregation order lifted, through the quiet restructuring of the middle schools, to the more controversial splitting up of the high school, Riverton citizens formally and informally discussed the motivations and likely consequences of these emerging policies. All of these conversations and public debates provided a social text that students read, discussed, and to varying degrees, internalized.

From 2000–2007, the time period in which the restructuring took place, articles and editorials about the future of Riverton schools appeared nearly every week in the local newspaper. When events drew attention to the restructuring process, such coverage occurred daily. Although the topics being discussed varied—such as the outcomes of student and parent surveys, the location of school zones, the demography of the schools, funding for the new school buildings, etc.—a few themes related to the quality and status of the three new high schools were consistently present. These included:

- Anxiety about the public schools becoming predominantly Black.
- An assumption that the new Union High School would be a less desirable place to work and attend.
- A concern that students at the new all-Black Union High School would be forgotten and neglected.

- Anticipation that students at the new Union High School would be lower performing.[1]

In short, the new Union High School, with its all-Black feeder schools, was marked repeatedly in the public discourse as a lesser school. Students who would attend that school were marked as lesser students—less capable academically, less likely to succeed, less safe to be around.

To illustrate the way these themes saturated the public discourse about the restructuring of Riverton schools, this chapter examines four key moments in the restructuring process. First, we look at the original discussions about the need for restructuring the district. These discussions were driven by concerns about white flight and the prospect of Riverton public schools becoming predominantly non-white. Second, we examine the public debate about the location of the new building for the West-Side high school. This debate surfaced a variety of parental anxieties, most notably the risk that geographic isolation would intensify the racial and social isolation of Union High students. Third, we examine teachers' expressions of preference regarding the school to which they would be assigned. These preferences revealed a variety of faculty anxieties about the relative status, safety, and working conditions at the three schools. Fourth, due to certain legal and bureaucratic restraints, the new Union High retained the charter for the district's only International Baccalaureate (IB) program.[2] The effort by some parents and administrators to have the program moved to one of the other schools surfaced racially coded anxieties about the safety and quality of the West-Side school in comparison to the other two schools.

The Rhetoric of Restructuring

The 1992 Supreme Court *Freeman v. Pitts* decision and some subsequent lower court decisions made it easier for school districts to have their desegregation orders lifted. In 1993 the Riverton school board tested the new legal waters by requesting permission to create a new elementary school in an overwhelmingly white part of town. When this request was granted in 1995, it took it as a sign that the courts were ready for a petition to release Riverton from federal oversight. In 1996 it began the process of applying for unitary status.

Initially, advocates for ending federal oversight worked primarily through private channels. Such advocacy, however, cannot be kept indefinitely from public view. The elementary school test case had drawn objections to it as a move towards de facto segregation. Anticipating intensified opposition to having the district-wide desegregation order lifted, predominantly white community leaders sought support for the petition from community leaders serving the predominantly African-American West Side. The concern of these white community leaders, it was later reported, was that Riverton public schools were becoming increasingly Black, and that eventually this would reach a tipping point where white families would move en masse to private schools, as had happened in other regions of the state. This in turn, they feared, would create an all-Black public school system and become a deterrent to attracting businesses to the town, depress property values, and ultimately undermine the tax base for all community services including schools. This was happening at a moment when local leaders were trying to persuade a large multinational manufacturing company to build a plant nearby.[3] Recognizing that opposition to having the desegregation order lifted was most likely to be organized and expressed by African-American community members, the white business leaders sought to persuade them that the current school demographic trajectory was not good for anyone in the town. They offered promises of infrastructure investment for the West Side of town in exchange for their support for the emerging restructuring plan.

African-American community leaders knew that there was a pattern of judges granting such petitions to have desegregation orders lifted. The U.S. Justice Department had long since ceased its active support of desegregation. Counsel for the NAACP Legal Defense Fund observed that "There seemed almost a fatigue with the cases . . . and a desire to get them finished." As one local lawyer publicly commented:

> Today the federal court seems more intent on returning local control than on ensuring educationally effective schools for the people who for far too long were discriminated against on the basis of race.

Sensing the inevitability of the end of the desegregation order, several prominent civil rights activists from the region, including a state senator and a federal judge, agreed to testify in favor of granting Riverton school district unitary status. They reported later that they did so in the hope that they could use the need for their support as leverage for securing state of the art educational facilities and other investments on the West Side of town.[4] A local civil rights lawyer who had operated on the national stage proclaimed, "This is the best thing for our community right now."

The support of these civil rights leaders shocked some members of the Riverton community. Rumors spread of backroom deals and pay-offs. It was predominantly West-Side parents who objected initially. A local minister on the West Side of town called out these leaders personally, and a local radio personality began to make the possibility of backroom deals a feature of his daily radio talk show. By 1998, when the federal judge granted Riverton unitary status, more than fifty Riverton citizens travelled over an hour away from town to attend the hearing and strenuously object. One parent was quoted in the papers as saying:

> I cannot understand why we want to settle for this. They have not desegregated the schools. Is George Wallace still standing in the school house doors?

Revealingly, the presiding judge delivered her decision to lift the desegregation order with an accompanying statement of ambivalence. In a comment reported in local and state newspapers, she said to the distressed parents and community members on the day of the decision:

> I grew up in this state in the '60s, in a small town . . . You can't know my views about segregation and how strongly I feel about our state and our history of racial injustice . . . You don't understand why I'm doing this, and you think I'm wrong. But I'm doing what I believe the law requires me to do.

What is important for this study is not whether backroom deals took place, but that at the earliest stages the lifting of the desegregation order was accompanied by a rhetoric of fear—fear that Riverton schools were becoming too Black, fear of the possibility that if a school became all-Black, this would have negative consequences, fear that the reason this was happening was corruption, not rational and fair policy making. The lifting of the desegregation order was narrated as an unfortunate retreat from a commitment to justice that was being forced upon the community—an acquiescence to the power of racist bias.

This was the story students heard in the papers, their churches, living rooms, and from peers from the earliest stages of the restructuring process. For students at Union High, both they and their school were marked as less desirable. Whether students resisted this designation or internalized it, it would become a part of their schooling experience and identity. For all students in the district, the narrative of the erosion of civil rights progress became a part of their schooling experience, contradicting the more optimistic lessons about the civil rights history presented in social studies classes. This was the beginning of the curricular effect of the school restructuring policy that was to come.

The Tipping Point

School and community leaders forwarded many rationales for the resegregation of Riverton public schools. One of the earliest was to cite the benefit of smaller schools. This justification was dropped relatively early when opponents of the restructuring pointed out that small schools research generally defines "small" as less than 400 students (Cotton, 1996; Fine, 2005; Klonsky, 1995; Klonsky & Klonsky, 2008; Meier, 1996; Wasley & Lear, 2001). The restructured high schools in Riverton were to have enrollments no less than 800 students.[5] This argument was briefly supplanted by claims that neighborhood schools were better for students, until the zoning lines were revealed: the new zoning lines had students living across the street from the new Union High attending schools across the river several miles away. Clearly family proximity to schools was not the priority of the restructuring plan.

It was variations on the "tipping point" scenario that adults in the community cited most consistently as a rationale for the restructuring. In 1958 social scientist Morton Grodzins introduced the concept of "racial tipping points" into public planning discourse. He predicted that "once the proportion of non-whites exceeds the limits of the neighborhood's tolerance for interracial living, whites move out" (p. 6). This concept was later used to refer to the proportion of students of color in a school district that will motivate white parents to either move to different school districts or enroll their children in private schools with a higher proportion of white students. The term long ago became a taken-for-granted part of public policy discourse and is circulated without citation.

No single proportion of white to non-white population that constitutes a "tipping point" has been consistently identified. In studies that identify such things, the figure ranges from 5% to 75% non-white population, and depends on the ideology and culture of the area in question, the income profile of a community, and the relative levels of comfort with racial diversity among the white population, among other things (Grodzins, 1958; Schelling, 1971). In Riverton, community leaders, educators, and parents most frequently cited 70% or more Black students as the salient figure. This also happened to be the percentage of non-white students in the high school at the time of the restructuring.

Of course most Riverton citizens were not familiar with the sociological research literature behind the concept of a racial "tipping point." The idea, however, had a common sense appeal. Part of that appeal seemed to lie in its ability to displace distasteful racial motivations for the restructuring onto others. It provided a frame in which people could maintain a principled opposition to increased racial segregation, and yet endorse the restructuring as a necessary evil. Several variations of the rationale circulated in the community. Some versions attributed the initial white flight from the Riverton public schools to the attitudes of more racist white parents in town. Their exodus in turn created conditions where remaining white parents had little choice but to find less racially isolating options for their children. Others focused on the increasing proportion of both Black *and* low-income students in the schools as a reason some families were choosing other schooling options. Still others cited the secondary consequences of these declining enrollments—such as fewer advanced courses and fewer extracurricular options—as the cause for the dynamic. Across these various justifications, the underlying story was consistent: as the population of students considered undesirable reached a certain threshold, more affluent and high-achieving students were leaving the Riverton public schools. A parent advocate for restructuring explained:

P5NWM: Of course schools should be integrated. Diversity is important. I would not put my children in an all-white school. I don't think anybody wants that. But I also don't want to put them in a school where there are only a few white students. That is what we are facing. As more white and affluent parents take their children out [of Union High], more parents *want* to take their kids out. Not just for racial reasons. The school funding also decreases as enrollment goes down, and there are less advanced courses. Lower academic standards as higher achieving students leave. Pretty soon everyone who can afford to leave will.

A more detailed version of the tipping point rationale was frequently offered by those working in the school system or who were involved with board and district politics. This version focused on the possibility that the more affluent neighborhoods north of the river would break away from the district, take their high-end tax base with them, and create their own school system. This scenario had played out in nearby larger cities, and the result was that the tax base of the remaining school district was drastically reduced, which in turn caused severe fiscal problems and reduction in services for the remaining urban school district. A Union High School teacher cited this as the reason he eventually became a supporter of the restructuring.

E3UWM: It's not a white-Black issue, very much it's a financial issue . . . I think the number one goal of the Board of Education, although they've never said this, was to stem the flow of students from the system. To keep those north of the river from forming their own schools and losing the tax base for Riverton and quickly becoming what Pine City schools has become, what Kingston city schools and some other inner cities have become—all minority schools. A lot of the people complain about the fact that Union's virtually all African-American. They don't seem to want to consider the fact that the entire system—from elementary to high school—perhaps would have been all African-American here five or ten years down the road. That—so that's one reason I changed my mind about being supportive of the restructuring process.

Economic motives were often included as part of the tipping point narrative of the restructuring. Respondents frequently mentioned the need to attract business investment and skilled professionals to the Riverton community for the sake of economic development. However, these comments assumed that the attractiveness of the school district depended on the racial demographics of the school. In this way apologists for the restructuring plan projected responsibility for the resegregation of the district onto the prejudices of imagined investors and migrating professionals. As one teacher who was opposed to the restructuring explained:

E4UWF: I think the city school system—which had been good—was losing white population. And I think that in order to attract people to the system, in order to attract people to the city, for industry, for college, for university professorships, whatever—I think that the city sent the . . . the city . . .

councilmen, the city chamber and all decided that . . . we needed to do something to pull white kids back into the school system. Because the county was filling up with our . . . white children.[6] And so I really . . . I think it was probably racially motivated, but that's what you call racial motivation.

This racial motivation was confirmed when the district created a 100% Black high school where there had not been one before. The district did not create a school attended by 100% low-income students. It created an all-Black school. And it did so, according to these interpretations, not because this was good for the students in that school, but for the sake of the comfort of *other people* who did not want their children in predominantly Black schools. In fact, the well-being of the students who would be enrolled in the all-Black school was rarely mentioned by anyone in our study, even those opposed to the restructuring plan.

The racial tipping point narratives were not just rumors circulating among parents, teachers, and citizens. They also influenced formal school policy making processes. The Restructuring Committee for Riverton City Schools High School[7] produced a publicly available report for the school board that made the following assertion:

> Members of the Committee—white and Black—have expressed profound concern at having a nearly all-Black high school, and we have diligently sought another realistic multiple school approach. . . . There is no realistic alternative approach to zoning three high schools using existing middle school lines. It would be highly disruptive to have zone lines different from those governing the middle schools. Moreover, the housing patterns in Riverton do not permit the drawing of zone lines for three schools without a nearly all-Black school.

Two things are important to note in this passage. First, the report naturalizes the creation of an all-Black school, calling it unavoidable. This claim is false, or at best misleading. It presumes it would be impossible to restructure the middle schools, something that the district could have chosen to do and had done previously under the desegregation order. Second, it frames the creation of an all-Black high school as an undesirable outcome. It does so by citing some committee members' concerns, underlining that the committee sought alternatives, and by feeling compelled to argue there were no viable alternatives to this scenario.

The committee report goes on to observe that segregation of Riverton schools was already taking place through the growth of predominantly white enrollment in local private high schools. The Committee Report concludes:

> The only solution to this larger problem is to reverse the outflow of white students from the City Schools. This can only be done by changing the

status quo—essentially by making the City Schools more attractive than the alternatives.

(p. 25)

Changing the status quo meant restructuring the district schools to create multiple high schools and corresponding feeder school systems, one strand of which would have 100% Black enrollment. Although the committee was divided on the issue, the following statement was included in the concluding pages of the document:

> Some feel that only by going to multiple high schools can the schools attract enough white students back into the system, and retain existing white students, to avoid the complete segregation of the system by having nearly all white students go to private or county schools.
>
> *(p. 37)*

The way the new schools would become more attractive to white students, it is implied, is by enrolling a higher proportion of white students. The overall proportion of white students in the district, however, was declining. The only way, committee members reasoned, to suddenly and significantly reverse that demographic trend was to raise the proportion of white students at some schools by concentrating a large number of Black students at a specific school site. This was contested and controversial. The report acknowledged that some committee members considered the multiple schools plan "a return to segregation" (p. 37). The report offered a compensatory hope that

> if the multiple schools are sufficiently successful, it may one day be possible to redraw zone lines to have three mixed race schools. Thus, having a nearly all-black high school could be seen as a temporary expedient leading toward a future fully-integrated City system.
>
> *(p. 25)*[8]

The recursive racist logic of these justifications for the resegregation of Riverton schools is important to note. The tipping point rationale cites the inevitable operation of racist ideologies as justification for policies that intensify institutionalized racial inequality. Rather than address the cause of the problem, this rationale recommended policy solutions that institutionalized the problem it purported to address. The tipping point argument was offered consistently by citizens who did not see themselves as racial segregationists, and certainly not as racist, but who nonetheless acquiesced to or supported the restructuring of the district.[9] Such a rationale, however, only makes sense if the consequences of the restructuring for the students at the newly resegregated school are ignored—if the well-being of the black students in the district is regarded as less significant than that of the white students. A Union High School teacher put the question to a focus group starkly:

E5UBF: So we are going to sacrifice the futures of half the black students in the city to [quote marks in the air] "save the district"? Who are we saving it for? We know who we are saving it for! What I would like to hear, what we will never hear, is someone advocating for a policy that will save the district by sacrificing the well-being of half the white students in the district.

For opponents of the restructuring, the tipping point argument undermined resistance by framing resegregation as inevitable. It reduced the number of persons willing to actively oppose the restructuring of the schools. And it made compromise and an effort to secure compensatory concessions seem the only viable political option.

On all sides of the issue, however, certain premises underlying the tipping point narrative were the same. The increasing proportion of Black students in the city schools was considered a problem. The creation of an all-Black school was regarded as undesirable. Nonetheless an all-Black school was going to be created despite no one thinking this was in the interests of the students who would be attending this school.

Forty Acres and a School

Once the school board had committed to splitting Union High School into three separate high schools—Northbrook High (on the northern side of town), Garner High (on the eastern side of town), and Union High (on the western side of town)—building sites were identified, architectural plans developed, and bids for construction solicited. The Northbrook and Garner sites were quickly identified. Each was forty acres in size and included new sports facilities and playing fields. The Union site, however, became a subject of controversy, which delayed its construction.

As mentioned in the previous chapter, the board considered a proposal to build the new Union High School in a city park on the far western side of town. Proponents of this plan offered it as a centerpiece of a more general urban renewal plan that would see the creation of middle-income housing around the school. The combination of a new school and affordable housing would draw white and middle-class citizens back into the schooling zone, thereby revitalizing the economy and political visibility of West-Side neighborhoods.

Opponents of this plan found this scenario unlikely. They felt no number of incentives were likely to entice white citizens to move into West-Side neighborhoods. And promises of urban renewal were regarded with skepticism. The idea that a new public school would revitalize western neighborhoods by attracting new homebuyers and business investment was considered a scam by real estate speculators at worst, wrongheaded at best. As one parent observed:

P6UBM: [T]heir point of view is, "Hey, we put this nice school there—that's going to draw other people down there—stores and neighborhood and people are going to start moving down there . . . But people don't move to a place simply because of a public school. They may take that into consideration. But, you know, when you supposedly are building three schools that are equal, which is their whole sales pitch is that we're going to divide it into three equal schools that are all the same, then why move to that area? If the schools are equal. So there's a flaw in their logic.

The debate about the location of the West-Side high school generated more public dialogue, especially among West-Side residents, than any of the previous aspects of the restructuring. By the time enough people were informed about the implications of the restructuring, the policy had been decided and construction had begun on two of the schools. The question of the location of the high school on the western side of town became the most visible issue about which citizens could effectively express their resentment toward the restructuring plan. It was also an issue on which there were clear indexes of fairness and equality—such as the size of the site and the school facilities. Two focus group participants bracket this latter issue concisely:

P7UBF: I wouldn't build Union at the old Union East site. Some think the old Union site is not large enough. The other schools got forty acres, so as to accommodate their new sports facilities. I would find a site that was comparable to Northbrook and Garner and build a comparable facility.
P8UBF: I don't agree with that. If the old Union High was big enough for all Riverton high school students, how could it not be big enough for one third of them? That don't make sense. People just want something to complain about. We need to focus on the . . . the quality, not the size, of the school.

What is significant for this study's purposes is that all sides of the debate about the school location presumed that the new Union High School would be the lowest status of the three schools. Advocacy for specific locations was consistently expressed as ways to redress the stigma people expected to be associated with an all-Black high school located on the West Side of town. For example, some interpreted resistance to the far west location as a form of prejudice against the West-Side community generally. As one teacher explained:

E6UBF: What's wrong with sending kids to the far West Side of town? We already send the rest of them waaaay out of the city. [Laughs] That's the way that I feel about it. WHY is it that a school couldn't come to the western side of the city? Why does it have to be sort of . . . "centrally" [used mocking tone] located where Union is? To me that says, you know, we can go way out almost to them over in Northbrook [laughs] but we can't even come to the West Side of town and build a school. That says . . . that the west is not good enough. And to me it . . . some of our own people are saying, "The West Side of town is not good enough." [Laughs]

Many others who advocated for a more central location cited the optics of the location as a pressing concern. Respondents frequently expressed apprehension that a school built on the far West Side of town would make it less visible and easier, therefore, to neglect. This group lobbied to have the new Union High School located on the site of the original Union High, where it would remain a central feature of life in Riverton. As one teacher summarized:

E4UWF: I personally never wanted them to build a new school at that park. It bothers me that we're going to have a Black high school and if we're going to have one—let's not put it out in the Boonies somewhere where everybody will forget about it. I want it right there on Maple Street where everybody sees it when they drive by. I want them to be very visible . . . They don't need as much land as the other two places because the school doesn't need to be as BIG as the other two schools.

A common motivating concern organized advocacy for both of the locations—a desire to counteract a stigmatization of the all-Black school that was considered inevitable. The consistent message throughout this public debate was that Union High was likely to be framed as a problem school or simply forgotten because it was all Black. Students were listening to this debate and could not fail to hear this message.

Despite the shared concern for the support and reputation of Union High on all sides, the debate about the location of the school divided the community zoned for the new Union High. Arguments about the location frequently became heated. Advocates for the park location were accused of corruption and collusion with real estate speculators. Advocates for retaining the old Union High site were criticized for a lack of sophistication and vision. Even the student walkout, which drew large numbers of students and adults, was not a unified community gesture. Many West-Side community leaders spoke against the walkout.

E7UBF: You've probably seen in the paper what it's been doing. It's divided the community because a small cluster of people wanted it out at the park site but it wasn't representative of the students and parents—which was a big division—which makes me very sad because for us to be trying to work together we don't need to be breaking up in little groups. Of course some of the same people who were kicking and screaming about they wanted to keep it on the site of the park have now changed their stand to have it at Union because I guess some of the community people have said, "You can do this but we don't support you. And you know, we vote—we're going to let you know we don't support you."

This inability to come to consensus about a location for the new Union High School delayed the construction of the new Union High campus. Construction proceeded on the other two campuses. Ribbons were cut on the Northbrook High and Garner High facilities in August of 2003 in time for students to begin attendance there that fall. Cost overruns on these two school sites caused the city and school district to expend funds intended for the construction of the new Union High site, causing further delays in the construction of the third high school.

Lacking a new school to attend, the district placed Union High students in the building that had formerly held ninth and tenth graders prior to the restructuring.[10] This meant that when the restructuring finally went into effect, the Northbrook and Garner students had new school facilities, but the Union students were attending school in one of the oldest buildings in the district. Compounding this, the Union High students inherited used band uniforms, sports uniforms, and other "Union High" branded equipment because the district could not justify the expense of purchasing new materials that had the same names and logos on them. The older school building and used uniforms and equipment reinforced the impression that Union High School was the neglected lower status high school in the district. As one student described:

S3UBM: We always felt Northbrook's jerseys were better than ours. When I came to Union, and first started playing football, I was like "our jerseys are used!" They looked BAD! All hanging off and stuff. It looked bad. You didn't have no swag. And Northbrook had new all-black fitted pro combat jerseys. Ours were all baggy. And the other team would talk to us about it. Even if we beat them, they would still say stuff about how we looked.

The most poignant signifier of the identity of the new Union High, however, lay with the history of the building the students were entering. It was the site of the old Oakstreet High School, the high school that African-American high school students attended during the era of de jure racial segregation in Riverton. Placing the newly constructed all-Black high school in this site was scandalous to many and underlined the fact that the district was—in part—racially resegregating. One of the older teachers who had attended Oakstreet High observed:

E8UBF: It's sad, I think. I enjoyed my time at Oakstreet. But that ... that was a long time ago. It was different then. We shouldn't be back here. It just goes to show how little progress we have really made.

To summarize, for well over three years the community discussed and debated how to respond to the lifting of the federal desegregation order. Students listened to these family and community conversations. These conversations were almost always organized around the premise that the creation of an all-Black high school would not be good for the students in that school, that it constituted a loss and a regression from hard won civil rights era achievements of racial equity in schools. On the day students entered the restructured schools, Garner and Northbrook students entered new buildings with new equipment and uniforms and joined an integrated student body. On that same day Union High students found themselves entering one of the oldest buildings in the district, one that used to be the site of a pre-civil rights era racially segregated school, joining an all-Black student body, and being issued used uniforms and equipment.

Ultimately the district built the new Union High School on the site of the old eleventh and twelfth grade building, the site more centrally located in town. The site was smaller than the forty acres allotted to the Northbrook and Garner schools. And the building was smaller, as the district anticipated lower enrollment at Union. Union students entered their new building three years after the original restructuring, in 2006. But by this time, Union had clearly been marked as the lesser school of the three.

Teacher Preferences

The West Side of town had the highest concentration of black population. It was a predominantly low-income neighborhood. It had several public housing projects. And it was an area of town that many white and middle-class citizens avoided. Although Riverton's population barely qualified it as an urban school district (less than 200,000 residents) and crime rates were relatively low, the West Side of town was an exotic, crime-ridden locale in the imagination of many Riverton citizens. A teacher observed that this sentiment existed in the teaching faculty. When asked why he thought Union was being built at the more central location, he explained:

E9UBM: Part of it is the teachers. Many have expressed an unwillingness to drive deep into the West Side to work . . . because if they work late or have an afterschool function, they are afraid to be there at night.
I: Do you think this is justified?
E9UBM: Well, I . . . [long pause] I would not tell a woman that concerns about assault are unfounded. It is right to be careful. But I . . . I don't think there is any reason to be more concerned about such things at Union. And I don't hear these concerns expressed about Garner or Northbrook.
I: Would you assign a teacher to Union if they expressed these concerns?
E9UBM: This . . . it's complicated. Because all three schools need good, highly qualified teachers. That has to be the priority. But if a teacher feels this way

about the community they are teaching in, if they are biased against the community, then they—how could they not be biased against the students?
I: By bias you mean . . .
E9UBM: I mean racism.

A Garner teacher corroborated that this feeling influenced some teachers' opposition to building Union on the far western side of town. Regarding her colleagues' preference not to work at the proposed site, she said:

E10GWF: If you've ever been down there—it's—and I use the term "ghetto." It's on the west end of town—that is a very poor part of town. You know, most people won't go to that end of town because they're afraid to go to that end of town. After dark—they won't go.

This aversion to working on the far western side of town was for many a part of a more general aversion to working anywhere on the West Side, with West-Side students, or in an all-Black school. Of the over fifty teachers interviewed for this study who were asked, only three listed Union as their first choice for school assignment. Several were adamant that they needed to be assigned to Northbrook or Garner. Two teachers reported they were prepared to leave the district or the teaching profession rather than accept a position at Union High or its feeder schools. One seasoned teacher confessed to weeping upon learning that she was assigned to Union High School after the restructuring.

E11UWF: I worked real hard to get to the place where I was that I didn't have to deal with a bunch of low-level math classes. And so I picked Northbrook . . . I had thirty years of teaching. I had more teaching years than anybody in either math department . . . And I will never forget to this day, and [voice starts to crack, pause] . . . the powers that be do not know what kind of hell they put all the teachers through. The tension and the . . . really . . . it never crossed my mind . . . and I mean this sincerely, it never ever once crossed my mind that I would get assigned to Union High School, which was my third choice . . . when I went in the office and I opened my envelope and it said, "Union High School" I felt like somebody had stabbed me with a knife . . . in the back. And I went back to my room, turned off all the lights, got in the corner in a ball and cried and cried and cried and cried.

It was reported that student teachers in a local teacher education program had similar responses to being placed for student teaching at Union or its feeder schools. Students in this program frequently expressed hope they would not be assigned to West-Side schools, even though the program did not permit them to choose the school to which they were assigned. An African-American student in the program described the strength of some reactions to such assignments:

E12UBM: When we got our envelopes [with their student teaching assignments], this girl in my row was crying. Her friend was hugging her. It was crazy. You'd think somebody died. She had been assigned to Union High. I was, like, what are you crying about? But for her, it was the worst thing that could happen to her. She was not the only one.

Teachers did not keep their responses to school assignments to themselves. They were publicly performed and discussed, thus contributing to the community discourse about the relative merits of the three high schools. Teachers complained to and consoled one another. They talked to family members and neighbors. A teacher who was assigned to Union High despite her preference to be assigned to Northbrook explained:

E13UWF: I think what they did to me had a lot more impact than the administrators ever will know because I was always one of these teachers—I did everything they asked me. I did Honor Society. I did graduation stuff. I did … you name it—this committee, that committee. I worked tirelessly. Hours and hours and hours … Everybody in the whole school walked around shocked. I mean this was a shock to everybody. Nobody ever expected … And I had people coming up to me and said, "You know what I learned from watching this? That there's no such thing as loyalty. The harder you work and the more you do the more you get dumped on."

The "dump" in this case was getting assigned to teach at Union High School. No teacher interviewed reported strong negative reactions to being assigned to Northbrook or Garner High. Aversion to working in West-Side schools was so prevalent, however, that the district had to offer extra incentives to get teachers to teach in the West-Side schools. The stigmatizing effect of such incentive pay was not lost on one teacher:

E14GWM: I don't know if you're aware of some of the new things that the super-intendent's been talking about as far as trying to get some teachers out there to the western cluster … offering them a longer contract period with more pay, you know, to get them to teach out there in some of the elementary schools and middle schools. I mean, that's the sort of thing that we need to do but … you know, I just … it says something's wrong. I just see that whole thing [the restructuring] as just being kind of a festering sore on the city school system.

Riverton administrators reported that some teachers did list Union High as their primary preference. And once the school opened most Union teachers quickly became committed to the school and its students. The administration and faculty were able to establish a relatively high level of morale. Fears of discipline problems proved to be unfounded. In fact Union High had lower rates of disciplinary referrals than the other two schools in the first two years. A teacher at Union familiar with discipline policy reported:

E15UBM: Teachers will say they don't want to go to Union because of the things that they have heard and not things that they really know. Because once you come in the doors of Union now, you will understand that the discipline will take place. If the kid is cutting up in class, we will get him out and we will make sure that that kid gets the message that he or she must do what they're told to do in the class.

This positive morale among teachers almost certainly influenced and was mirrored by many of the students. Teachers and students frequently expressed a desire to "prove people wrong" about Union High.

Positive assessments about discipline and respectfulness, however, were extended in only a qualified way to academics. Union High teachers expressed earnest commitments to holding high expectations for students, acted on those commitments, celebrated accomplishments, and discussed the pace of instruction with each other almost constantly. Nonetheless, Union teachers uniformly regretted that the restructuring had happened and frequently described west-side schools as focused on remedial educational work. They lamented the low levels of subject matter mastery students acquired in middle schools. West-Side middle school teachers in turn lamented the low levels of reading and mathematics skills students brought with them from elementary school. Even in Advanced Placement and honors classes, teachers described their classes as operating at lower levels of performance than they did before the restructuring. Teachers in the advanced classes routinely told students that they needed to work harder to keep up with Northbrook and Garner students. One African-American parent reported that when he visited the all-Black middle school on the West Side, a teacher there who knew him to be an educated professional, advised him not to enroll his child in the school.

P9NBM: I wasn't thrilled with the North-Side middle school we were zoned for. I listened to teachers over there talk about students from the West Side. You know what they called them? They referred to them as "bus kids." Their parents worked or didn't have a car, so they had to ride the . But the white kids, most of them, were dropped off by their parents. Bus kids! You could write a dissertation on just what that word meant. So I considered enrolling my son at the West-Side middle school. I talked to a teacher there. She was Black and she lived over there. And she told me—took me aside and said, "You don't want to put your son in here. The learning is very low level.

You'd be better off attending another cluster if you can." It was upsetting. "I am just trying to help," she said. What hope do we have if even our Black teachers have given up on our kids?

Some of these comments made by teachers, such as concerns about safety or preference for where they work, were personal opinions. Others, such as impressions of lower levels of academic performance in West-Side schools were supported by empirical evidence. Students in West-Side schools consistently scored 10–15% less on standardized tests than did students in the other zones. For the purposes of this study, the veracity of these views is less important than their existence. Opinions, justified or not, can be real in their consequences.

This is especially true where teachers and the public perception of educational issues are concerned. Teachers are members of the community. They attend churches, synagogues, temples, and mosques. They are members of civic organizations. They are neighbors and friends. In moderately sized towns like Riverton almost everyone knows a teacher and teachers are often the most trusted source of information about what is going on in schools. So many teachers in Riverton did not want to work in west-side schools and even those that did had concerns that West-Side schools were not performing at the level of the other two clusters, which inevitably contributed to broader discourses in Riverton that framed Union High and its feeder schools as the least desirable of the three school zones. Students heard, read, and participated in this community discourse. Additionally, students spent six to eight hours a day among teachers. They overheard teachers' conversations in the hall. They asked perceptive questions and discerned the sentiments of their teachers even when they did not explicitly state them. Teacher opinions about the structuring influenced students both directly and indirectly.

International Baccalaureate Program

One of the most publicly discussed curricular controversies associated with the restructuring concerned the IB program, a prestigious and highly structured college-bound curriculum for only the most advanced students.[11] Prior to the restructuring, the unified Union High School campus offered an IB program that featured advanced level courses in world literature, modern foreign languages, social sciences, experimental sciences, mathematics, theories of knowledge, and electives such as art and psychology. Participating students were required to design experiments, write extended essays, do historical research using original documents, and participate in at least 150 hours of individually designed and thoroughly reflected upon volunteer service. The IB program enjoyed high status in the school community. It was more than a curriculum; it was an identity and source of pride, not unlike being a star athlete. And the parents of IB students included some of the people most active in local school politics.

The IB curriculum was originally conceived as a standardized course of study for the children of people working at embassies and in other forms of foreign service. The advanced curriculum and corresponding assessments were designed to ensure that the children of professionals working abroad had access to education that would prepare and qualify them for admission to prestigious universities. The program eventually expanded into more provincial markets, where parents and educators wanted to provide the option of a challenging curriculum for students with ambitions to attend prestigious universities. Riverton school district founded its IB program as part of an early effort to stem the movement of high-achieving students to local private schools. A small group of students at Union High were enrolled and they generally took their classes together during their junior and senior years. Ninety-five percent of these students were white before the restructuring took place.

The IB program at Union became the subject of controversy during the restructuring process. The headquarters of the International Baccalaureate organization is located in Geneva, Switzerland, and it requires schools to apply for participation. Schools must demonstrate an ability to pay for and sustain specialized training for IB course instructors, for curriculum materials, and for the summative tests required for student credit. They must demonstrate student interest. And they must agree to abide by the rules set down in the IB charter for their program. This latter parameter is what created complications for the district. The charter states, among other things, that the program must be located at one campus, cannot be transferred between campuses, and that additional IB programs cannot be established in a district until the first has demonstrated success in the form of students consistently passing IB tests and earning an IB diploma.

In the initial stages of the restructuring of Riverton's high schools, there seemed to be an assumption among central administrators and community stakeholders that the IB program could be placed at any of the three new schools. Despite warnings from the IB program coordinator, Riverton administrators planned to locate the IB program at Northbrook or Garner, because that was where all of the students in the IB program were zoned.

E16GWM: I knew it wouldn't be that easy. I kept telling them to call the main office, but they seemed too busy with other things with the restructuring. They just couldn't believe it was going to be a problem.

The program charter listed "Union High School" as the site of the IB program. Since the school stayed in one of the old buildings that housed Union High and retained the name "Union High," the IB office in New York ruled that the program had to stay at "Union High School." The district repeatedly protested and petitioned the decision, but to no avail.

News of this quickly spread through the community of IB parents. This meant that IB-enrolled students, most of whom were white and all of whom were zoned for the other two schools, would have to electively enroll at Union High in order to continue in the advanced IB curriculum. For many this required weighing the benefits and status of enrollment in the IB program against their aversion to attending an all-Black school on the West Side of town. Parents did not initially accept the choice being presented to them. The ensuing effort by parents to have the program moved to another school surfaced racially coded anxieties about the safety and quality of the West-Side schools in comparison to the other two schools.

Parents made a variety of arguments about the new arrangement. Privately, parents expressed an unwillingness to enroll their students at Union because they regarded it as a safety risk or they feared their children would feel isolated and separated from their friends. Publicly they objected to the irrationality of locating the program where there were no students currently enrolled and where, it was often added, there were unlikely to be students enrolled in the future. After the restructuring, one parent of a former IB student offered a widely shared sentiment:

S4NWM: The whole thing was a complete fiasco. It was the death of the IB program really. They still have it at Union High, but it is not the same. The students it was meant for moved on. And the students in it now are not—and this may sound bad—but they are not at the same level. Ask the teachers. They may not say it to you. But they say it to us. It won't last much longer over there.[12]

Some teachers were willing to express a sense of fatalism about the future of the IB program. One long-time IB instructor was quoted by the local paper as saying:

Almost all of the IB students were coming from Garner neighborhoods and north of the river, and if you build a brand new school in the middle of that, it doesn't take a genius to figure out what's going to happen to the program at Union High.

Once it became clear that the IB charter couldn't be moved, parents argued for IB programs at every school. The cost of additional charters and training three sets of instructors for the IB program were deemed too expensive by Riverton school district administration. And it was not clear that the IB organization would grant additional charters if enrollments and graduation rates in the original program diminished precipitously. The district struck a compromise in which juniors in the IB program at the unified high school would be permitted to enroll at Union their senior year to complete their IB diploma. Students at Garner and Northbrook interested in the pre-IB courses, also considered an elite curriculum, would be bussed to Union High in the morning to take pre-IB classes there, but be returned to their primary campuses in the afternoon where they could participate in non-IB coursework and extracurricular activities at their home school. Six of the sixteen students previously enrolled in IB elected to transfer full time to Union High where they took classes with one Union student enrolled in the program. The pre-IB classes were predominantly composed of transfer enrollments. By the second year, all Northbrook and Garner students withdrew from the IB program and students taking the bussing option to pre-IB courses significantly declined.[13]

That first year the bussing arrangement created a circumstance in which the all-Black high school in town was host to some of the most advanced academic classes in the district. Some of the most highly qualified teachers at Union High were assigned to teach these classes. Union High students did not enroll in these classes because they either lacked the prerequisites for the program or they had been discouraged from doing so. Instead white students were brought in from outside to take this curriculum. These students did not see themselves as a part of the Union campus and interacted very little with Union students. This arrangement brought into high relief what had been true even before the restructuring—the IB program was de facto racially segregated. It underscored the widely circulated impression that Union High students were not as academically accomplished as students at Northbrook or Garner. And the unwillingness of IB parents to enroll their children full time at Union reinforced the idea that people saw Union High and the West-Side zone as a place to be avoided. Interest in IB curriculum among Northbrook and Garner students evaporated relatively quickly. Within three years there were no students from those schools electing to be bussed into the Union IB or pre-IB program.

IB curriculum was maintained at Union High by merging it with Advanced Placement (AP) courses.[14] The initial appeal of the IB curriculum, however, was that it was more demanding than the more common AP courses which led to concerns voiced by IB-trained teachers that the IB curriculum was becoming "watered down." In order to increase enrollments, students were permitted to take single IB courses without pursuing the full course of study that would lead to an IB diploma. As a consequence, the number of IB diplomas dropped significantly, thus making it even more unlikely that a new charter could be started elsewhere.

Based on these considerations, the IB coordinator at Union High began to publicly advocate for ending the program. He made the case at board meetings and on a call-in radio program popular with many Union High parents that the costs did not justify the benefit. Only a few students at Union High were prepared for the courses, he alleged, and the costs of providing IB curriculum to those students was not fair to the other students in the school and district. He recommended in an interview with the local paper:

> At this point, it would be better to have AP courses at all three campuses. They count for college credit, are more flexible, and are far less expensive to the district.[15]

The IB coordinator's remarks galvanized West-Side educational leaders who objected to the low expectations being expressed for Union High students. James Herbard, a school board member representing the West-Side cluster of schools was reported in the local paper as saying:

> "We have fallen into this trap of accepting excuses for when these schools are low-functioning. This lame excuse is being offered when the problem is lack of challenging kids and not expecting them to perform on a higher level," he said. Herbard said the problem doesn't end with IB. Setting lower expectations for Black students has a ripple effect throughout the school system, beginning at the elementary school level. "It's created this sort of brain drain," Herbard said. "You've got all these smart little kids running around the elementary schools, and all of a sudden when they get to Middle School, they disappear."

Parents of Union High students, including many whose children were not IB students, wrote a letter to Riverton district administrators; it was quoted at length in the local paper. The letter objected to the talk about eliminating the IB program at Union High. This program was the one feature of Union High that distinguished it academically, they argued, in a context that disadvantaged Union in almost every other way. They explicitly mentioned the resegregation of the schools as a necessary consideration when considering the future of the IB program at Union.

> Our concern is that this program will be made available to students at the other city district high schools, but eliminated from Union High School . . . . Such action would be grossly unfair to the student population living on the western side of Riverton. That Union High School is now racially identifiable makes this all the more crucial; for denial of the IB program to students attending Union also means outright denial of the program to a specific population group, in this case, African-American students.

Eventually the IB program was retained at Union High and remains there over ten years later. Educational equity advocates could consider this a small victory for West-Side students. But the victory had an undertow. Although the IB program remained at Union High, the debates about the location and future of the IB program surfaced and circulated some of the most negative public statements about the quality and climate of Union High School. From the anxieties of white parents unwilling to send their children to Union High, to the spectacle of bussing white students over to take special advanced classes at Union High for which Union students were not considered eligible, to teachers making comments that Union students were not performing as well as their peers at other schools would, to West-Side parents publicly inventorying the low expectations others had of their children—all of these reinforced the pervasive narrative that Union High and its feeder schools were the least of the three school zones in town.

Summary and Transition

The public dialogue about the new Union High School was relentlessly negative. Even when Union High was being defended, this happened against a backdrop of assumptions that Union was or was perceived to be a low performing or dangerous school, and thus repeated and reminded listeners of those assumptions. Official documents such as the committee report that recommended restructuring the district, school board discussions, and newspaper articles reveal that the creation of an all-Black high school was intended from the beginning of the restructuring process. Advocates for the restructuring offered promises of compensatory developments that would offset these negative consequences, revealing that local leaders—from federal judges and state senators to city council members and local ministers—understood the restructuring was not in the best interests of students zoned for Union High School.

The dialogue among Riverton citizens revealed a similar pattern. The tipping point argument that persuaded many supporters of desegregation that restructuring the district was necessary presumed that an all-Black school was an undesirable outcome. Why else would it be necessary to cite a threat to the property tax base of the district to justify the creation of such a school? This rationale warned that all Riverton schools were likely to become predominantly Black, low performing, and lacking in public support if something was not done to retain white enrollment. Many seemed to assume, however, that exactly these outcomes would occur at the new Union High. This justification for the restructuring, therefore, essentially treated the welfare of Union students as if they did not matter—as acceptable casualties.

The debates about the location of the new Union High School surfaced related anxieties about the stigmatization and neglect of West-Side schools. Advocates for the far west location were seeking a means of urban renewal, which they believed would transform the poverty and the negative image of West-Side neighborhoods. Advocates for the more central location feared Union High would be neglected if placed that far out of town, forsaking students to low expectations and low levels of funding. Placing Union students in the old Oakstreet High School building—the site of the all-Black school before desegregation took place—and giving them used equipment, textbooks, and uniforms when the other two schools had new facilities and equipment underscored this threat of neglect for everyone in the community.

Teachers expressing a preference to work at Northbrook or Garner, complaining when this did not happen, or expressing sympathy for their colleagues assigned to Union, also contributed to a discourse that pathologized West-Side schools. Even teachers committed to working at Union and its feeder schools regularly expressed concerns about the low level of academic performance at their schools. Similar concerns fueled the controversy about the International Baccalaureate program, which provided a window into the pervasiveness of the assumption that Union High School would be an academically low-performing school. The public debates about the location of the IB program consisted of the repeated articulation of the view that Union students were not worthy of the district's most advanced curricular program. The resurfacing of debates about the future of the IB program approximately every two years serves to reinforce this view into the present.

More than these four issues precipitated disparaging comments about schools in the West-Side zone. Similar conversations took place around the location of the secondary vocational education program, the publication of school test score averages, the lack of a physics course at Union High, etc. When a fight happened at a basketball game hosted at Union High, the story was reported in the newspaper as part of globalized concerns about discipline at Union High. However when a sexual assault happened at the Northbrook campus, no such globalized concerns about discipline issues at Northbrook High were mentioned by the news media. This disparity was noted and objected to in editorials by West-Side residents. When one of the middle schools in the Northbrook zone became over-enrolled, the district redrew zone lines in a way that transferred only Black students out of that zone and into the Union High zone. This drew national media coverage and a preliminary investigation by the U.S. Justice Department, but was allowed to stand.

Considered individually, any one of these issues might be considered of marginal significance. Taken collectively, as a pattern, they provide evidence of a pervasive social discourse in Riverton that framed Union High and its students as lesser in quality and status than the other two high schools and their students, or at risk for being treated as such. The phenomenon being described is more than an aggregate of individual comments. These thematic concerns existed at a level above individual thought and bias. They provided a taken-for-granted vocabulary and set of background assumptions that framed conversations about education in Riverton. After a certain point the new segregation became a fait accompli. It was not possible to propose that the district desegregate again. And it was difficult to mention Union High without conjuring thoughts of pathology or stigma.

The conversations about Union High were influenced by and reinforced more global habits of thought and action, such as pervasive racism and bias against low-income communities. Negative expectations and images of Union High circulated across and through social groups, and were expressed repeatedly without significant alteration, almost as if they had a life of their own. They organized activity and had material consequences—such as the creation of new school buildings, the establishment of zoning lines that moved student bodies around the district, and uneven distribution of resources between the schools. These material consequences, in turn, took on symbolic significance—such as the way housing Union High students in the old Oakstreet High School building while other students went to new buildings reinforced an impression of neglect and underlined the racial segregation taking place. In this way, the symbolic components of resegregation compounded the material components and vice versa, creating a multilayered and noxious social context that enveloped students as they attended school.

All of this provides the setting for this book's main argument—that the resegregation process functioned as a kind of curriculum for students. The restructuring of the school system, including all of the public and private conversations that preceded and followed it, the symbolic significance of various material inequities, and the material impact of those inequities, provided a kind of social text that students read, interpreted, and took in various ways to heart. The effect on students was more than just that of overhearing a few untoward remarks about Union High. They found that everywhere they turned the resegregation of Riverton schools was sending them messages about the relative worth of students based on their race, class, and the location of their home.

Notes

1 Identification of these themes were based on a content analysis of local newspaper coverage of the restructuring process from 2000–2007. The presence of these concerns in the community discourse was consistently corroborated by a content analysis of interviews and key policy documents related to the restructuring.
2 A high track college preparatory curriculum generally considered more advanced than either honors or AP classes. (See: http://www.ibo.org/)
3 They were ultimately successful in this effort.
4 In retrospect, fifteen years later, these same community leaders have acknowledged that few of these promises were kept.
5 Actual enrollments would eventually diverge with Northbrook High exceeding enrollments of 1,200 and Union High enrollments frequently dipping below 700.
6 The county school system, which was separate from the city school system and served more outlying rural areas, was majority white. Families moving outside of the city schooling zone so as to enroll their children in the county school system accounted for a significant portion of the "white flight" out of Riverton schools.
7 This committee was convened by the Riverton school board and included school board members, district administrators, teachers, parents, the PTA president, a representative of the local NAACP, a representative of the Chamber of Commerce, local clergy, and other community members.
8 A subsequent restructuring of this sort never came to pass. This possibility was never mentioned again in any of our interviews or the public documents we examined. The hoped for return of white private school students to the district happened only slightly and briefly before the demographic trend towards lower proportions of white students resumed. As of this writing, Northbrook is ~30% white, Garner is ~20% white, and Union remains less than 1% white.

9   Respondents citing this rationale were predominantly, but not exclusively, white.

10 This decision left open the possibility of either renovating the old eleventh and twelfth grade building or tearing it down and building a new school on that land.

11 More information about the program can be found at: http://www.ibo.org/

12 This prediction turned out not to be accurate. The IB program continues at Union High over twelve years later.

13 There was one exception to this pattern. A student frustrated with the lack of advanced curriculum in the county schools transferred to Union High in order to enroll in the IB program the second year the school was open—after the exodus of the Northbridge and Garner students. Consequently this young woman was the only white student in the IB classes and during her senior year was the only white student in the entire school. Both the student and her parents reported very positive experiences with the school and the student's mother became a vigorous advocate for maintaining the IB program at Union High.

14 Advanced Placement courses are another internationally market-standardized curriculum designed to simulate lower division undergraduate courses. Many universities will grant college credit to students who pass AP courses with high marks.

15 This teacher later recanted his position on the issue and became an advocate for a strong IB program at Union High.

Bibliography

Cotton, K. (1996). *School size, school climate, and student performance*, Close-up No. 20. Portland, OR: Northwest Regional Educational Laboratory.

Fine, M. (2005). Not in our name: reclaiming the democratic vision of small school reform. *Rethinking Schools, 19*(4), 11–14.

Freeman v. Pitts, No. 503 U.S. 467 (1992). Retrieved August 28, 2015 from https://www.law.cornell.edu/supremecourt/text/503/467

Grodzins, M. (1958). *The metropolitan area as a racial problem*. Pittsburgh: University of Pittsburgh Press.

Klonsky, M. (1995). Small schools: the numbers tell a story. A review of the research and current experiences. ERIC Digest. 385 (517).

Klonsky, M., & Klonsky, S. (2008). *Small schools: public school reform meets the ownership society*. New York: Routledge.

Meier, D. (1996). The big benefits of smallness. *Educational Leadership, 54*(1), 12–15.

Meier, D. (2005). Creating democratic schools. *Rethinking Schools, 19*(4), 28–29.

Schelling, T. C. (1971). Dynamic models of segregation. *Journal of Mathematical Sociology, 1* (July), 143–186.

Wasley, P. A., & Lear, R. J. (2001). Small schools, real gains. *Educational Leadership, 58*(6), 22–27.

3

THE CHILDREN ARE WATCHING

Demography as Social Text

main point
argument

The level of public conversation about the restructuring of Riverton public schools increased steadily from the earliest reports about the lifting of the desegregation order until Union High was finally built over five years later. As the circle of conversation widened, school-age children could not help but hear and be influenced by what they heard. The ideas and attitudes thus acquired provided lenses through which they came to understand the changes they were experiencing in the schools. Students, especially the older students, understood that the worries about the effects of the restructuring were worries about what it would do to them.

Students didn't just bear witness to these conversations. They also participated in them. They talked to parents and teachers. They talked to their friends at other schools. They saw the other schools' facilities at athletic and competitive academic events, so comparisons of the three high schools were inevitable and frequent in their conversations. Reflection on the differences between the schools prompted discussions about why they were separated in this manner, leading to speculation about the purpose for the restructuring. Students, much more than the non-educator adults in the community, were confronted with the stark demographic differences between the schools. It affected their social lives and their futures even more than it did that of the teachers. Students noticed how they had been divided across the city and worked out their own interpretations of the hierarchical arrangement among the newly-created schools.

This study focused primarily on high school students, who were frequently quite vocal about the restructuring process. Over 200 students were interviewed in the course of the study, many of them multiple times. Their comments about the restructuring process were analyzed for thematic content.[1] In what follows, we identify, illustrate, and consider the significance of some of those themes. Overall, we found a great deal of consistency in students' interpretations of the new school arrangement. The resegregation of Riverton schools—more precisely, the conscious enactment of this segregation or acquiescence to it by adults in the community—was communicating a variety of messages to them and they were listening.

Patterns and Precedents

At some level, the resegregation of the high schools was nothing new for the students of Riverton. In the years preceding the high school split, the middle schools had already been restructured in similar ways. The feeder school for the new Union High was 97% Black. The others were more racially diverse. These enrollment distributions at the new middle schools, however, did not precipitate significant political controversy as long as their students were destined for a common high school. Still, the students who attended the restructured West-Side middle schools recognized that something problematic was happening to their schools.

S5UBF: And to me it just didn't start in high school. This goes back to when they decided to split the middle schools up. To me, this is where it traces back to. Because—they are our feeder schools and you can look and tell when they split the middle schools up, you just—

S2UBM: [Joins in almost simultaneously] You knew how it was going.

S5UBF:You knew how it was going to go when they split the high schools up. So it's, to me, it's like—basically the same. It's like, it started. This wasn't something that just happened in the high schools. It happened in the middle schools also.

Notice that these students had tracked the resegregation of their middle school and saw it as presaging the resegregation of the high schools. As Chapter 2 showed, they were right about this.[2]

Students searched for plausible explanations of the changes that did not involve race. For example, students mentioned thinking early in the process that the new buildings were needed to alleviate overcrowding at the old Union High campuses. However, it appeared that something had gone wrong because classes in the new schools were still overcrowded. And occasionally students observed that enrollment numbers from upcoming middle school groups indicated this problem was likely to grow worse. Students also considered the possibility that the new zoning arrangement would save money through reduced transportation costs. But, given that many West-Side students actually rode buses that travelled past Union High School on their way to Northbrook, fuel economy seemed an implausible explanation. Unable to find believable economic rationales for the restructuring, all but a few of the students we interviewed turned to the demography and school location in order to explain the new arrangements. Viewed in this way, the distinctive class and race profiles of the schools and the school identities and reputations that these profiles precipitated seemed to students to have been imposed on them intentionally. Student speculation about the motivations for this led them to conclude, inevitably but often reluctantly, that many leaders in the community had lowered expectations and less care for Black students generally and for those of the West-Side community in particular.

> S5UBF: We already knew when we got a middle school, by the time we hit between the seventh and eighth grade, they were already debating on splitting the high schools up. So when they're already debating about splitting the high schools up, right then and there you know there's some other stuff going on. I don't care—under the table, over the table—wherever. They was going to have—they was setting up what each high school was going to *have*. And I—you can—you figured that out. You knew where each school—you just basically knew, when they split up, you can see. You can just see it, because they decided right then and there. They were like, "Okay," you know, "This has this—." They already—to me when they decided to split, they knew the demographics of the school and what the school was going to have.

Students frequently presumed that the racial division of the schools had been part of a calculated plan that was implemented slowly, but steadily, over time. Again, subsequent interviews with district leaders and analysis of district documents confirmed these suspicions. School district leaders did intentionally plan to create an all-Black school, and knew that the size, reputation, and achievement levels of the three schools would not be equal.

The accuracy of these student interpretations, however, is less significant than the students thinking this at all. The restructuring did not just change the building in which they attended the schools. It did not just change the reputation of the school in the minds of adults. It changed the meaning of that schooling space for the children who attended there. Before the restructuring, students entered schools where racial stratification did not appear to be an intentional feature of the structure of the school district.[3] Their school was one where opportunities for white and Black students were at least equally physically proximate. After the restructuring, the racial stratification became a much more central part of the identity of the schools for students, especially in the West-Side feeder zone. Equal opportunities were no longer physically within reach. Some opportunities were across town and would require changing residence and sorting through bureaucratic barriers to access. In some cases they would not be accessible at all. After the restructuring students walked into schools in which they felt that racist intent surrounded them in the bricks and mortar, the course offerings, the books and uniforms they were supplied with, and the way they were regarded by members of the community.

Demographic Awareness

Every student interviewed knew that the restructuring had not happened in a racially balanced manner and had developed opinions about this fact. Students had a rough idea of the racial demographics of all three schools. Northbrook, for example, was always designated by students as the "whitest" school. Union was known to be nearly 100% Black. And Garner was most frequently considered "mixed." Students often compared these to the demographics of the formerly unified Union High, which some of them had attended in previous years.

S8NWM: What were the ratios at [the former] Union? It was still pretty startling—like seventy-five–twenty-five I think was what it was? Like, Black was seventy-five, white was twenty, and then "other" was five, so it still was very predominantly Black when we went to [the former] Union. . . . But, I remember when we first got to Northbrook, white was in the majority or as close to it—

S9NWF: And now Black is the majority.

S8NWM: Black is the majority now here too.

From its founding, Northbrook never had less than 50% enrollment of Black students. Nonetheless, Northbrook quickly became identified as "the white school" by many students, especially by students at Garner and Union. Comments made by both Black and white students, however, revealed that Black students were often framed as outsiders or visitors there. Recognizing this, a Black school board member commented that he was more concerned about the welfare of Black students at Northbrook than at the new, racially isolated, Union High.

E17UBM: They know they are not wanted. They are taking the brunt of this restructuring the most. Our kids have more discipline problems north of the river than they do at Union. You think that is an accident? It's bad—toxic over there. Toxic for them.

This discourse of outsidership is illustrated in the following conversation among a group of white students about overcrowding and racial demographics.[4] Students mistakenly attributed crowded classes to the enrollment of students from out of zone at Northbrook and considered possible solutions.

S4NWM: There's already zoning problems, but we just need to zone, you know, and have some kind of standard to it so that you don't have these kids that go here that aren't supposed to go here or that don't go here that are supposed to go here, or—you know? That kind of thing. I think they should be a lot more strict with where you live.

S11NWF: I thought they did that to make all of the schools, like, racially equal.

S4NWM: I'm not sure.

S12NWF: Me neither. How's our school?

S4NWM: We're fifty/fifty, Garner HS is fifty/fifty. It's just Union that's somehow all Black.

S13NWM: But they're doing the zoning over, though. Since the new Union is being built, they have to—they say they're doing the zoning over. So a lot of Black people are going to be gone from Northbrook.

Note the recognition that Union "somehow" being "all Black" was something the student felt required explanation. Also note that the reference to students "not supposed to be here" is initially a reference to students attending out of zone. The initial solution proposed is to be more "strict" with enforcing zoning lines. However, another student suggests the overcrowding problem will soon be addressed by a change to the zone lines—suggesting it is not out-of-zone attendance that is the problem. This student presumed that it was Black students who would be zoned out of Northbrook and sent to Union High, the all-Black school. There would be no geographic reason for this presumption. There were as many white students as Black students at Northbrook whose residence was closer to Union High. The comment suggests a presumption that Black students were outsiders to the Northbrook school community, and would therefore be the most likely to go if enrollments were reduced. The student turned out to have been correct in this prediction. Three years later the school board approved a second rezoning that shifted approximately 800 Black students from Northbrook and Garner feeder zones to the Union cluster of schools. No white students were affected by these zoning changes.[5]

Northbrook High School students, however, did not seem to covet identification as "the white school." Students there, both white and Black, were sensitive to that designation and often refuted this misnomer when it came up in the interviews. "They say we are white" one white Northbrook student said of her school in a tone that suggested confusion, "but we're not. We're not even in the majority" (S14NWF). Referring to her friends at Union High, a Black Northbrook student similarly commented on this misidentification:

S15NBF: They say we are white over here. We're the white school. But that's not what I see.

I: What do you see?

S15NBF: [Laughs] I see Black people.

I: Why do you think your friends say this is a white school?

S15NBF: My Union friends. Nobody here says that. . . . I don't know why they say it. I guess 'cause they're all Black, we look white compared to them?

Garner students also tracked the demography of the schools. Students there embraced the designation of their school as racially "mixed" and often used the term "integrated" to describe their school. There was a sense of continuity with the former Union High in this regard. As one young woman commented:

S16GBF: It's like we are the—the new Union really, not Union, not the school called Union.
I: Why is that?
S16GBF: Because we are, like, integrated. Union is all Black. The old Union was integrated. We are like that.

Although there was broad embrace of a multiracial identity at Garner, there were discussions about more subtle aspects of the racial identification of the high school. Several students mentioned that the quad outside the cafeteria was occupied primarily by Black students during the lunch hour as evidence that Garner was culturally more Black. The character of the band was also a topic of conversation. The old Union High's marching band performed in the high knee-lift style of historically Black colleges and universities, which was considered a marker of a Black school. The new Union High band performed in this style as well, whereas the Northbrook band performed the corps style marching characteristic of predominantly white universities.[6] Garner's first band director organized a corps style band, signifying to students a school identification with white cultural aesthetics. Three years after the school opened, Garner got a new band director who favored the high knee-lift style. Over that same time period the school's demography had shifted from 60% Black to nearly 70% Black. Some students interpreted this shift in band style as a reflection of the shifting demographic identity of the school. The principal at the time of the hire, however, reported that this was not a consideration.

Consciousness of the demography of the schools was most acute at the new Union High School. Students there had, on average, more detailed and strongly held opinions about the racial balance among the schools. Most students didn't want to believe that race was the only reason Union High was all Black. As one senior reacted, "I don't want to think that it was race—that would be too terrible" (S5UBM). Students could see that some Black students were enrolled at the other two schools, which complicated their view of things. Nonetheless, a view of the racial identity of the schools was widely shared.

I: How would you describe the three schools?
S18UBF: Northbrook's the white school. Garner is mixed. We are the Black school.

S19UBF: [Shaking head] There are Black kids at North. It's mixed, too.

S18UBF: Not as many.

S20UBM: It's on the white side of town.

S19UBF: There are Black families live there, too. Mr. Franklin [the Black Principal] lives there.

S18UBF: Not as many.

S20UBM: Whatever, we are a Black school. And people say Northbrook is white—even though Black students go there.

Union being an all-Black school was the most salient aspect of the identity of Union for the great majority of the Union students we interviewed. It was mentioned more frequently and commented upon at greater length. It was not however, the only distinguishing characteristic of the school. Students there also described their school as being identified with the western side of town, as having a strong sense of community or family, as being athletically competitive, as being lower income. Students were aware that others thought of Union High as a less desirable school, but students who mentioned this almost always expressed resistance to this characterization, saying things like "They don't know us" and "People just believe bad things they hear. They should come and see for themselves" (S21UBF). Students occasionally vocalized their struggle against the idea that the restructuring might affect their future. Responding to another student's comment that it seemed like the board wanted Union High students to fail, a Union Senior explained why she didn't like to think that way:

S5UBF: It looks like that, but you hate to say it. But you don't want us to think that your race is holding you back because I never ever want to think that. 'Cause in life I believe I want to achieve regardless where—race, where school, wherever I go to. But they make it seem like, it's just like—it makes it a more racial issue because they knew when they split up, they knew. It's like you knew the demographics [places hands before her face] of your city. If you know the demographics of your city, you automatically know, "Well, the schools will be equally split." No they won't! If you look at the race—and the financial areas of it, it's not making sense. It doesn't make sense. And that's what you hate to say. It seems like a racial issue. But it's a racial—it's like a racial and more of a financial and demographic—it's like a demographics thing.

Here we see a student self-consciously attempting to keep at bay the conclusion that community leaders deliberately set Union High students up to fail by zoning it to be all Black and to have more low-income students in it. The student recognizes that such thoughts are enervating because they put her success and well-being outside of her own control. The demographic evidence of the situation, however, seems to overwhelm her resistance as she speaks. She doesn't want to conclude that the demography of the new school zones were chosen knowing it would disadvantage Union High students, but how else can she interpret the facts of her experience?

Not all the students at Union High were reluctant to attribute malice to school district leaders. Many students seem to have expected the racial segregation of the schools to happen, and presumed it was intentional. But some students expressed surprise that Northbrook and Garner had as many Black students as it did.

S22UBF: Some of 'em have made, like predictions. Like, last year they were saying that they was going to start—when new Union was being built, they was goin' to start rezoning all the Garner, Northbrook, and Union folks. And some of 'em said they was goin'—when they built Northbrook and Garner they wasn't intending on so many African-American kids to go there. They wanted—they wanted it to be for [stops and gropes for word; a peer prompts her] for—Caucasian kids. [Laughs]

I: White kids—yes?

S22UBF: They didn't expect so many Black people to go to their school and now they see how—it's like a lot of Black folks that go to Garner High. I know they ain't expecting a lot of Black folks to go to Garner. And it's a lot of white folks at Northbrook, but over here we just all—Black. It's like 98% Black over here. I personally think that that is the main reason they did that. They just wanted to sep—segregate us all again.

There can be little doubt that the demography of Riverton's three high schools was on the minds of students as they attended their new schools. Not only did they hear and read about adults talking about these differences, students were having their own conversations about it, too. Students saw the demographic differences between the schools and correctly inferred that this kind of distribution could not have been accidental. This led to speculation about the possible intent behind the restructuring. Lacking any believable narrative from the district, students asked themselves why district leaders would do something like this and why the community would let them.

The Shadow of Intentionality

As recounted in Chapters 1 and 2, the district offered rationales for the restructuring. Early in the process, before the schools were built, they claimed the new arrangement would provide smaller schools or schools closer to students' residential neighborhoods. By the time students were attending the schools, however, these claims were obviously false. Eventually dropping efforts to rationalize the rezoning,[7] the district persisted in denying that the restructuring had anything to do with the racial demographics of the schools. The district asserted publicly on multiple occasions that the rezoning was "color-blind." The zones, they alleged, were the result of natural neighborhood divisions. A consultant they hired to assist with developing the rezoning plan testified at a public meeting:

> I am an expert with the U.S. Department of Justice on equity and school issues nationally; you'll find that this planning first of all is done with a demographic across the board that is color-blind. It isn't separating Black students from the white students . . . if I had smelled an aura of trying to create a segregated school district, I wouldn't be standing here.

Few community members were persuaded by these denials, however, probably because the claim that the creation of a 100% Black school was a necessary consequence of geography was plainly unbelievable.[8] Zoning lines are a human contrivance and could have been drawn otherwise. A visiting public speaker pointed out that the possibility that one of the three schools randomly ended up 100% Black was less than the chance of an individual being struck by lightning twice in one year. The lack of alternative explanations, coupled with a long history of institutionalized racism in the region, left only one reasonable interpretation of the increased racial segregation in the district—it was intentional.

Students were aware of the district's denial that racial demography influenced the restructuring. At times it appeared some Union High students wanted to believe these claims, perhaps because it would be painful to think that the adults in the community harbored such hostility that they would try to isolate them in a segregated school. How could it not be painful to consider that possibility? But given the evidence, believing the restructuring was free of racist animus was a struggle for students as the following student comments reveal:

S23UBF: Some people think they did it to split up the races—like send all the Black people over there, all the white people to the new schools. But—that might be a reason. It might not be. 'Cause the school board said that was not a reason.

<div align="center">~~~</div>

S24UBM: But looking at the way the schools are positioned and where they're being located, it's kind of hard not to think that—that it's to segregate the schools. But—and then I've heard a lot of people say that it's for the development of the community—for the communities.

<div align="center">~~~</div>

S25UBF: I thought that the reason that they wanted to split up the schools was because they thought it would bring a larger population, but I really feel like they did it to split up Black and white kids. . . . I feel like they wanted to separate Black and white kids. And they didn't really—if you think about it, they really didn't do it. But then again, as I think about it, they did.

Some students invoked the strict legal definitions of *de jure* segregation when interpreting the demography of their school. Lacking the concept of *de facto* segregation, these students underscored that their school couldn't be considered segregated because it wasn't legally being forced to segregate. One Union senior, for example, mentioned a conversation with his 25-year-old sister about the impending rezoning:

S26UBM: She said to me that they're going to try to go back to segregating and all that. . . . If it happens—the people that started it—they will have to pay for it—somehow.

Note that, although attending an all-Black Union High, he referred to "segregation" as something that might yet happen. If it ever did take place, he was confident there would be repercussions. This is a distinction that many adults and policy makers held onto in the community. The fact that there were no all-white schools was cited as evidence that the schools were not racially segregated. However, this was not even the former legal standard for considering a district segregated. The *Green Factors* specified that the creation of any racially identifiable school violated the prohibition against racial segregation. Beyond the legal definitions, the analysis of policy documents and adult discourse in the community revealed that the community did deliberately create an all-Black school.

What is significant for our purposes is that in the face of the intentional creation of an all-Black school, some students felt the need to insist that, whatever was happening to Union High, it was not segregation—not the raw form of racial oppression they had read about in history text books. Students did not want to believe they were being subject to a kind of institutionalized racism that their grandparents had struggled against. This is illustrated in a comment by another student who insisted that the current demography of Union High was temporary, that it would eventually become more integrated, because the alternative was too appalling to consider.

S27UBM: Well, I still think it going to be equal because—they can't segregate us. You know. They can't—they can't do like they did back in the days. It ain't going down like that.

These students held on to the notion that legal recourse would ultimately protect their school and educational experiences from race-based discriminatory action. A decade later, we now know that the courts have not provided such protection in Riverton or anywhere else resegregation of schools is occurring.

Students' word choices at times also revealed a struggle with interpreting the significance of school demography. For example students often used the verb "separate" instead of "segregate" to describe what was happening in their schools. At times students' tones suggested this was just an arbitrary substitution of a synonym. On other occasions, the term "segregation" seemed to carry too much sting, as in this exchange:

S6UBF: If you really want to know, we say it's a—they try to get whites on one side—on one side and Blacks on one side. That's really what they're trying to do.
S7UBF: It seems like we're going back to segregation.
S17UBF: Well, I don't know about that. They're trying to keep the Blacks on their side of town—OUR side. I think that's how it is. I mean, I just think they're trying to separate everybody.
S6UBF: What you're saying is the same thing—segregating keeps people on their own side of town. She's just using different words.

This reticence to directly describe the restructuring of Riverton schools as a deliberate and indefinite racial resegregation of the district is significant, because it indicates that at least some students were struggling with the negative psychological impact of the resegregation.

Most students interviewed for this study, however, did not deny that their schools were resegregating, nor that this was intentional. Many students saw the deliberate racism of white community members as driving the reorganization of the district. As one young woman explained:

S27UBF: I feel like since a lot of people that's in the system are white—not all of them, but a lot of them are—I feel like, you know, some of them are racist and things. Like, that they know that they have control in the say-so over—you know. "Well, we can split them up." You know. "We have the say-so in the schools, so we'll just try and do it." And I feel like they're doing it slowly. And people don't want to recognize that. They think it's just the, you know, "Expand Riverton." I don't think it's all about that—'cause you could expand it in another way.

This student did not turn away from the racial resegregation that was unfolding around her. She named it. This acknowledgment required an accompanying explanation of the unfairness she saw. She, like many others, attributed the racially unbalanced demography of her school to the racist motivations of white community leaders. The resigned tone with which she made these attributions suggested that this acknowledgement provided no relief from the psychic burden of the demographic changes to her school. It simply meant that she experienced the message of exclusion differently. She attended a school every day that she believed was consciously constructed as an act of hostility towards her and other Black students.

Discussions of the racial demography of the schools almost always led to conversations about the racist intentions behind the restructuring of the schools. The two issues were bound together in the imagination of the students. In focus groups, we often asked students how their school might be improved. At Union, the most frequent answer was to desegregate the schools, to return to the racial integration that existed before the restructuring. The racism revealed by the resegregation, however, made this seem unlikely to happen to the following students.

I: What would you tell them to do to make Union better?
S28UBM: [Very quietly] Not sep—not separating Black people from white people.
S29UBF: [Calls from across the room] I really want to know, why did they split
　　the schools up? . . . [Answers her own question] We Black, they white!
S33UBF: [Cuts in to clarify] Because some people, you know, the white
　　people—um—parents—probably don't want them around us because we—
　　you know how some whites are like—don't like Black people because of
　　racism and stuff like that. That's probably why.

The first student speaker says racially integrating his school is the first way he could think to improve it. His response reveals both his consciousness of the school's demography as a salient feature of his educational experience and a sense that attending a racially diverse school would be preferable. This response immediately precipitated the second student's rhetorical question—why did this happen? A question to which she and the third student felt they had an answer: racism. Specifically, this student mentions the racism of white parents, which turned out to be a common theme. Students did not simply attribute the resegregation of their schools to corrupt racist politicians. More often they saw it as a consequence of a pervasive racism among local white parents who didn't want their children going to school with Black children.

S29UBF: I took [Technology School] my ninth grade year and like, you know,
　　they have Garner, Union, and Northbrook classes over there. And like—the
　　ones I talked to . . . [takes a peer's perspective] "I didn't want the schools to
　　split up." They didn't like the school splitting up. So—it's really not the
　　students. It's the city board. It's the parents. [Pauses] Mainly the parents,
　　because they elect the board. So that's the way it is.

Resegregation Again

Many students we interviewed doubted that the initial restructuring of the schools would slake the racist desires they saw driving school policy. Rather than a single racist policy, they saw this racism as a continuing active force in determining their school experience. As such, they expected schools to become even more racially segregated. The opening of the new building for Union High, scheduled to be finished three years after the initial restructuring, was frequently cited as the moment the next stage of the district's resegregation would take place. A senior at Union described the expected trajectory for the demography of the three schools.

S20UBM: I believe that the new Union they build—I think they are building it to further—separate the schools because once—like, where Union is at now—it's mostly a Black community over there. So when they go to rezone at the new Union, all the Black—most of the Black kids—at Northbrook and Garner will be going to Union.

On another occasion a younger student explained:

S30UBF: All these kids on the West Side—that's not their neighborhood. The same kids who walk to school—they're going to have to catch the bus from this school all the way over there. So it's really not a neighborhood. And if you look at—they tried to split it up—to send the kids to Northbrook who stay on West End. But when they rezone—when it's the new school that opens—all them kids are going to go right back—to the new Union. And that's what they tried to do. That was their first intention—just to make it seem like that way. But then, after the years passed, they're going to send them right back to new Union—when it opens.

Notice how the latter student says the district will send Black students at Northbrook and Garner "back" to Union, as if that is where they belong. The students she refers to had never attended Union. Students all over the district were bussed long distances, so these students were not unique in that regard. Neither geography nor history actually distinguished them as more suitable for Union High. Their race and the income level of their neighborhood, however, did. Her remark implies that she thought West End students would be moved to a zoning status for which they were somehow more suited or destined. Even in voicing a critique of the racism underlying the district's policy, this student naturalized the idea that these low-income Black students belonged at the new Union High. The district's polices were shaping her conceptions of race, place, and belonging.

Union students often had very detailed knowledge, usually accurate, of how zoning lines would fall. Their analysis of the demographic reasons for the particulars often consisted of a combination of racial and class considerations. One student offered a breakdown of every housing project and some section eight apartment complexes that would be included in the new Union zone, including ones where students attending Garner and Northbrook lived. He did this well before the new zoning plans were publicly announced:

S18UBF: People from Oaklawn Acres are going to be at Union. Also, McKinney
    Apartments, Briarstone, Kingston Villa, and Colonial Hills.
I: Are they putting more Blacks at this school?
S18UBF: Yeah.
S31UBM: [Voice of surprise] No—No way.

Some students considered it unimaginable that the district would be permitted to rezone again in the direction of further resegregation, as the comment of disbelief illustrates. Of course, this is exactly what transpired. On May 3, 2007 the rezoning plan was approved by the school board in a three to five vote. Every street and housing section named by Union students nearly fourteen months before the rezoning plan was adopted were in fact rezoned to Union.

Not only did students name neighborhoods and housing developments likely to be included in the Union zone, they often named the ones that would be zoned elsewhere. Again, it was income level and racial demography that informed their predictions. One student mentioned a middle-class mixed-race neighborhood known as Postoak Hills:

S32UBF: Like Postoak Hills? That's a nice neighborhood, therefore that nice
    neighborhood goes to Garner. You see what I'm saying? They wouldn't zone
    Colonial Hills to come—to Union. But they will zone [Housing Project 1]
    or—no offense or [Housing Project 2] or [Housing Project 3]—you know,
    to come to Union because—look at what side of town they on.
S33UBM: You won't hear of them zoning [Housing Project 4] to go to
    Northbrook. [Outburst of laughter from students.]
S32UBF: Exactly. I'm surprised they zoned West End to go to Northbrook, but
    I guess they must've ran out of lines and places for them to go and they're
    just puttin' them somewhere.

These students also talked about the students far south of the city who were bussed across the entire city to attend the school in the far north even though they were closer to Garner and that students in nice neighborhoods closer to Union ended up at Garner. All this was evidence for them that the district leadership knew where each subdivision was and who lived there, and that this would influence where students were zoned.

Notably, students considered it inevitable that most students in public housing projects would be zoned for Union. The one exception to this pattern—students from West End attending Northbrook—did not disconfirm the students' discernment of racist intent. Instead, they concluded it must have taken place because there was just no more room for these students anywhere

the placement of students in the other school

else. The use of language like "just put them somewhere" indicated how Union students read the way district leadership felt about West-Side students. These students were not valued. Their placement at Northbrook was not made to advantage them academically. Nor was it made to bring the positive value of diversity to Northbrook. Instead, they were placed wherever there was room for the leftover students. West End students were leftovers.

This theme that Black students placed at Northbrook or Garner were demographic detritus arose repeatedly in our interviews.[9] Given the racist intent students saw behind the creation of an all-Black school, they were often at a loss for how to explain why the other two schools had so many Black students in them. Some adults considered this a positive achievement—at least they had preserved integration at two school zones in the face of the tipping point threat. But to most Union students, the most salient feature of their experience was being in a Black-only school and the racist recoil from them that this represented. Since Union students knew they were no different from Black students at Northbrook or Garner, they often concluded the placement of Black students at those schools was a mistake, an imperfect execution of racist intent, one that would be corrected in another round of restructuring. When these predictions came true, student fears were confirmed, and the number of students denying that the district had deliberately resegregated dropped dramatically.

In this way the opening of a new school building for Union High students, which should have been an occasion for celebration or at least represent a compensatory move towards some kind of equity, became instead a symbol of the community's will to racially resegregate the schools. When Union students entered the new building, there was a pleasure taken in the newness of the building and associated equipment. But the shine did not obscure the fact that the move to a new building was also a move further into an apartheid school system.

White Students

So far we have primarily cited the comments of Union High students. It is not surprising that Union students had more to say about the demographics of the district, since their demographic profile was the most different from the previously unified mega high school. The conversation about the resegregation of Riverton schools was not limited to Union students, however, nor was it confined to the Black students at Garner and Northbrook. The white students we interviewed also had opinions on the matter. Although there was more buy-in to the idea that the restructuring needed to happen among white students, less pointed and detailed critique of the zoning lines, and less skepticism about the neighborhood schools argument, the majority of white students we interviewed were critical of the restructuring policy, often because of its racial justice implications. As one young man at Northbrook High observed:

S8NWM: First of all, I don't see why they felt such a big need for change. And also I thought it was—it would have been so much better if they had kept it as Union. It would have showed that [our state] wasn't so quick [female participant interjects, "Yeah!"] to split back up. If they had actually stayed in the mega high school for even just like ten more years, it would have shown that we don't care if we have an order[10]—you know—"We've done this, we like it, we'll keep doing it." But instead, as soon as we got out of the court order they split again. So that just kind of represented us badly, too, there.

White students at Garner and Northbrook frequently commented on the unfairness of the demography and sense of shame that the district had broken up the old Union High so they could make a whiter school. Comments such as "It makes us look bad," (S34GWM) and "I don't see why they did it. It was fine the way it was before," (S35GWF) were common in our interviews.

Again, there was frequently an expression of surprise that the district could get away with a transparently unjust policy. White students, like several of the Black students interviewed in the early years of the study, assumed there was an external authority that was monitoring schools and would guarantee some minimal form of racial justice. As one student said, "It's not real segregation, because that's . . . it's like they'd get in trouble for that" (S36NWF). Other white students had less faith in the legal system, as the comments from this Garner student illustrated:

S34GWM: It's almost like they found a way around the system to segregate things again but not have to make it equal across the board—because Northbrook, which is the majority white, has got the most advantages. They've got the most money. . . . Right now Union doesn't even have a school. You know. They're going to Union West—a falling apart school and that's an all-Black school. It's almost like they resegregated things and they just found a way to get around the system.

This student's comment reveals a presumption that there is a "system" in place that would prevent resegregation of schools, but that Riverton school district found a loophole in this system that enabled it to do something that should be prohibited. In fact, the laws that had effectively prohibited racial segregation in schools had been dismantled by the time of Riverton's restructuring of its schools. There was no such "system" in place any longer and schools all over the nation were resegregating.

A few white students also anticipated the further racial segregation of the district. Like students at Union, they often interpreted the resegregation of the district as continuous with a regional and national history of racial injustice.

S34GWM: I personally think that it's more segregated now than it's ever been and hopefully it'll never be this bad again but . . . in a couple of years, the way that it's looking like, Garner's going to be pretty much all Black and then so is Union. And then Northbrook is going to end up being all white . . . . And that's just segregating the whole city—the whole town—more than it already is. And it's bad enough since we live in [a state known for its segregationist history] and that's how it is. That's how it's always been down here. And it needs to change sometime—at least shortly.

White students at Northbrook and Garner were, of course, in conversation with Black students there and to a lesser extent at Union. They also read the same newspapers, saw the same TV news. And many of their parents were critical of the district's restructuring policy. So it should not be surprising that they observed the restructuring of Riverton schools and came to many of the same conclusions as the Black students—that it was racially motivated, unfair and unjust, and that the segregation was likely to get worse.

Summary and Transition

Riverton students faced the brute fact of their school demographics every day. Conversations in the adult community—at home, in the newspapers and television news, school pronouncements—circulated around them daily. Consequently, they could not help but notice and seek to make sense of the changes brought on by the restructuring of the school district. Students questioned teachers and parents about it. They talked with each other about it. They speculated about the motivations behind the changes and considered the implications for themselves and the community.

Most students in our study regarded with skepticism the district's denials that race had been a consideration when district zone lines were drawn. Some students wanted to believe the district's claims—"I don't want to think that it was race—that would be too terrible!"—but found it increasingly difficult to accept the official narrative. Others didn't want to call it racial segregation, because they associated that term with pre-civil rights era racial apartheid and they did not want to think they were going to be subjected to such treatment. "They can't—they can't do like they did back in the days." Most high school students we interviewed, however, recognized that the creation of an all-Black attendance zone and the shift of an additional 800 Black students to that zone could not have happened unintentionally.

The shadow of this intentionality fell over all students' experiences. Even those who didn't want to believe it nonetheless felt compelled to wrestle with the possibility that racism was driving the restructuring process. For those who saw intentional racial bias in the restructuring, their criticism varied in its level of detail and sophistication. Like the "lads" in Paul Willis' (1981) famous study

Learning to Labor, these students had astute but partial critiques of the district's restructuring policy. All expressed disappointment and concern about the demographics of the new zoning. Most correctly identified racial motivations behind the restructuring and a few accurately predicted both the fact and form of further racial segregation to come. Even the transfer to the new Union High building was interpreted as cover for a further racial resegregation of the district. Students in Riverton high schools read the social text of the resegregation of their district constantly and critically. They either suspected or were convinced that something deeply problematic and officially unacknowledged was happening to Riverton schools.

When asked, students would acknowledge that racist disparities existed in the schooling system prior to the restructuring. However, the burdensome concern that racist intent lurked behind every design feature of the schools was present with a greater scope and intensity after the resegregation of the schools. Our study shows that students at Union saw themselves surrounded by institutional malevolence, in large part because of the demographic imbalance of the high schools. The schooling arrangement marked them as less respectable, less capable, less worthy of care and investment, than other students in the district. This implicit message spilled over the zoning boundaries, and communicated a similar lack of value to Black students at Garner and Northbrook. The presence of Black students at these schools was not seen as desired, but rather as a mistake or as an unavoidable but regrettable necessity. Black students were described, and at times described themselves, as not belonging at Northbrook. This message was reinforced when 800 Black students were moved out of the Northbrook and Garner feeder zones in the last phase of rezoning.

Students were not passive recipients of these messages. They named what was taking place. They objected and argued against it. They were a part of community discourses with a long history of resistance to racist disrespect. But whether students denied, accepted, or condemned the motivations of policy makers, the resegregation of the district still conveyed a message to the students.

In the next chapter we look beyond demography to a host of other more intimate and specific signifiers that Union High was considered the least of the three schools and that Union High students were considered lesser than their Garner and Northbrook counterparts. We look more closely at the students' interpretations of these features of their schooling experience and what it was teaching them about their world and their place in it.

Notes

1 See the Preface for a more detailed account of the study's methodology and theoretical assumptions.
2 The School Restructuring Committee Report, for example, cited the already restructured zones of the middle school as one of the primary reasons that the high schools had to be zoned as they were.

3 There was, of course, racial stratification in the tracked curriculum, with lower proportions of Black students in the courses with the higher academic press. But this was not a feature of the entire school identity and did not lead to stigmatization as a result of affiliation with the school.

4 In the initial years of the restructuring, average class sizes were neither larger nor smaller at Northbrook. The primary cause of the perception of overcrowding was probably that classrooms were physically smaller in the new school building.

5 Due to shifting demographics and continuing white flight, Black enrollment at Northbrook remained greater than 50% even after this second rezoning.

6 These styles, of course, do not correlate perfectly with the enrollment demography at various universities. The two band styles draw influences from the same sources and some band directors incorporate elements from both band styles. Still, the style "high stepping" and the "corps" style for marching bands remain recognizably distinct enough to serve as signifiers of different cultural traditions throughout the United States. For more information on these styles, see: Price, Kernodle, & Maxile, 2011.

7 Arguably, the desire to increase the proportion of white students in some schools as a means to prevent a wealthy white neighborhood seceding from the district or as a way of attracting foreign businesses to town constituted a rationalization for the restructuring. However, it was not one the district chose to espouse publicly or in official press releases. It is worth noting that only a few students mentioned these as possible reasons for the school restructuring. No student specifically mentioned the tipping point argument that circulated so widely among parents and educators.

8 Those that read the initial restructuring report could see that the creation of an all-Black school was intentional.

9 More will be said about this in the next chapter.

10 He is referring here to a federal court desegregation order.

Bibliography

Price, E. G., Kernodle, T. L., & H. J. Maxile (Eds.). (2011). *The encyclopedia of African American music* (Vol. 1). Santa Barbara, CA: Greenwood.

Steele, C. M., Spencer, S. J., & Aronson, J. (2002). Contending with group image: the psychology of stereotype and social identity threat. In M. Zanna (Ed.), *Advances in experimental social psychology* (Vol. 34, pp. 379–440). New York, NY: Academic Press.

Sue, D. W. (Ed.). (2010). *Microaggressions and marginality: manifestation, dynamics, and impact.* Hoboken, NJ: Wiley.

Willis, P. E. (1981). *Learning to labor: how working class kids get working class jobs.* New York: Columbia University Press.

4

GHETTO WEST

Students Read Other Signifiers of Stratification

As we saw in Chapter 3, the unbalanced demographics of the school zones conveyed an implicit message to students at Union that their high school was the least desirable school of the three in the district. It also was interpreted by some students as implying that Black children or West-Side children were unwanted at the other two schools. It was not, however, just demographics of the new school zones that communicated something problematic to Union High students. Daily life in the restructured Riverton schools provided many other social texts for students to interpret. Students discussed teacher attitudes about the school, differences in the quality and size of the new physical plant for the third high school, comments made by students at other schools, athletic and band uniforms, differences in fund-raising capacity and many other personal experiences. The messages students took from these various aspects of the restructuring were highly consistent and reinforced the message that Union High was considered unsafe and undesirable, that its students lacked academic ambition, and that the community was not interested in investing in the school.

Despite the obvious structural inequalities working against students assigned to the new all-Black school, our study shows how the differences that emerged between the schools—size, academic performance, reputation—were frequently interpreted as consequences of deficits in the Union students themselves. Union students were framed as being "less" than others, as lacking motivation or ability, or as lacking community and cultural values that support learning. This interpretation, in turn, became a social fact with which Union High students were forced to contend. Either students accepted the interpretation and consequently lowered their expectations for themselves or they resisted this portrayal of them as less-than, but then spent significant social and psychological effort fending off this negative portrayal.

In this way, the structural inequality of the schools was compounded and amplified by a discursive inequality that accompanied the resegregation of the schools. Even if the schools had created materially "separate but equal" schools—which they did not—the stratified status of the three schools had consequences for students' educational experiences. The ubiquitous message that the students served by Union High were somehow less than other students in the system influenced Union students' experiences in ways that made equality impossible to attain within the restructuring plan.

Are You Going With Us?

Once the decision to restructure the high schools was finalized, construction on the Garner and Northbrook buildings began early in the fall of 2001. Students, however, were notified of their new school assignments in the late spring, near the end of that school year. Those who had been paying attention knew that student assignments at the high schools would follow the pattern established with the restructuring of the middle schools. For such people, the revelation that the district would be creating a school whose enrollment would be 100% Black students confirmed with stark finality the anticipation that the district was racially resegregating. However, for those who had not been paying close attention, the creation of a high school whose enrollment would be 100% Black was a surprise. To many it was an outrage.

Public awareness of the exclusively Black enrollment at the new Union High School dawned slowly. When students were notified individually of what school they would be attending, overall enrollment patterns at each of the schools was not announced by the district. It was several weeks into the summer before it became general public knowledge that Riverton schools—once a model for racial desegregation—was regressing toward its racially segregated past by creating a feeder zone in which Black students would never attend classes with white students from kindergarten through twelfth grade.

Students discerned the high school enrollment pattern more quickly than the general public. They compared school assignments with friends and surmised what was happening while school was still in session that spring. The difference between the three high schools became a frequent topic of conversation the last few weeks they were all together at one high school. The establishment of a status hierarchy between the schools began almost immediately. Students recalled awkward conversations with one another about their school assignments the last month they were at the old Union High. Comments such as the following were common:

S2UBM: She said, "Oh, you got stuck over there." And I said, "What is that supposed to mean?"

~~~

S20UBM: Yeah, I knew I was going to Union, to Union West, but it was like—I don't know. The kids assigned to Northbrook and Garner felt they got better. I don't think they did. Well, maybe. But they were acting all superior.

~~~

S15NBF: It was hard, because friends were being separated. I was in ninth grade and one of my best friends was going to Union. I felt sorry for him at the time. It was—bad. But we're still friends.

Students also reported feeling something important was slipping away. The most common sentiment expressed by students was a sense of regret that the unified "Union High" identity would be lost and forgotten. There was regret about the anticipated loss of community-wide support for a single high school with winning traditions in many extracurricular areas from football to choir. Students worried about the divisive rivalries that might emerge between new high schools, rivalries that might take on racial overtones, and pit friends against friends. As one Garner High student put it:

S35GWF: I just hope students don't forget that we were all one, together. I think they will forget.

Some of the most poignant moments of the last month at the Union mega-school came when students asked teachers at which school they would be working. Students knew that teachers had been given the option to express a ranked preference for the school they would attend. Once those preferences had been submitted, but before the assignments had been announced, students began asking teachers where they were going. Teachers reported that this question was particularly charged when students zoned for the West-Side school zone asked their favorite teachers, "Are you going with us?" There was already a sense that something unjust was happening and the students zoned for the West-Side schools were watching to see if the adults in their lives would stand by them. Teachers recalled these questions vividly.

E5UBF: It was messed up. Teachers weren't talking about it with each other. Not at first. Then students started asking. It was hard. I had asked to be assigned to Northbrook, because that is where I live. But—I told students I didn't know where I would be assigned, and this was true. I hated what they were doing [breaking up the school]. But the students asking was the worst. They didn't have a choice.

Some teachers described their choice as a personal struggle. For teachers who thought the district policy was objectionable, expressing a preference for a school became a decision about whether to be complicit with an unjust policy. One very popular Black teacher reflected on this kind of deliberation:

E10UBF: I was going to apply to Garner. It made sense for a lot of reasons. But as I thought about it, I—they [West-Side students] were going—they were going to feel left behind. It hurt my heart. I prayed about it. [Pause] I prayed a lot. I turned my form in late. I told the district I wanted to be at Union. So when students asked, I said I am going to the Union.

I: How did they respond?

E10UBF: [Pause] "Excitement" is not the right word. Some hugged me when I told them. They were happy. But it was more like relief.

Presuming her interpretation of the students' response was accurate, this comment raises the question, why would the students feel relief? What does it mean that students might feel anxious about the school to which they were to be assigned or relief that they would be accompanied by their favorite teachers?

For some teachers the decision about school preference was more complicated. One white teacher reported that her preference for working at Union was complicated by her status as a certified International Baccalaureate (IB) instructor. The IB program was going to be located at Union[1] and yet no students assigned to Union were in the IB program. In order to keep the program viable, the district offered to bus students from Northbrook and Garner to Union High for half days so they could complete their IB diploma, yet remain officially enrolled at their home schools. This meant the new Union High, with its all-Black enrollment, would be hosting small, advanced curriculum courses on its site for white students bussed in from other schools. The teacher said:

E2GWF: It was unacceptable. Having an all-white IB class in an all-Black school, and bussing the white students in to take advantage of the advanced curriculum, but not having Union students in the class? What would that say? You are not good enough for this? I wanted to teach there, but I knew they would assign me to the IB program. IB training is expensive. They had invested in me. Why pay to train someone else. I told the district I would not do it. I told my husband that I would quit and we would have to do without the income before I would participate in something so—gross. So I applied to Garner, where both my regular and AP classes would be mixed.

When students asked her which school she had requested, this teacher declined to discuss the topic. She felt it was not professionally appropriate to discuss teacher building assignments before they were officially announced. "No good is served if students know their school was your second choice; best to wait till we know, I thought."

Students, however, came to their own conclusions based on what they could find out. Some teachers told students which schools they requested or where they thought they were going. Others declined to say. Overall, students observed that few teachers were willing to tell them that they had asked to be assigned to the new Union High. One Union student recollected:

S3UBM: I didn't hear of any teacher who said they asked for Union. Except Coach Jeffers. Maybe some of the teachers did, but—seemed like they all wanted to go to Northbrook or Garner.

As we saw in Chapter 2, this student's assessment paralleled the findings of this study. The overwhelming majority of teachers interviewed reported that, when the district initially solicited teacher input, they chose a school other than Union as their preferred assignment.

Once the restructuring happened, this narrative lingered on in student conversations. Several years after the restructuring students still occasionally commented that most Union teachers "didn't want to be here." Such remarks were precipitated by many things, such as the inability to hire a teacher for a particular class, teacher transfers out of Union, or, teachers comparing Union student performance unfavorably to other schools in an effort to motivate harder work. In one case, a student witnessed a new teacher being brought to tears and consequently leaving for the day, requiring other teachers to cover her class. He considered her discomfort with Union students an extreme version of a more common feeling and observed "most of them asked to be assigned to other schools, but they got Union" (S33UBM).

Our interviews suggest that teacher ambivalence about being assigned to Union moderated over time. Although many teachers expressed a preference for a school other than Union prior to the restructuring, three years after the restructuring most Union teachers expressed high levels of commitment to Union High. Nonetheless, despite these relatively high levels of commitment, stories about teachers being assigned to Union against their will persisted at the school. Whether or not these stories were true, this narrative about teacher preferences circulated among students and was a part of students' experience of Union as a stigmatized space. This experience was a direct consequence of the resegregation.

School Facilities

After the demographics of the schools, the differences in building facilities were among the most visible signifiers of the inequality of the restructuring process. As already indicated, the racial division of students occurred first in the middle schools. Students attending the middle schools in the north and east feeder zones were housed in the newest middle school buildings. For high school they moved to brand new buildings complete with state-of-the-art athletic facilities. This was in stark contrast with the West-Side students who attended the oldest middle school building in the system (built in 1965). Once in high school, they were placed in the fifty-year-old building on Oak Street (built in 1954) that many of their older family members had once attended as a segregated school. Their outdoor athletic facilities were all located on the former Union High eleventh and twelfth grade campus, 1.8 miles away (or twenty-two blocks), to which athletes had to provide their own transportation. Construction of the new Union High building at times left the existing athletic facilities without electricity (affecting hours of practice with no lighting on the fields) or running water.

These incongruities reinforced the idea that the new Union High was being neglected and that its students were less valued. Students interpreted this as one of the reasons even Black students living in the western zone tried to get into Northbrook and Garner—they wanted to attend a school with a new building.

S37UBF: Like for people who stay over here—they use like, other people's addresses to get to go to other schools 'cause for instance there's this person— somebody that stays next to me and they go to Northbrook. But, the only reason they go to Northbrook is because they use their Grandma's address so they can get over there.

I: Why do they do that?

S37UBF: Because they think that that school is supposed to be better just 'cause it's newer than this one.

The assumption that people associate better education with a new building and thus will be motivated to transfer to that school was not just a child's idle speculation. This same effect was anticipated by the district. The May 2000 Restructuring Committee Report explicitly cited the creation of new buildings as one of the ways they recommended that the district could stem the white flight out of the district.

> The City Schools' experience proves that the public perceives new schools as better schools and one of the attractions of a multiple school approach . . . is the expected impact of new schools on enrollment. Failing to build new will significantly reduce the enrollment impact and benefits of multiple schools.
>
> *(Restructuring Committee Report, 2000, pp. 28–29)*

At the time of the report, the system's facilities plan projected new high schools for the north and east areas, plus a new eastern middle school. The old high school and middle school buildings were projected for renovation for the western zone's two secondary level schools. The Restructuring Committee

Report noted the obvious inequity in this arrangement, leading them to conclude that only renovating the western schools could not be considered fair. "Ultimately, the West Middle School zone should have either a new high school or middle school—at least" (Restructuring Committee Report, 2000, p. 29).

Interestingly, although the district leaders considered the marketing appeal of a new school on parents they were trying to attract back into the district, they did not consider the converse effect that placing students in an old building would have on the reputation of the new Union High School or on the experience of students therein. Union students used adjectives like "ghetto," "broke-down," "old," and "raggedy" to describe their facilities.

S38UBM: It [the restructuring] was to try to put all the Black people in one school and put the white folks in the other two schools.

I: Say more about how you understand that taking place.

S38UBM: Well, they might think the white folks couldn't learn as well in the class with us. They probably thought they was better than us—and they kept us in the raggedy school.

I: Have you had conversations about that with . . . friends at Northbrook and friends at Garner?

S38UBM: Yes ma'am . . . they think that, "We've got a new school." All they think is they're better than us. And—they kept us in this raggedy school.

Union students were not just concerned about the material fact of the inequality of their schooling facilities. They were equally, if not more, concerned about its symbolic impact. The delay in construction of a new building, for example, signified to many students that the education of western cluster students was not a district priority.

S39UBF: It's kind of like they putting us on the back burner. They feel like they went over there and built these new schools for these other people, but they can't build us one. They didn't even have to rebuild me a school. They could've went over there and renovated it. . . . I would've been so happy if they just did that.

Even as their new building was being completed, students continued to sense that Union High School students were regarded as less than those attending the other schools. The delays, even if not intended to do so, communicated to Union students that they were somehow not as good as the students attending the integrated schools.

Union students frequently reported feeling looked down upon by students at the other high schools because of the old school building they were in. The old school building and its history as the site of the pre-civil rights era segregated school combined with the racial identity of Union High and the reputation of West-Side neighborhoods to reinforce a negative view of Union and its students. The term "Ghetto West" emerged in student discourse across all three zones to refer to the holistic pathologization of the western feeder zone. When Union High students used this term, it could be read as a complaint about unfair treatment, or at least as an equivocal gesture of resistance. But when others called Union "ghetto," the term seemed to stereotype Union students as well as their school.

I: You actually heard the term "ghetto school"?
S38UBM: Everybody said that. "Ghetto West." . . . "Ghetto West." That kind of hurt my feelings, you know?
I: Why do they say something like that?
S38UBM: 'Cause how old our school looks and there—our population of Black people. You know. We don't have any white people here, then so we've got to be ghetto 'cause we Black. . . . we on the *West Side*."

This student acknowledges that Union's reputation as a "problem" school is overdetermined by multiple factors. The lower status of the school would likely have emerged based just on its racial and regional identity, but the three years Union students spent housed at the Oakstreet site exacerbated their stigmatization.

The status difference between schools affected relationships, especially between students who lived near each other but were assigned to different schools. Being assigned to different schools put physical and social distance between students who were previously close. This distance was not a simple difference, but was hierarchical. It was often experienced as a rejection based on the relative status of schools, as one Union student described:

S40UBM: I think it caused tension between students, too, because when I was in ninth grade I had a lot of friends and now they're going to Northbrook—they don't—talk to me or anything. You know—they like changed—because of the rezoning. And it caused a lot of problems when they—[does not finish sentence.]
I: What changed them?
S40UBM: I believe because of the new school they built they thought they were probably a little like—higher. We were beneath them or something, you know, because they got a new school or whatever. And since we still in the same old school we don't—probably don't mean much—are less than the other two schools—you know? That's my thought.

The strain put on relationships between students who attended different school zones was at times complicated. It was not just that the buildings they attended were different, nor even that Union's facilities represented an attitude of neglect by the district. Students were also having very different schooling experiences.

Union students were attending an all-Black school in a fifty-year-old building, but Garner and Northbrook students were attending new schools that remained racially integrated. Consequently, Garner and Northbrook students often failed to empathize with the feelings of isolation expressed by Union students. Union student complaints were at times interpreted as exaggerated, or as an expression of lack of character or racial self-loathing. One Black student at Garner remarked that she found complaints from West-Side students and parents tiresome. Commenting on fears expressed by Union students that the second round of rezoning would further segregate the district, she complained that Union students and parents were being too negative about the restructuring.

S41GBF: People want to consider as with Union being a new school that once they rezone, it's going to be more Black students at Union instead of having more Blacks at Garner or Northbrook. They want to consider, once they rezone [a second time], that Northbrook is gonna be a whole white school, Garner is going to be a mixture of Black and white, and Union is going to be a whole Black school. But I feel as though that's not really going to happen. You probably still might have your whites at Union. You probably still will have your Blacks at Northbrook. But I guess because of the culture and the race—that's why we have so many problems. . . . they just won't come together and be like, "I think this is going to turn out great!" They just want to consider us [Black people] as negative and everything like that.

This student mistakenly assumed that there were white students at Union High and that there would still be white students at Union after the second restructuring. In fact there was only one white student at Union the first two years the school was open and a handful of students who only came for the IB classes but were never enrolled at Union. She also attributed the complaints of Union High students to a form of internalized racism. In this way, even the protests of Union students to their unequal treatment became signifiers of their lower status and lack of worth.

Other students at Garner and Northbrook were not quite so pointed in their remarks. However, their comments confirmed fears that the lower quality of the Union school facility contributed to a lower opinion of Union students. For example, Garner students frequently commented on the degree to which the Union students had been treated unfairly regarding their building. These comments often generated a counter-response—a rationalization of the district's decision based on the expectation that Union students would ruin a new building if they got one. The following quote came from a focus group with four Black students, however some version of this interpretation of the district's actions were repeated by other students, both white and Black, at Garner and Northbrook.

S42GBF: They're glad that they're getting part of—a new school too. 'Cause like, at first it seemed like they were getting left out with, you know, the new schools or whatever and not getting—that was an old school or whatever. But they're glad that they're getting a new school now you know.

S43GBF: [Subdued tone] I've heard what [S42GBF] said too, but I also heard that they were kind of worried about if they were going to mess up the new school and make it look really bad and if they would—if the community was just wasting their money—fixing up a new school for them.

S41GBF: Well, I have heard that sometimes people want to criticize Union, talking about that Union has *bad* children at their school, but I don't think so. But, they'll come along with the new building. I think everybody will be fine because they'll get to do as much as Northbrook and Garner does.

One Garner junior listed the pejorative stereotypes of western zone students that she felt contributed to a belief that Union students would ruin a new building. These stereotypes of West-Side students, she believed, were behind a reluctance on the part of the leadership to provide Union with a renovated or new school facility. This student also felt these views were false and concluded by defending Union students:

S44GBF: I think it's because the fact that most people that go to Union stay on the West Side. [Holding back laughter] Because the West Side, not to be funny but the West-Side girls got the reputation of being ghetto and they're kutchin' [laughter] and the um West-Side boys got the reputation that they'll shoot you—not to say that they will, but that's just their reputation so when they say that it's going to be an all-Black school I kind of think like when they were arguing about them building Union a new school I kind of think that they didn't want to give them a new school because they figured that it was all Black kids and they probably were going to mess the school up anyway like they weren't going to care when that's not the case. I mean, of course some people were going to think like that but then some people are actually going to school to get their education . . . and they not trying to just mess up their environment.

Our archival research revealed no such rationale for the delay in the building construction in formal policy documents or in interviews among teachers and district administrators.[2] Early in the restructuring process, well before construction started on Garner and Northbrook, the City had committed to building three new high schools. For the purposes of this study, however, the intentions of district administrators matter less than the effect of their actions on student experience. The district may or may not have delayed the construction of a new Union High because some thought less of the students there. However, that is the message many students *took* from the delay. This message was then amplified in the echo chamber of student discourse, intensifying the isolation experienced by students at Union High.

Older students contrasted the status hierarchy between the schools and the corresponding disparagement of West-Side students to their experience in the previously unified high school. Acute divisions between students, they claimed, did not happen at Union High.

S45UBF: Well, I think—some people's attitudes have changed 'cause they going to a new school and they think they better than us now since they got a new building. So—they have a new attitude.

I: How do you pick up on—attitudes?

S45UBF: Like, you could talk to somebody, like, that you used to go to school with, and then they go to like Garner or Northbrook and they're a totally different person. They don't want to speak to you 'cause you go to Union— which is an old building.

I: So, you're saying that they associate the students with the type of building you're going to?

S45UBF: Yes.

S37UBF: They also base it on the side of town you on. Just because we're on the West Side they consider us to be, you know, alley and loud and bad and rude and—you know, all that little stuff right there.

I: Was it like that when the Union was all one big Union?

S37UBF: I mean, no. Everybody had their little groups. Like, if you didn't want to hang with this crowd you didn't hang with them. It wasn't like, "Oh," you know, "We ain't going to talk . . . they on left hallway." You know—all that. It wasn't like that 'cause—I don't know. They was all together. It was one school. It was *Union*.

The delay in the construction of a new school, and the temporary housing of Union students in the old building that had been the site of the pre-civil rights era Black school ultimately had a doubled effect. The inferior facilities provided to Union students had direct effects on learning through poorer lab equipment, distracting maintenance issues, and sub-par athletic facilities. Of comparable if not greater significance were the symbolic effects of the delays and placement in the old Oakstreet High School building. Students at other schools saw it, interpreted it, and then represented their school back to Union students as a marker of their own lesser status. The status differential between the schools put a strain on student relationships and left Union students feeling isolated, neglected, and shunned.

Pervasive societal racism and classism probably made it inevitable that an all-Black school serving a lower income population would be stigmatized in the district. However, the inferiority of Union High facilities contributed to this experience of inequality. It very visibly underlined the lower status of

Union students in the minds of those within and outside the western school cluster. The two could not be separated in the experience of Union students. As one Union student phrased it:

S46UBM: Out of all the high schools we are looked at as the bottom. As where all the bad students go to. Like the students who graduate from Union will never go on to do anything in life. But they don't know. There's no difference. [Pause] The only difference is they don't give us the resources—because they think we're bad. We're bad because we're Black. Because we are on the West Side.

Other Signifiers of Lesser Status

There were other daily indignities that reinforced the message that Union students were considered less worthy of investment than their counterparts at other schools. Several students remarked on the differences in the types and quality of uniforms provided to band members and athletes. Quite often athletes had no spirit packs.[3] Union students had old athletic equipment leftover from the unified Union High. Students at the other two schools got new uniforms and new extensive spirit packs. This was one of the first differences the younger students noticed about the schools, possibly because attending games gave them a picture of what it was like at the new schools. One student who was on the basketball team was especially aware of these differences:

S3UBM: Garner gets, like, new jerseys like every year. At Union we be using the same jerseys for the same, like, past two or three years. . . . Every time you see Garner play us in a different year they got new stuff on. And we come by there with the same old stuff on. And then they be like, "Oh! Look at Union! They so old!" And everybody and the fans be like, "Oh Northbrook the tight brass! They're tight!" And everybody be looking at us like we are the joke of the game. All while we at the game—they'd be like, "Dog! That stuff old on 'em or what!" And then they be like, "Northbrook—Fresh!" "Garner stuff—Fresh!"

Teachers confirmed this inequity. One of the coaches reported having to wear home colors even when playing on the road, because the away-game uniforms were in such bad shape.

E15UBM: But yeah, it definitely—almost to the point of embarrassment—kind of a sense of shame to where here you are, you're trying to compete and you can't even look presentable sometimes. You know, like I'm going to have to call a coach Monday that we're playing and be like, "Hey, can we wear red? I know we're supposed to wear white, but our whites are so bad. Is there any way that we can wear red for the game?" And, you know, it's just—it's just pitiful sometimes in that sense. It's just not fair to these kids. You know, they didn't do anything to deserve this. And I just hate it and it really aggravates me.

Retaining the name, the colors, and the mascot of the old Union High for one of the new schools achieved cost savings for the district by avoiding the need to purchase new letterhead, logos, and uniforms. It is probably safe to assume that the new equipment, uniforms, marquis, etc. at Garner and Northbrook were intended to be a part of the marketing of those schools that conveyed improved educational opportunity so as to attract white private school students back into the public schools. However, little thought seems to have been given to the likelihood that providing one school out of the three with older, used equipment would have the converse effect; it would give the perception of neglect and diminished opportunity.

Similar remarks were made about uniforms for other sports teams and the marching band. Peers' comments at the games drew attention to other school comparisons, including references to the building, demography, even test scores. These differences were used to taunt Union High that it was not trying hard enough and just could not build up its program. This was a continual source of frustration and was one more indication to Union students that they did not have comparable support in the ways the other schools did.

Students also noticed related inequities in parent boosterism and community donations. Many observed that the restructuring created unequal access to a resource crucial to their extracurricular programs—community wealth. The western school zone included many of the lowest income areas of the district and none of the highest income areas, which made fundraising for various school activities more difficult. This disparity was confirmed by the school principal who observed that the most active parents in the Parent Teacher Association (PTA) at the unified Union school were almost exclusively from the northern and eastern zones. They had also been predominantly white. The new Union High had difficulty forming a viable PTA the first few years after the restructuring. The school's first Athletics Booster Club fundraiser actually lost money due to poor attendance. One teacher of twenty-five years who had attended Oakstreet High School before the district's desegregation explained:

E8UBF: Parents on the West Side used to be very active—when I was in school. They were present for everything. Cooked for us. Sewed for us. We had fundraisers for student trips and—Parents were *active*. Then the schools desegregated. And while that was good, good in many ways, it killed our parent involvement. The white parents pushed the Black parents out of that. Pretty soon the West-Side parents just let them deal with it. For thirty years. Now nobody knows what to do. The tradition of involvement has been lost.[4]

West-Side students noticed that despite the district's rhetoric of equality, stark differences in the potential for fundraising existed between schools. This was a concern because the existence of some educational opportunities, especially extracurricular programs, depended on parent and community donations. As with the other differences between schools, the students believed that community leaders knew this would occur. How could they not know that lower income neighborhoods wouldn't be able to provide as much supplemental funding to schools? And since these leaders let this happen, students inferred that the community did not care as much about them or the survival of their programs.

Students at Union often attributed the lower status of their school to the lack of wealth in the western zone and the corresponding inability to secure community investments in the school. Students saw this as a problem that would continue even after Union had a new building, making it unlikely that students would ever transfer voluntarily back to Union in large numbers.

S47UBM: I feel that if we had the funding to do whatever we felt we needed to do, most people would come back because that's the better—place to be. We just ain't got that much funding.

The lack of supplementary funding for the schools created material disadvantages. At times it also took on symbolic significance to students. The lack of funds created the appearance of neglect that then was attributed to a lack of moral character on the part of Union students and families.

S48GBF: And like what I was trying to say—the school was built around in certain places—Union—in poor surroundings, Garner and Northbrook in a better wealthy environment. So they think—you know. Yeah, they think, "Well okay, these schools are better because they're built in better environments. They're built by white folks. So they're going to have money so it's going to be better." You know, they're gonna take care of their stuff. Where at Union—not as much, not as many people have, you know, money and materials to put into the school like they can put into Northbrook and Garner. That's basically what it is. People just basin' it on race—and where you live—that's all.

Notice that the student suggests that people think wealthier neighborhoods are "gonna take care of their stuff." This echoed the rumors cited earlier that the district was not building Union a school because the district was afraid students would not take care of it. The student did not accept this narrative, but instead generated a counter narrative to explain how others might come to this conclusion. From her point of view the district had set Union High school up for failure. They had created conditions where Union would not be able to raise funds, and then blamed the community for the resulting poor performance and appearance of the school. She also tied the perception of superiority not just to wealth, but also to whiteness—"They're built by white people."

Other Union High School students made similar comments about the way racist and classist perceptions of Union High students contributed to a lack of community investment, which in turn produced effects that reinforced those perceptions. This created a vicious cycle of disinvestment according to the following student:

S27UBM: They think they know how we treat stuff, you know, like just because our school look like—we didn't put it like this, you know. It was already like, rain [there were leaks in parts of the building], the conditions, stuff like that . . . . And then they're like, they won't send us no money because they come over here and look at our school they think that they going to buy us something, we're going to mess it up. We didn't put it that way.

Again, this freshman student objected to the idea that Union High students were responsible for the condition of their school or deserve the poorer facilities they have. His objection, in this case, had the tone of a plea. It was less an accusation directed at the district than an act of psychological self-defense against pervasive messages of lesser worth and a request that the listener recognize the injustice of the conditions he and his schoolmates faced.

Psychic Self-Defense and the Burden of Racial Macroaggressions

The interpretive displacement of blame for educational inequality from institutional policies that create the inequality to the character of students and families of color is a familiar feature of racist discourses. Such pathologization of the victims of systemic racism is well documented in schooling processes (Valencia, 1997; Woodson, 2013) and in general (Du Bois, Gates, & Oliver, 1999; Fanon, 2008; Gilroy, 2000; Harney & Moten, 2013; Weheliye, 2014). It is, therefore, not surprising to see deficit theories operating as a part of the Riverton resegregation. Neither is it surprising that some students took this message to heart and either pathologized Union students or themselves.

What is significant is how many students resisted these pathologizing discourses. Union students worked against the grain of the message that they had been assigned to inferior facilities because they were "bad Black kids" and from the West Side by generating counter-interpretations of their schooling conditions. Richard Delgado (1989), in his famous essay "Storytelling for Oppositionists," points out that the critical reinterpretation of oppressive circumstances is a long-standing and important practice of resistance among societal "outgroups."

The member of an outgroup gains [from counter storytelling], first, psychic self-preservation. A principal cause of the demoralization of

> marginalized groups is self-condemnation. They internalize the images that society thrusts on them—they believe that their lowly position is their own fault. The therapy is to tell stories. By becoming acquainted with the facts of their own historic oppression—with the violence, murder, deceit, co-optation, and connivance that have caused their desperate estate—members of outgroups gain healing.
>
> *(Delgado, 1989, p. 2437)*

Students at Union engaged in this counter storytelling resistance by frequently locating the blame for the educational disparities they faced in the false racist assumptions others harbored about them, their school, and their community. These racist assumptions inspired inequitable policy decisions, which in turn produced actual inequality, thus reinforcing racist assumptions about them and constituting a materially self-fulfilling prophecy. Students' counter-narratives were a form of psychological defense against the self-perpetuating message that West-Side students were inherently flawed and less worthy of investment.

Students' counter-stories, however, could not completely insulate them from the corrosive curricular messages of the resegregation. The material inequalities and malignant neglect they faced remained, even when it was not converted into a form of self-condemnation. Students' alternative—and arguably more accurate—reading of the social dynamics at the school constituted a different form of message to students. Rather than communicate that they were personally flawed, it communicated that they were surrounded by a pervasive institutional hostility. This message, while perhaps preferable to internalized self-condemnation, constitutes its own form of burden and cannot be considered an appropriate or acceptable message to be communicating to children in schools.

There is a vast amount of evidence that such environmental messages of hostility have ill effects on both children and adults. Social psychologist Darrel Wing Sue offers the term "racial microaggressions" to describe the symbolic performance of racial hierarchy in interpersonal interactions. Sue describes racial microaggressions as "brief, everyday exchanges that send denigrating messages to certain individuals because of their group membership" (Sue, 2010, p. xvi). Sue and others have documented the damaging psychological impact of such messages, whether or not recipients of those messages consciously consent to their dehumanizing content (David, 2014; Steele, Spencer, & Aronson, 2002; Sue, 2010). Solorzano, Ceja, and Yosso (2000), in a study of the educational experiences of African-American College students, concluded "that the cumulative effects of racial microaggressions can be devastating" (p. 72).

The question raised by this study is, what happens when the racist microaggressions are not just a feature of "brief, every day exchanges" between individuals, but are a persistent feature of the institutional and material arrangements in which we live and reside? Such arrangements have measurable effects on things like learning outcomes and drop-out rates. However, these arrangements are also freighted with symbolic content that has emotional effects. This study demonstrates that structural inequalities of resegregated schools send denigrating messages to certain students because of their group membership in ways similar to interpersonal microaggressions. Might we call these institution-level dehumanizing messages *macroaggressions* (Huber & Solorazano, 2015; Matias & Liou, 2015; Smith, Allen, and Danley, 2007)? And what are we to make of the fact that these symbolic assaults are a consequence of the design of institutions whose purpose is to care for children?[5]

We may assume that the architects of the resegregation of Riverton schools would claim that these hidden curricular messages were unintentional or perhaps deny the validity of student complaints altogether. One salient feature of microaggressions according to Sue (2005) is that they are enabled by a conspiracy of silence. They are inherently ambiguous and thus easy to deny, making it difficult to hold anyone accountable for them.

> Microaggressions (a) tend to be subtle, indirect, and unintentional, (b) are most likely to emerge not when a behavior would look prejudicial, but when other rationales can be offered for prejudicial behavior, and (c) occur when Whites pretend not to notice differences, thereby justifying that "color" was not involved in the actions taken. Color blindness is a major form of microinvalidation because it denies the racial and experiential reality of people of color and provides an excuse to White people to claim that they are not prejudiced.
>
> *(Sue et al., 2007, p. 278.)*

Individual microaggressions, such as verbal slights, are rarely conclusive evidence of racism. And if confronted, the utterer of the comment is likely to deny racist intent and claim other motivations for his or her remark.

Similarly, each of these features became manifest in the text of the resegregation faced by Riverton students. For example, a particular teacher's preference to work at Northbrook High School could not be conclusively attributed to unconscious racist aversion. When confronted about the obvious racial imbalance of the schools' demography, the district insisted that its zoning plan was "color-blind." When asked about the failure to construct a new building for Union High students or provide them with new uniforms as had been done for the other schools, the district had rationales. The community could not come to a consensus about a building site for the new Union High. It made no sense to buy new uniforms when the district had perfectly good uniforms with the "Union" name on them. There was always a reason for the apparent inequity.

This meant students attended school every day exposed to material conditions that undermined their success and discursive conditions that made it difficult to hold anyone responsible for these conditions. Additionally, these discursive conditions prevented adult educators from acknowledging the gravity of their situation and helping students formulate a constructive response to it. Even if students didn't internalize a message that they deserved this neglect, they nonetheless got the message that others thought they were less worthy and were willing to put them in harm's way. They also got the message that, to a considerable extent, they were facing these conditions alone.

Summary and Transition

The demographic differences between the schools were only one of many signifiers of the lower status accorded to Union High School in the Riverton community. Almost every feature of the schooling process—the age and quality of school buildings, band and athletic uniforms, teachers assigned or not assigned to their school, fundraising for extracurricular activities, etc.—was interpreted at some point by Union High students as being influenced by unjust racial politics. This in turn became a part of the broader message that students in the western feeder zone were lacking in moral character, lacking in intellectual capacity, less likely to be successful, and for all these reasons, less worthy of investment.

Unlike the much younger students in Kenneth and Mamie Clark's (1950) doll studies, the older Union High School students interviewed for this study did not simply internalize a negative message about themselves. Most objected to the messages. They rehearsed arguments about its unfairness. They offered counter-narratives that critiqued the moral character of district leaders and the political majority driving policy. Still, the dehumanizing spirit behind the stigmatization of their school permeated their educational experience. It conveyed a message that they were surrounded by institutionalized racist hostility.

Differences in facilities and uniforms, however, were not the only, or even the most, educationally significant signifiers of racist hostility that Union students faced. After the restructuring Union students faced reduced curricular offerings caused in part by lower enrollments, which were caused in part by the stigmatization of Union High. As one student put it:

S84UBF: While they're so busy worried about a *building* they need to be trying to check to see if we gonna have the right—enough computers, enough books and stuff, enough teachers—while they're worried about a building.
S5UBF: Enough students.

In the next chapter, we look at another commonplace signifier of the lower status accorded to Union High. We examine the differences in curricular options available to students at different high schools, and how those differences had a mix of substantive and symbolic influence on Union High students' experience.

Notes

1 As recounted in Chapter 2, the national IB chartering organization required the IB program in Riverton to remain at the school named "Union High" because this was also the name of the original unified high school that originally received the charter. This happened over the strenuous objections of Riverton district administrators, who had proposed to relocate the program to Northbrook High School.

2 Which is not to say such motivations didn't exist, simply that they were not explicitly expressed in policy documents, board meeting minutes, or interviews with university researchers.

3 Spirit packs are the matching sets of sweat pants, shirts, caps, socks, etc. with school logos on them.

4 There is a large literature on the social capital that was lost in Black communities as a result of desegregation. For example see: Fultz, 2004; Haney, 1978; Hudson & Holmes, 1994; Ladson-Billings, 2004; Walker, 1996.

5 The term "macroaggression" has been introduced into the CRT literature by scholars such as Huber and Solorzano (2015), who define it as follows:

> We define macroaggressions as the set of beliefs and/or ideologies guided by white supremacy, that justify actual or potential structural arrangements that legitimate the interests and/or positions of a dominant group over non-dominant groups. Thus, the macroaggression names the ideological foundation that justifies the institutional racism, from which visual microaggressions emerge.
>
> *(p. 232)*

This use of the term essentially makes "macroaggressions" a synonym for ideology. Although related, our use of the term here is actually closer to that of Smith, Allen, and Danley (2007), who emphasize the psychological effects of the symbolic content of institutionalized racism. They write: "Racial macroaggressions are largescale, systems-related stressors that are widespread, sometimes becoming highly publicized, race-related, traumatic events. For example, the 1963 Birmingham church bombing or 'driving-while-Black' restrictions would classify as racial macroaggressions" (p. 610). Our use of the term macroaggression here stays close to Sue's (2010) definition of microaggression, by pointing to the denigrating racist messages conveyed in personal interactions, but also to the denigrating racist messages conveyed by institutional arrangements. Sue's use of the term is not just descriptive, it carries with it ethical implications. We have an ethical responsibility to recognize and avoid sending microaggressive messages to one another. Similarly, we have a responsibility collectively to avoid sending macroaggressive messages to one another, and certainly to our children in the design and operation of our schools.

Bibliography

Clark, K. B., & Clark, M. P. (1950). Emotional factors in racial identification and preferences in Negro children. *The Journal of Negro Children, 19*(3), 341–350.

David, E. J. R. (Ed.). (2014). *Internalized oppression: the psychology of marginalized groups.* New York, NY: Springer.

Delgado, R. (1989). Storytelling for oppositionists and others: a plea for narrative. *Michigan Law Review, 87*(8), 2411–2441. http://doi.org/10.2307/1289308

Du Bois, W. E. B., Gates, H. L., & Oliver, T. H. (1999). *The souls of Black folk: authoritative text, contexts, criticism.* New York: W.W. Norton.

Fanon, F. (2008). *Black skin, white masks.* New York: Grove Press.

Fultz, M. (2004). The displacement of Black educators post-*Brown*: an overview and analysis. *History of Education Quarterly, 44*(1), 11–45.

Gilroy, P. (2000). *The black Atlantic: modernity and double consciousness.* Cambridge, MA: Harvard University Press.

Haney, J. E. (1978). The effects of the *Brown* decision on black educators. *Journal of Negro Education, 47*(1), 88–95.

Harney, S., & Moten, F. (2013). *The undercommons: fugitive planning & black study.* Wivenhoe: Minor Compositions.

Huber, L., & Solorzano, D. G. (2015). Visualizing everyday racism. *Qualitative inquiry, 21*(3), 223–238.

Hudson, M. J., & Holmes, B. J. (1994). Missing teachers, impaired communities: the unanticipated consequences of *Brown v. Board of Education* on the African American teaching force at the precollegiate level. *Journal of Negro Education, 63*(3), 388–393.

Ladson-Billings, G. (2004). Landing on the wrong note: the price we paid for *Brown*. *Educational Researcher, 33*(7), 3–13.

Matias, C., & Liou, D. (2015). Tending to the Heart of Communities of Color. *Urban Education, 50*(5), 601–625.

Patterson, J. T. (2002). *Brown v. Board of Education: a civil rights milestone and its troubled legacy.* Oxford: Oxford University Press.

Smith, W. A., Allen, W. R., & Danley, L. L. (2007). "Assume the position . . . you fit the description": psychosocial experiences and racial battle fatigue among African American male college students. *American Behavioral Scientist, 51*(4), 551–578.

Solorzano, D., Ceja, M., & Yosso, T. (2000). Critical race theory, racial microaggressions, and campus racial climate: the experiences of African American college students. *Journal of Negro Education, 69*(1/2), 60–73.

Steele, C. M., Spencer, S. J., & Aronson, J. (2002). Contending with group image: the psychology of stereotype and social identity threat. In M. Zanna (Ed.), *Advances in experimental social psychology* (Vol. 34, pp. 379–440). New York, NY: Academic Press.

Sue, D. W. (2005). Racism and the conspiracy of silence: presidential address. *The Counseling Psychologist, 33*(1), 100–114. http://doi.org/10.1177/0011000004270686

Sue, D. W. (Ed.). (2010). *Microaggressions and marginality: manifestation, dynamics, and impact.* Hoboken, NJ: Wiley.

Sue, D. W., Capodilupo, C. M., Torino, G. C., Bucceri, J. M., Holder, A.M.B., Nadal, K. L., & Esquilin, M. (2007). Racial microaggressions in everyday life: implications for clinical practice. *American Psychologist, 62*(4), 271–286.

Valencia, R. R. (Ed.). (1997). *The evolution of deficit thinking: educational thought and practice.* London; Washington, DC: Falmer Press.

Walker, V. S. (1996). *Their highest potential: an African American school community in the segregated South.* Chapel Hill: University of North Carolina Press.

Weheliye, A. G. (2014). *Habeas viscus: racializing assemblages, biopolitics, and black feminist theories of the human.* Durham, NC: Duke University Press.

Woodson, C. G. (2013). *The mis-education of the Negro.* New York: Tribeca Books.

5

CAUGHT IN THE CURRICULAR NET

Material and Symbolic Entanglements of Resegregation

Most research on the effects of racial segregation examines its influence on students' access to social capital in the form of grades, test scores, literacy levels, high school diplomas, college admissions, etc. (Guryan, 2004; Kainz & Pan, 2014; Lutz, 2011; Mickelson, Bottia, & Lambert, 2013; Orfield & Frankenberg, 2014; Reardon & Owens, 2014; Reber, 2010; Ryan, 2010). Sometimes such studies examine the actual material effects of segregation on students and their families, in the form of long-term employment and income levels, health statistics, rates of incarceration (Johnson, 2011; Mickelson & Nkomo, 2012). This study was designed to complement that research by documenting the qualitative effects racial resegregation of schools has on students' experience. Specifically, we have examined the symbolic messages that resegregation communicated to students about their capacities, worth, and place in the community.

It would be a mistake, however, to draw a bright line between the material and symbolic effects of resegregation on students. And it would be a greater mistake to act as if one form of analysis comes at the expense of the other, as often occurs in debates between critical theorists who emphasize the material economic bases of racial hierarchy and post-structuralists who emphasize the discursive bases of racist oppression.[1] The semiotics of the marginalization of Union High and its students was a complex weave of material economic disadvantage, constricted access to various forms of cultural capital, symbolic stigmatization, and personal psychological effects. Each of these, and their interactions, in turn became phenomena students could reflect upon and further interpret, so that materiality, action, and meaning became layered one upon another.

In this way a material semiotic[2] net of racism, of which the resegregation of Riverton schools was a part, closed around Union students. Nowhere were these complex interactions more apparent than in students' interpretations of the changes in learning opportunities wrought by the resegregation. Students were placed in materially inferior facilities and provided with materially inferior equipment. They watched as this contributed to symbolic effects such as a decline in the reputation of their new school before it even opened. This decline, in turn contributed to the material effect of enrollments dipping below expectations, which in turn caused reductions in elective and extracurricular offerings. The restructuring also created an imbalance of high-performing students, which caused differences in test scores between the three high schools, triggering a shift in curricular emphasis from advanced courses to remedial courses at Union. Both of these effects contributed to a further decline in the school's reputation, which in turn deterred teachers and academically ambitious students from coming to Union. These dynamics, along with what students felt were unfair public media representations of Union High, contributed to an increasing feeling of isolation and hopelessness for Union students. Even if they knew it was wrong, even if they believed they did not deserve what was happening, the losses of curricular opportunity were real. The institutional dynamic causing this real loss often appeared overwhelmingly large, complex, and unstoppable, which undermined student morale and motivation.

Instructional Materials

Some of the earliest and most frequent comments students made about the explicit curricular effects of the resegregation regarded inequities in instructional materials such as educational technology and textbooks. There were clear material inequities in the technology available to teachers and students, as the new schools came outfitted with new computers, audio-visual equipment, and smartboards. Multiple teachers at all three schools and two principals confirmed that the technology inequity was real. According to a Union High language arts teacher this could be seen most clearly in the kind of equipment available in classrooms.

E18UWF: Garner and Northbrook ... I have seen the technology that those teachers have. I've seen, for example, just that they have dry erase boards that they can write on. I don't. I have one dry erase board that I can't even use because it's so old and can't be erased anymore. ... at this point, as a teacher, I've seen how the other classrooms are managed just in terms of, as I said, the technology, the materials that they have, the fact that they have—every room has a computer that's hooked up to a television so that they can use an LCD projector. We have to schedule an LCD projector through our library and take turns. Every teacher at those schools— they just put a CD in their computer and can bring up a PowerPoint with no problem.

Inequitable access to instructional technology impacted students' education both practically—through its use—and symbolically—in that old technology was another signifier of Union's lower status in the district.

A central district administrator rationalized that Union would get that new technology when its new building was constructed, because it would be fitted for the appropriate network connections. For this administrator, the delay in Union getting access to new technology was simply a matter of practical technological necessity. It did not seem to occur to him that new technology was not just instrumental, but also symbolic in its impact. For Union students and teachers, however, the lack of the latest technology was further indication of district neglect. The perception of neglect had real effects on student experience and morale.

There were also material shortages of textbooks. These shortages occurred at all three high schools. Students, however, could only see the shortfalls at their own schools. This lack was interpreted as a signifier of neglect at Union High in a way that it was not at the other three schools. Union students persistently remarked that they were getting fewer or lower quality instructional materials than the other schools. As one Union student commented:

S27UBM: It's not fair. We don't have a new school building. We don't even have the books and computers the other students have.

A lack of textbooks was a persistent theme in Union student comments. Students reported having too few textbooks for classes or delays in their delivery.

S5UBF: Books was a huge problem. Textbooks. . . . Like in Pre-Calculus we didn't have our books at the beginning of the year. We had to wait until near the end of the *first 6 weeks*—the middle to the end of the first six weeks before we even had our Pre-Cal books.

Students often interpreted the lack of textbooks not only as a sign of neglect but as an indication that the district's white leadership intended to set Union High School up for failure. It reinforced the perception of a pervasive racial hostility toward West-Side students. A freshman at Union remarked:

S49UBM: Well that—[my parents] told me that they're trying to put it all like it used to be. Just 'cause the white folk don't care about us. They want—they want to set us up for—failure. You know? And we ain't got no books over here or nothing. We don't have no books, we ain't going to learn. We don't learn, we're going to sell drugs. If we gonna sell—if we sell drugs, we gonna be held in jail.

I: Okay—you're saying that you don't have any books—is that for a specific class?

S49UBM: Like, all classes—we don't have that many new textbooks. So, we had to use—everybody had to use the same textbook every class period. [Means textbooks remain in classrooms and are used by multiple classes.] Then we have problems studying 'cause we don't have any textbooks to take home.

[Other students mumbled agreement. Teacher intervened to pursue his point.]

Teacher: In the other schools, did they have textbooks to take home?

S49UBM: Yeah.

Teacher: How do you know?

S49UBM: I talked to people over there. They have their own textbooks. It was to take home. . . . We don't have that many to take home.

Given the other forms of inequality faced by Union students—older building, racial isolation, lower income population, less instructional technology and older equipment—the textbook shortages further reinforced the impression of institutionalized racist inequality between the schools. In these students' views, the textbook shortages were happening "'cause the white folk don't care about us." Towards the end of the interview, when the classroom teacher asked the focus group what would be different at Union if white students attended there, one student replied matter-of-factly, "We would have more books" (S50UBF).

Even ten years after the initial restructuring, after multiple new textbook adoptions had taken place and no apparent material inequality of instructional technology remained, Union students still often mentioned having inferior textbooks as one of the ways Union High was treated unfairly. It was discursively sustained in the imaginations of students in part by a context characterized by other forms of inequality—both material and reputational.

Diversity

Students also frequently mentioned the lack of diversity at Union High as one of the curricular effects of the resegregation. Seniors attending the new Union High the first year it opened found themselves in a school that was nearly all Black, a stark difference from their earlier experience in a racially integrated high school. Freshman entering Union High that year and every year thereafter saw a familiar sight—an all-Black school population. A few years after the restructuring there were students graduating from Union High who had never attended a school with more than one or two white people.

This racial isolation was a concern to teachers at Union. They remarked repeatedly that Union students would have to get jobs working with and for white people. They wondered how Union students were to learn the cross-cultural and code-switching skills necessary for such jobs if they were never around white people. One teacher observed that not only were Union students not exposed to white people, but that some students grew up never leaving the western side of town. Noticing the interviewer's surprise, she said this was more common than some might think. She recounted a recent occasion that illustrated her point:

E28UBF: I took a young woman to the mall with me the other day, just five miles away, and she said had never been there before. They only shop at the Piggly Wiggly store [a local grocery] and the thrift [shop], she said. It was a new experience for her. She was fifteen.

Economics compounded the racial isolation experienced by some students at Union High. Many students and families didn't have cars and Riverton lacked reliable public transportation. This, and discomfort moving into social spaces where money was required to participate and where their clothing or linguistic performances elicited scorn and harassment, kept some Union students in their home neighborhoods.

Several teachers had attended Riverton schools when they desegregated. They recalled the challenges of that transition and the possibilities it opened up in their lives. For a few, the integration of Riverton public schools had led to their first immersive experience with large numbers of white persons and their first sustained social interactions as peers with white people. One such teacher, a coach at Union, explained the importance of these experiences to his later life.

E21UBM: I had not been to a white person's house before high school. But I was on the football team and the track team that first year [after integration]. So I got to know people, my white teammates, got invited over. It was important—to experience that. My first job was working for a friend's, a white friend's, father, at an office supply store. Those experiences and connections, they opened doors. There is no way I would have gone to the [local majority white] University if it—if I hadn't gone to Union—an integrated school. I wouldn't be here today, talking to you. I worry for some of our students that they won't have that. I don't know where they will get it if not at school. At 18, when they are applying for a job or for college, it is too late.

Union students shared these concerns about the social education they were getting. The older students who had attended the unified Union High were able to compare their earlier experiences to the new school configurations. Students fitting this description universally considered the lack of diversity at the new Union High to be a serious drawback. A diverse student body had its inherent pleasures, a few pointed out. It made school "fun." More importantly, diversity provided the opportunity to learn things that would be instrumental in later life.

S21UBF: And at [the unified] Union you were with everybody in the entire city of Riverton that went to high school. So, I mean, you got exposed to like a lot more diversity and—it was just—more fun.

S51UBM: Well another disadvantage, going back to what [S2UBM] said, yes, the neighborhood schools will be good because you won't have to adjust, but they will also be a hindrance in later on in life 'cause you will soon have to adjust one day and—

S2UBM: [Cuts in] You wouldn't know how to interact with other people.

S51UBM: —you wouldn't know how to interact with other people—like when you go to college or when you get on the job site. You wouldn't know how to react with other people.

S5UBF: Diversity. Diversity.

S2UBM: Diversity.

Students mentioned all manner of "diversity" including regional diversity, religious diversity, and just diversity of interests. One student remarked that she would be happy if they just had some new Black students transfer to the school, as opposed to attending school with the same students from first grade through twelfth, signaling a concern about a geographic kind of isolation. However, primarily students were referring to concerns about racial diversity. Racial diversity was what was most conspicuously lacking at Union High. When asked why this was a source of worry, students gave variations on the same answer. They needed the opportunity to learn how to "associate" and "talk" with people from differing backgrounds:

S52UBM: Yeah I agree with her. I think that well—if we do meet different people, it'll teach us how to interact and not just keep to ourselves. It'll teach us how to meet different people and how to—associate with them.

S53UBF: It'll teach us how to associate with other races instead of just the same.

S6UBF: Union is a majority Black school. An African-American school. Where when it was just one big high school, you know, we had all kinds of people . . .

S54UBM: Yeah. You just seeing your own race—during your whole—high school life. You probably won't even be prepared like when you go to get a job or something—you know, like how to socialize with somebody that's different from you. And 'cause you've been with your one race for a long time you won't know how to um like you know talk to—talk to—act towards another—

S6UBF: —culture.

S54UBM: Culture.

S6UBF: You're not culturally diverse.

Students and teachers at Union High clearly considered a racially diverse student body to be a source of learning opportunities. They felt such diversity made it possible to acquire the cultural capital necessary to thrive in a racially stratified society. There is considerable research that supports this view. Scholars have documented correlations between the ability to linguistically code switch and employability (e.g. Akinnaso & Ajirotutu, 1982; Baugh, 1983; Cocchiara, Bell, & Casper, 2014; Lippi-Green, 1997; Robbins, 1988; Terrell & Terrell, 1984). There is also research that suggests integrated schools provide other important learning opportunities such as developing the skills necessary for democratic citizenship (Gurin et al., 2002); enhanced subject matter learning (Caldas & Bankston, 1999; Johnson, 2011; Orfield & Whitla, 2001) and different developments of self-concept (Taylor, 2012). The reality of such benefits have been the basis for desegregation and affirmative action jurisprudence for decades (Welner, 2006). As civil rights activist Mark D. Rosenbaum observed:

> Is it possible to learn calculus in a segregated school? Of course it is. . . . Is it possible to learn how the world operates and to think creatively about the rich diversity of cultures in this country? It is impossible.
>
> *(Rich, 2012)*

Integration has by no means been a panacea for the suffering caused by racial stratification and segregation. Its effects have been mixed and complicated (Dumas, 2014a, 2014b; Ladson-Billings, 2004; Reardon & Owens, 2014; Taylor, 2012). However, the benefits of a more diverse student population perceived by students was not mere self-deception. The lack of diversity at the new Union constituted a loss of access to certain kinds of schooling experiences. This curricular loss was doubled because students were conscious of it as a loss, and thus the lack of diversity at Union also became a signifier of something more pervasive. The lack of diversity became a symbol of a general indifference to the educational needs of Union students.

This understanding of the racial diversity at the school as a curriculum resource being willfully denied to them was most apparent when Union students mused about the need to get white students to enroll in their school as a means of securing this kind of diversity curriculum for themselves. The zones were already strangely drawn, some students reasoned, and Black students were already being bussed from the West Side over to Northbrook High. They wondered aloud why the converse did not also take place:

S27UBF: If they can send West End Black kids and different neighborhoods of Black kids all the way to Northbrook for it to be a mixed race, then why can't you send some white kids over here then, since you want to rezone it in a weird way? Why not rezone other—other areas with white kids in it to send them to Union?

The same idea was proposed in a different focus group. This time students cited the bussing of white students from Northbrook to Union as evidence that such a thing could be done.

S17UBF: If they had to like bus kids over to this side of town, I don't see what would be the problem. They bus kids from Northbrook . . . for a whole semester to come for two periods. So I think—so they can bus kids over here for an entire day of school. Because like—I don't understand the zoning lines. Its kids that live like—right across the road, right up here. They go to Northbrook. But they have the Black kids over here zoned for Northbrook, but why aren't the white kids over there being zoned for Union? That's what I don't understand. . . . I feel like when it comes to diversity, we're just getting the short end of the stick.

Although there was obvious confusion over the zone lines, the pressing issue for most students was the outcome of the zoning process—the lack of diversity at Union. They recognized a contradiction in district policy. If the district was allowing white students to transfer so they could enjoy the benefits of the International Baccalaureate (IB) curriculum, then, as a student sardonically asked, "Why *can't* white people be brought to Union" so that Union students could gain the educational benefit of attending a racially diverse school?

S5UBF: We have white people come here too. We love white people! You know? And—I don't have a problem. We—we *want* other people here. [Peers agree in background.] I just don't understand why they did—how they just split us up that way.

Students posing such rhetorical questions were often the same students who in other moments would offer explanations of the resegregation that attributed it to pervasive racism in the community. In other words, when posing such questions students actually understood why there were no white students at their school, or at least they had well-founded suspicions. However, they felt compelled to constantly point to the irrationality and unfairness of the situation in which they found themselves.

Students were penetrating in their analysis and emotions often ran high. A Union junior offered a particularly incisive and passionate critique of the language used to describe the demography of the school and the way those language choices obscured what was actually happening to her education. She asked why people constantly spoke about the presence of Black students at Union as if that was the bad thing happening to the school. She considered that to be a part of the racism driving the resegregation.

S17UBF: They're putting it like, they're just saying, "It's all Black kids. It's all Black kids." Why aren't you saying that it's "No white kids"? Don't just say, "It's all Black kids." [Hits desk to emphasize each word.] Speak about the people that aren't here. They always just say who's here, who's here, who's here. But—when you say who's here, they're here so what's the problem?

That's not the problem ... it doesn't upset me about the point of being around all Black people because when I go home, my grandmother is an African-American, so I will be at home with an African-American. My family members are Black. The people in my community are Black ... Everywhere you go there are Black people so it's not about that. The point that I just don't like—I think they're giving us the short end of the stick on diversity ... I feel like this should be—it should be more diverse than this. If there are not any white people here, I think there should be Asian— something! Anything—you know. But it should be more than one race attending this high school because other schools—they have racial diversity. That's what I'm screaming. It's not about all Black kids being here because I'm used to Black people.

This student identified and critiqued a problematic discursive formation that often afflicts public discussions about racial segregation in schools. The issue is often framed as if it is the exclusive presence of Black and Latino students that is a problem. This framing implies that the presence of Black students is a source of negative effects. More significantly, it erases the operative principle actually driving the resegregation—the aversion of whites to enter majority Black spaces. It is the absence of racial diversity in her school, the young woman argues, that constitutes a negative effect on her education, not the presence of Black students.

Consider the levels of racist signification this student was parsing, because it indicates that students were aware of the multilayered nature of the racial discourse formations around them. Not only did she read the lack of diversity as a detriment to her education. Not only did she read that lack of diversity as a symptom of a broader racist aversion among white persons to attend school with Black students. She also read the way the community conceptualized segregation as the presence of an all-Black student enrollment without naming the absence of whites as part of the problem facing Union High students. Based on what we found in our study, she was correct on all three counts.

International Baccalaureate Courses

One of the most visible explicit curricular effects of the restructuring process was the controversy that emerged around the district's IB program. As was recounted in Chapter 2, the IB program is an advanced college-preparatory curriculum made available by an international organization based in Switzerland. Districts apply and pay to participate in the program. They must abide by the terms of a charter in order to have continued access to the curriculum as well as the exams that certify student achievement.

All but a few of the students participating in the district's IB program were zoned for either Northbrook or Garner. The district leaders therefore believed that it would be able to transfer this advanced curricular program to one of those schools and made plans accordingly. The IB chartering organization, however, denied the transfer proposal and ruled that the IB program had to remain at the school with the name on the charter, causing distress among IB students, their parents, and district administrators. This may seem to have been a benefit to the Union High students and in some ways it was. It insured that a certain kind of advanced curriculum would remain proximate to them. However, initially the curriculum was only physically near Union students, because only a few of them had the prerequisites necessary to enroll in these courses. The first year a few seniors in the IB program who were zoned for other schools were permitted to attend Union to finish their IB diplomas. By the second year however, the IB eligible students zoned for Northbrook and Garner withdrew from the program to attend school in their assigned zones. Low enrollments forced the IB courses to be merged with other advanced courses to keep them viable.

A similar dynamic played out for the pre-IB courses as well, also considered an elite curriculum. In response to parent demands, the district made funds available to bus students in from other high schools for half-days to take the courses to keep enrollment up. Parents of these students, however, were unwilling to register them full time at Union High. In this way, the IB program's location at Union High became a glaring public signifier of the academic disparities between Union and the other two schools. The implication was that most Union students were not good enough to take the IB courses and that students from other schools really didn't want to be at Union.

This disparaging message was not just conveyed by enrollments in the IB courses. Apparently West-Side students felt discouraged from enrolling in the program. Union students recalled hearing negative messages about their ability to complete the IB program in "recruitment" meetings held at their middle school. A high-achieving Union student describes her memory of the pitch:

S56UBF: All of the eighth graders were put in the cafeteria. And—at least at—down at Oakstreet Middle, that's when they told us, it wasn't an, "Y'all get in it" thing. It was like, [imitates rough, male voice] "It's going to be hard. Don't get in it! It's going to be hard. Don't get in it!" That's what they . . . that's how it was when they came down to Oakstreet. I guess because they didn't *expect* many of us to come, to do it better—as good as—the kids from Garner and Northbrook would do. I was a little upset, but I still went to a counselor. I went to our counselor down at Oakstreet and I talked to her about it. And she signed me up for all my classes—where I could . . . take the IB stuff or whatever.

This student was speaking of signing up for the pre-IB courses in the ninth and tenth grades, which enabled her to enroll in IB courses in the eleventh and twelfth grades. Once in the IB courses she was able to compare her experiences with students who had attended middle school in the north feeder zone, but who had been rezoned for Union High in the second restructuring and realized how different they were. A student who had attended a North-Side middle school described this very different recruitment experience. Unlike her peers from Oakstreet Middle School, she had been strongly encouraged to enroll in the IB program:

S1UBF: To what S56UBF was saying—that's just how—you could see just how—segregated they are 'cause she said they went to Oakstreet, it was like, "Oh, it's going to be hard," —all like that. When they came to Northbrook MS, the girl was like, [imitates a girly student voice] "Oh, you've got to get into the IB program. It's a lot of opportunities!" You know, "You could do it!" You know, doing this getting up all of your spirits and stuff like—[changes to her own voice] "Oh, okay! I can go to IB program and just—," you know, get all these scholarships and everything. I mean, it was the total opposite what they told S55UBF.

Another student who attended the North-Side middle school corroborated this account of the enthusiastic tone of the IB program recruitment she received. She interpreted the more encouraging presentation of the IB program as a consequence of her classmates being white.

S57UBF: [Sighs] Well, I took class with a whole bunch of white people . . . They didn't say what they said at Oakstreet. No. No. No. It was like, [shifts to an upbeat tone] "The smart, smart kids—y'all come and be in IB and AP classes! Go get those scholarships! Get that! Get that! Get into a good college! Go get into Harvard and Princeton!" and all that. "Go and get in that class!" [Quiets voice] They didn't say what they told those people. No.
S2UBM: It seems like they were trying to discourage Oakstreet students from entering the program—while encouraging the students headed to Northbrook and Garner.

The idea that the IB program belonged to white students and therefore belonged at the school most identified with its white population—Northbrook High—was a consistent theme in the student discussions about this advanced curriculum.

Teachers corroborated these student observations and reported that the practice of recruiting to the IB was complicated during the restructuring process. Initially most teachers and administrators believed the IB program would go to Northbrook High, which provided an incentive to discourage West-Side students from signing up for the program based on regional accessibility. When it became clear that the IB program would stay at Union, this inspired some educators to recruit more vigorously from Oakstreet, in order to help the program survive. At the same time, others who advocated ending the program entirely discouraged students from signing up for the program. A former IB program director called into local radio programs to make the case that West-Side students were not adequately prepared for the IB curriculum and that the resources spent on the program could be better spent on other things. The resulting mixed messages had the unsurprising effect of depressing enrollments of West-Side students in the pipeline of pre-IB courses that led to the IB program.

S58UBM: And I know what she's talking about because like, when I was down there, there was like—"Y'all, it ain't what y'all's used to," and all this stuff . . . like they was just saying, it's not for us. And then, so everyone was like, "Well, we ain't going to get in." When I got to ninth grade, it was like three or four of us that were from Oakstreet that got into the IB program [referring to the pre-IB classes].
I: Only three or four out of the whole school?
S2UBM: All we had from Oakstreet was three or four.

The restructuring of Riverton schools occurred in such a way that the location of the IB program at Union, rather than being a sign of possibility and college aspiration, instead became a signifier of the lack of possibilities for Union students. Confusion about the future of the program created conditions in which some educators felt compelled to publicly express low expectations of West-Side students, sometimes directly to the students themselves. In this way, the proximity but lack of access to the IB program became a form of hidden curriculum that reinforced the message that Union High students were less fit for advanced curriculum than were Garner and Northbrook students. This message folded seamlessly into the community conversation about the relative quality of the three high schools and more universal racist assumptions about all-Black schools. One student imagined what this would look like from the outside:

S17UBF: But if someone just came and they were from Canada—anywhere, you know, they came to Riverton and they looked at this school and they looked at Northbrook, and Garner, and Givens County High [large mostly white county school], you know—they wouldn't think that this school has the IB Program, with the surroundings and all that, you know. With—if they came and looked at our student body they wouldn't probably think that we—that we were the only school that has the IB program.

Similar views about the location of the IB program circulated among parents and students at the other high schools. Parents of IB students at Northbrook were heard more than once referring to Union High as "the school for geniuses and deviants." The "geniuses" were the bussed in IB students, all of whom were white except for one Asian-American student and one Black student. "The deviants," while not specified, was likely a reference to a stereotype of everyone else at Union. Two Northbrook students who were bussed the first year to Union for pre-IB courses were considerably kinder in their remarks. They acknowledged the overall unfairness of the new zoning plan, but similarly felt the IB program belonged at Northbrook where more people "wanted" to take the courses:

S59NWM: It's like having, when they rezoned, like what she said—it's unequal rezoning and stuff like that. Like, really the Black—like having to be like Union—like it's all Black—
S60NWF: Yeah, it's kind of segregated.
S59NWM: Yeah, and like Garner is like, the middle school or whatever. But like Northbrook is mostly white so it would make more sense to put the IB program where people want to take it instead of having all those Northbrook people come over here to take the classes and it's only a few that want it at Union.

Notice that these students explicitly linked the whiteness of Northbrook with a demand for the IB curriculum. It was invisible to the Northbrook students that West-Side students had been discouraged from signing up for pre-IB courses. Therefore, they interpreted the low number of students from the western zone in the IB program as an expression of interest or a consequence of their ability. In this way racist discourses in one context produced effects that reinforced racist deficit theories in another context, which in turn was cited as a justification for policies that would have exacerbated the structural curricular inequalities faced by Union students. A focus group of Northbrook students who were bussed the first year to Union for IB classes, expressed frustration that the IB program could not be moved to Northbrook, where they felt students wanted it more.

S59NWM: The restructuring program just completely wiped out IB.
S60NWF: I know.
S61NWF: Yes.
S59NWM: Because, I mean, no offense to Union or anything, but the students that are still here do not care about the IB program with the exception of maybe … Seven, eight. [Laughs] And none of them are doing the IB program next year. The actual IB program! And I think it's just sort of a waste … and it's just a waste because—*I know* that there will be a lot more people who would take it if it was at Northbrook because—
S62NWF: [Softly] Yeah.

The unwillingness of white students from the north feeder zone to attend a majority Black school combined with the persistent message that Union students were not fit for the IB program caused enrollments in the program to drop. This, in turn, caused changes to the content and method of delivery of the IB curriculum. The school could not afford to offer advanced level courses with extremely small enrollments. The primary strategy used to overcome the smaller enrollments was to combine IB, Advanced Placement (AP), and Honors course sections together into single classes, a seemingly simple strategy made difficult by the compromises it forced teachers to make in the various programs' content.[3] When asked about the effects of the restructuring on curricular options, including IB classes, one teacher replied that it was "Terrible."

E22UWF: Because last year I tried AP English and we had seven students. This year AP/IB are being combined. I don't know how you can teach the two together because they're so different. So our kids suffer in that way—the courses being combined and all that.

Teachers were willing to do the extra work to offer combined courses, because they knew the alternative was not to have AP or IB courses at all. All three teachers we interviewed who were teaching such combined courses felt that the most advanced students were shortchanged by these course mergers. The more advanced IB content was often turned into independent study assignments, so as to accommodate the need to spend extra time on the Honors and AP curriculum. Students experienced this as an unfortunate reduction in the quality of the courses:

S63UBF: Like they said, the IB and the AP and the Honors—the difference in the levels of those classes—because of the enrollment number at this school we have to, like they said, crowd the classes together. Students have to be in an Advanced Placement class with Honors students, which should be on two different levels—I personally believe.

S64UBF: The classes kind of changed. They kind of had to combine classes when it came down to your—I want to say your ability to learn and your willingness to do your work ... Like the Honors students, and the IB students and the AP students—we were all put into one class because there were not enough students to have separate classes. And that was kind of disappointing to a lot of the students when that happened, especially the IB students because, well that's such an advanced program ... They don't want to have to slow down for Honors students or AP students.

The lower enrollments not only forced course mergers, they also caused a reduction in the number of advanced courses offered. This constraint on the advanced curriculum at Union was something teachers often expressed concern about.

E23UBF: There's not enough students enrolled in the pre-IB/AP in the—there weren't enough students to form both AP Chemistry and AP Biology for our school . . . AP Biology didn't make it. So we just have AP Chemistry.

Union was also unable to offer an AP or IB Physics course. As a consequence of these gaps and other scheduling constraints, students were often unable to earn IB diplomas, and were thus limited to including a few ad hoc AP and IB courses on their transcript. Again, students across the district took notice of these limitations. Former IB students at Northbrook and their parents described it as the unfortunate collapse of the once strong IB program, reinforcing and expressing the more general discourse that framed Union as the least of the three high schools. When asked which school she would prefer to attend, a high-achieving Union student cited lack of AP courses at Union as a reason for wishing she had attended Northbrook.

S27UBF: The reason my first choice would be Northbrook is because by what I hear, by what my teachers tell me, like—I'm an Advanced Placement student. And a lot of classes I was supposed to take, I wasn't able to take 'em because it wasn't enough students to be in a class here and some of the teachers that used to teach it had moved to Northbrook and Garner. So no one could teach it—here. And like, enough students wasn't here to get in the class for them to even try to hire someone to teach the class. . . . So I would go there first, basically, for the courses—education-wise.

Students, of course, did transfer to Northbrook for these reasons—usually high-achieving students. Parents with the means to do so established addresses in the north and east feeder zones to advance the academic ambitions of their children. This led to what one Union teacher referred to as a "brain drain" at Union.

The fate of the IB program provides a window into the cascade of curricular effects caused by the resegregation of Riverton schools. An elite advanced curriculum program located at Union High School should have provided access to more challenging learning opportunities for Union students. But pre-existing tracking in the school system meant students at the new Union high did not have the prerequisites necessary to enroll in IB courses. So this curriculum was not initially available to them. IB classes were initially composed primarily of white transfer students from other zones. Similarly, pre-IB students were bussed part time to Union to take advantage of the pre-IB curriculum. When that transfer enrollment declined, the courses were merged with less advanced courses. Students were aware of how this reduced the rigor of the IB course of study. In this way, a program that should have been a source of pride and status for Union High instead was transformed into a symbol of its lesser status and the lower capacities of its students. Since the students bussing in for the IB and pre-IB courses almost all identified as white, and Union was otherwise an all-Black school, the racial optics of this reinforced racist stereotypes that Black students were less academically capable than white students. In this we see two layers of curriculum inequity. First, Union students lacked access to the IB curriculum. Second, this lack of access served as a reinforcement of the hidden curricular message that Union students were less capable and less valued by the school system.

This material-discursive reproduction of curricular inequality in the school system acquired further layers. The inconvenience of bussing combined with low opinions about Union High inspired an exodus of the transfer IB students. This required Union to merge the IB diploma courses with other less advanced courses in order to maintain economically viable enrollments, which in turn caused a reduction in the quality and rigor of the IB curriculum instruction. Low enrollments also made it impossible to offer some IB courses. Lack of courses made it difficult for Union students to complete the full IB diploma requirements. The consequent decline in IB diploma awards was interpreted by students, teachers, parents, and administrators at other schools as evidence of a lack of interest and ability among Union students. Teachers reported that this led to renewed calls for ending the program and annual debates in the public media about whether the continued cost of the IB program at Union could be justified. In this way the negative reputation of Union caused material changes to the curriculum offerings, which resulted in reduced outcomes, and this reinforced a negative reputation of the school.[4]

This vicious self-reinforcing cycle of declining reputation, declining enrollments, and declining curricular options was not limited to IB and AP curricular tracks. It also manifested in the general curriculum. The circulation of negative stories about Union High in the community as a whole led to smaller enrollments at Union and increased enrollments at Garner and Northbrook. Smaller enrollments at Union meant reductions in elective curriculum offerings and scheduling flexibility. Students followed this dynamic. They were particularly sensitive to the way Union High was represented in the public discourse. They recognized the impact of these representations on enrollments and the consequences of low enrollments on their educational options. The whole dynamic appeared to set Union High and its students up for failure.

Representations of Union High

Students frequently expressed concern about how the new Union High was represented in community conversations. Many students saw racial bias and other forms of prejudice in those representations. "Putting Union down" and "bad Black kids" were phrases repeated frequently by Union High students to describe the way they felt they were depicted by others and by the local news. This was experienced as a drastic change from the way high school students were regarded when everyone went to the same high school. Before the restructuring, the impression of the high school was generally positive and no group of students was repeatedly singled out as being "bad." After the restructuring, Union students felt singled out for criticism and disrespect.

S65UBM: I just have to say just—people always talking about how bad—things are over here. . . . It's still the same, but just hearing what everybody has to say. So there's just—it gets on my nerves a little bit though. No! [Laughs slightly to show he was joking, then smiles and brightens his tone] Not for me—I really don't care, 'cause I know—I know what be going on here. But from there, it's just—irritating to hear.

S66UBF: People will talk. I hear people talk negatively about Union a lot. But, I feel like if they don't go here, they really don't have anything to say because they don't know—what goes on here just like we don't know what goes on there. So I feel like they can't judge—our school.

S67UBM: [Softly to cut in] There's been a lot more bad things happening at Garner and Northbrook than here. We really haven't had anything bad here.

The final observation was thematically present in student conversations about Union's negative reputation. Students felt not only that Union wasn't a bad place, but that it had less problems with student conflict and discipline than the other two schools. Administrators and board members confirmed that the rate of disciplinary referrals were higher at the other two high schools than at Union during the first three years after the school restructuring.[5]

According to students from all three schools, the new Union High was often associated with violence. Union students consistently mentioned this reputation for violence and fighting as they tried to explain why they had been segregated out from other students, why their school enrollment continued to be so small, and why—unlike the other schools—students with other backgrounds (race, ethnicity and/or class) did not enroll in their school. With equal frequency, and often a sense of outrage and distress, they would insist on the unfairness of this reputation.

In the second year after the restructuring, there was a fight at Northbrook High that involved an assault with a knife. That same year the police arrested a murderer near the Garner campus and a Garner student was an accomplice to the crime. These events received momentary coverage in the news media, but the events lingered much longer in the minds of Union students. They constituted clear evidence to Union students that Union's reputation for violence was not based on facts, but was the consequence of racist and classist prejudice.

S68UBM: Things I heard is that people—this side of town seems to get into more trouble or like to cause more incidents so to say. And, like, they try to separate people who cause things from people who don't.

S17UBF: Whatever. At Northbrook High they had a stabbing. At Garner High they picked up a murderer, where we might have a couple of fistfights over here. We haven't had anything drastic—like no murder suspect gets picked up at our school. And then not only did the person kill somebody, he killed an old person.

S68UBM: That's the same thing I was saying.

S17UBF: Yeah! They looking at the wrong school. They look down—.

S69UBF: We just have normal school problems.

S17UBF: Yeah—they look down on Union. But, if you'll just look back at the stuff that has happened since Northbrook and Garner have been built, they've had way—it's like the stuff is so more—it's just—so out there. Crazy stuff. Stabbing people. We don't stab people. We might get into an argument in the hallway.

S69UBF: Like normal school stuff.

S17UBF: Yeah, if—Yeah! If we do have problems with somebody, we don't—I mean that—we don't do stuff like that.

Students at the other high schools corroborated both that Union had a reputation for violence, but that the number and severity of violent incidents seemed higher at Northbrook. One Northbrook senior, a white student who had attended Union High at the grade ten and eleven campus before the restructuring, recalled there being less fights at the unified high school.

S10NWM: I don't remember behavior being as much of a problem. . . . I still don't remember—the fights. I mean, it just seems here, it's a lot more. I don't know. There just seems like behavior is more of an issue here than it was there . . . at Union.

This student seemed confounded at the amount of fighting present at Northbrook—something he did not recall seeing at the old Union High. Somehow, the fighting and other discipline problems had become worse at Northbrook. He and his peers then mentioned several events, including the stabbing that year, which required police intervention and included arrests:

S12NWF: . . . like the stabbing. And I know that, like the last day of school— last semester, throughout the exams. Well, we were exempt, but I came back up here to bring like pictures to [a teacher]. There had already been like a huge fight. People had like splattered all of the papers—all of their folders all over the floors—everywhere. There had been a huge fight in the courtyard. There were cops—and other cops there making them—and it was just this huge thing. All the teachers were out there. People got arrested. Somebody even got arrested today.

S11NWF: Like [S10NWM] said, there was more violence. [All start to talk at once.]

S12NWF: There's even more stuff here and we're supposed to be the nice school.

S11NWF: Yeah, I know, and that's weird because that's why people move. Like, people in private schools didn't want to go to Union because they're like scared of the violence. And there—it seems like there is more of it here than there was there.

The student noted the irony that it was "safety" concerns that prevented some parents from enrolling their students at the unified Union school and feelings of safety that attracted students from private schools to Northbrook, when disciplinary incidents at Northbrook seemed to be more frequent and more severe. Garner students also complained that many in the community "view Northbrook as the school that's the 'safe place'" and unfairly regard the other schools as "dangerous," despite reports they heard from students and relatives that worked at the other schools that disciplinary infractions at Northbrook were frequent and sometimes severe.

Students repeatedly attributed the resilience of Union's reputation for violence and Northbrook's reputation for safety to biased media representations. Union students alleged that the other two schools were somehow protected from negative media, while negative events at Union would be blown out of proportion by local news outlets.

S70UBF: I mean, the students say it. They always want to act like we the lower class school in the newspaper and stuff like that.

S71UBF: And also like if Garner and Northbrook was to do something— something terribly goes wrong at their school, they won't hear about it in the newspaper. But if something goes wrong over here—like the smallest little thing—they want to put it in the paper or put it on the news and just put us out like we're the worst school they've ever thought of.

Students reflected on this unequal treatment in detail. An incident occurred during Union High's third year in which an unauthorized adult came onto school grounds, entered the building, and was quickly escorted off. The news coverage of this event emphasized the man's criminal record and gave the impression that such threatening events were more likely because of the higher rate of crime in West-Side neighborhoods, where the school was located. Citing this case, a student drew a contrast to events occurring at other schools.

S72UBF: Okay. Like just say for instance an issue takes place at Union. Just say for instance our security officer caught somebody coming out of our back door that don't supposed to be—he trespasses at Union. The media will put that on the TV and expose it as it being a bad issue. As far as Northbrook— say for instance that girl stabbed that student. She was in the paper—don't get me wrong. But on the Channel 4 news, the news cast put it on for like two minutes. It wasn't even on there that long. You blink you eye—it was off. But—if something like that happened at Union, they'll discuss it and they'll talk about it and they'll talk about it. Discussion'll be on the TV like it's just real, real bad. They'll take stuff out of proportion—if anything like that was to happen at Union.

Union students almost always had ready examples of perceived media bias. It was a topic they had clearly discussed or heard discussed. And there was an urgency in the way in which they cited the under-reporting of violence at other schools. Our research provided an opportunity to speak back to the misrepresentations of their school and themselves. They wanted to set the record straight.

Students also reported the converse effects. Not only did they feel the local media exaggerated bad news about Union High, they thought it also under-reported good news about the school. Students often stated that the accomplishments of Union students were not celebrated in the local media as consistently or vigorously as the accomplishments of Northbrook or Garner students. One student, who for several years had participated in and led community service activities noted this lacuna in representations of Union High.

S26UBM: On the media subject, they're always publicizing what—I mean if something bad happens on the West Side of town. But there are other good things that happen on the West Side of town, because the ROTC Program is volunteering with the Habitat for Humanity to go on out building houses for the low-income people and they're pulling in SGA, art classes, and anybody else that wants to go. And they go—I believe it's this Saturday. And, I got a team down there called First Hands and they go out with the Boy Scouts—teach classes with them and help them out.

According to this student, these community service programs were rarely featured in news reports. His tone was matter-of-fact. He said he felt secure that there were good things happening in his part of the city even if the greater community did not know it, so he did not take the negative media to heart. Still, as other students pointed out, such portrayal, even if not intentional, ultimately affected their school in damaging ways that they felt powerless to allay.

Students interpreted these negative representations to be a consequence of a pervasive societal racism. Union was not being framed as violent just because the school was located near several public housing projects. It was regarded as violent and unsafe because it was an all-Black school, and Black students were assumed to be more violent.

S69UBF: Probably the worst thing that we probably had was a fight and—this whole year, well we've hardly—we probably had about one ... which was today, and that was like, the only fight we've had this year. And last year, I mean like we probably had no more—like two or three out of the whole year. So, I mean, people just say we're bad 'cause we're Black and we're in an all-Black school, but—but that's not really true. We're—just like any other school.

Students consistently pushed back at the racism they saw animating the negative representations of Union High. The unfairness of these representations was obvious to them, as were the negative consequences for their school. Students often seemed incredulous that the community had so quickly labeled their school as an undesirable place.

More poignantly, several students pointed to the way the racial integration of the other high schools protected them from this kind of racist stereotyping. Being in a school with white students provided a kind of protection from their entire school and everybody in it being pathologized simply because they were Black. The following student shared her impression that the presence of white students at Garner and Northbrook provided insulation from negative press for the schools.

S27UBF: A lot of people that go to Garner and Northbrook, they—some of them actually stay on the West Side. Some of them stay near the West Side. They act just as worse as anybody that goes here. They fight just as much. But you never hear about that because they're mixed in with white students and they're not going to put those schools out there like that. But—if something's real bad happening at Union with all these Black kids over here—it's going to be in the newspaper or on the news. Because we Black. And I don't feel like it should be like that. I feel like if Union was still as big as it was and all the white kids and Black kids or whatever was mixed in here, we wouldn't have that much SAID about us if anything were to happen over here.

Similarly, the following student shared her impression that Northbrook's status as a "white" school protected its reputation even when a stabbing occurred at the school.

S17UBF: The perception of Union is so bad 'cause the students and you know, everybody says that, you know, "the bad kids at Union." But you know, even if they just say "bad kids" that's automatically saying "Black kids" because you know the school is a Black school, but—okay. But, if it was white kids here, then the bad kids could be white and Black—you know what I'm saying? I mean, and then it seems like the problem like if something goes on at our school it's like, "Oh gosh!" It's such a big deal. Like the whole little stabbing at Northbrook? It made the newspaper and everything. But was it a big deal? No—that wasn't a big deal. Just a little girl got *stabbed*—*at her high school!* At—[almost whispers] *at school*?! But it wasn't a big deal then. It wasn't a big deal. She just got stabbed. Do you know if that would've happened here? That would have like made [Neighboring city] News. For us, they would still be talking about that now.

There was a plaintive tone to this student's observation that implied she wished the evidence mattered in the face of the racist stereotyping of Union High, but that she knew it didn't. The limited media coverage of the stabbing confirmed her view on the matter. Union students would always be considered the "bad kids" and that was a coded term that really meant "Black." The similarity in responses across interview groups indicated an understanding for many Union students that things were stacked against them in ways they could not change.

This dynamic did not just affect Union students. Black students at the other schools, especially those who lived on the western side of town and near the western feeder zone, felt implicated in the racist stereotypes. A Black student at Garner explained how the stabbing at Northbrook High seemed to reinforce stereotypes about Black people. The resegregation of the schools seemed to intensify this racial stereotyping in her opinion, reinforcing a feeling that Black students didn't belong at Garner or Northbrook.

S73GBF: And I kind of think that that stabbing probably could play into this whole thing because, who were the ones getting stabbed? Well, it was a Black person who stabbed her and a Black person who got stabbed. So it's like, "Oh, well we don't need these people over here because it's very—." And it's bad that that's the perception. And then we watched this movie in here about "Bowling for Columbine," and they were talking about how it's always the Black male and all of this and stuff.[6] And—that is an issue. And I just kind of think that—by having the schools like this it kind of promotes that. And, I just think that, you know, there are some issues that are probably beyond our control. You're not going to make somebody think that, "Yeah, Black people are okay." And that's why the ones that are okay have to, you know, just—show that there are some that are okay. And it's not like every Black person is out to get you or may mug you or whatever, but—I just think that there are some issues and that this zoning thing is not—helping any of it. I mean, it just makes it worse—the fact that it's so—unequal.

Several things are worthy of note in this student's comment. First, she refers to a pervasive discourse that suggested Black students didn't belong at Northbrook or Garner (despite Black students being in the majority at both schools), a theme documented in the previous chapter. The stabbing incident, she says, contributed to this discourse. She then asserts that the unequal restructuring of the schools was the more fundamental cause of this hostility to Black students. Finally, she directly states how overwhelming the whole tangle of events, district policies, and racist views seemed. She expresses resignation that all these things were "beyond our control." She adds: "You're not going to make somebody think that, "Yeah, Black people are okay.""

Union students were closely tracking representations of their school in local conversations and in the media. These representations, even though they generally had off-campus origins, were nonetheless a part of the curriculum of the resegregation. The resegregation of Riverton schools created an all-Black Union High School, which inevitably became a target for racist disparagement in the context of a society still saturated by racist discourses. This pervasive derision taught students things. Sometimes it taught them explicitly and directly that they were neither wanted nor respected. At other times, it taught them how vulnerable they were to racist hostility, how such hostility could reshape their daily experiences and future, and how adults seemed unable or unwilling to stop it.

Test Scores

It was not just the racial resegregation of Union High that made it a target for disparagement. The school was also class segregated. It had a higher percentage of students from low-income households.[7] This, predictably, contributed to stratifications in test scores. It has long been known that the income of a student's household is one of the strongest predictors of achievement test scores (Bowles & Gintis, 2002; Brooks-Gunn & Duncan, 1997; Coleman et al., 1966; Duncan, Brooks-Gunn, & Klebanov, 1994; Herrnstein & Murray, 1994; Jacoby & Glauberman, 1995; Lareau, 2003). Even if the school board members and district administrators did not read this scholarship, in 2000 the local newspaper provided an analysis of how the test scores at the new high schools were likely to compare based on a composite analysis of the scores of students at their feeder middle schools. Northbrook would perform above the state average. Union would perform in the bottom 2% of the state. And Garner would perform roughly in the middle. District officials knew they were creating a schooling arrangement that would result in stratified test score performance.

The newspaper predictions bore out. The test scores, as a result, became one of the chief indexes of Union's status as a poor performing school and Union students as defective. Nothing educationally had changed. The same students in the district were making scores similar to the ones they made before the restructuring of the schools. However, the concentration of low-performing students at one school created conditions whereby this would become a central feature of their personal and school identity. Students noticed and struggled to describe this effect. A senior who recalled life in the unified high school offered the following analysis:

S1UBF: You know how they would rank your school as who's doing bad and the percentage that's doing good. Now they look at Union as everyone over here is doing bad. But the only reason it seems like that is because we had more people here—before. And you can always see—[if] it's a lot of people here, of course it's going to be more doing good than doing bad. But now all they see is that kids is doing bad because—[changes voice tone] they *been* doing bad! You just wasn't able to see it because there was a lot of people here. So I think it makes us look really bad because it's not a lot of people and they always try and rate who's doing good and who's doing bad and who be in the most trouble.

Teachers confirmed that the concentration of low test scores at Union High contributed to the labeling of the school as a bad place to be.

E22UWF: Right now they look down—I mean Union is looked upon as the bottom of the heap—you know, anything that goes here. So we have to work to change that. And that starts with the academics.
I: Do you feel that—where does that come from?
E22UWF: Just from people commenting about Union. You know, when you see things in the papers. The score cards—we're the worst of the worst of the worst. Yeah.

Union High teachers and parents corroborated the reports of negative representations of Union students in the media and general public discourse. They also expressed concerns about its corrosive effects on school morale. A white teacher with more than two decades of experience expressed resignation about the inevitability of the negative stereotype that enclosed Union and its students.

E24UWF: Union High may have not had excellent publicity before [the restructuring] but, when you take all of—I hate calling them "good students" or who make good grades or whatever, but—and take them over to the other schools of course Union is going to get the spotlight.. . . . Does it mean that every Black school is going to–have terrible test scores and—and violence? No, it doesn't! But it seems to be the stigma that it was going to get. I mean in this community [the West Side] I can see that they wouldn't want that to happen, because it would just put the spotlight on Union and make this look like a community that's built on violence or that's built on, you know, a "don't care" attitude—"We don't care that we graduate high school, we'll just stay here" kind of attitude–when *all* of the students certainly don't feel that way.

The pathologizing effects of creating a school with a higher concentration of low-income and low-performing students was exacerbated by the requirements of the federal No Child Left Behind legislation (NCLB), which required that schools be ranked according to their test score performance. It also required that parents be notified when schools failed to make minimum scores designated as Annual Yearly Progress (AYP) goals. The theory of change behind the legislation was that poor student performance was hidden and that making it public would enable communities to hold their schools accountable for improvements (NCLB, 2003). This optimistic view, however, presumes that community members believe all students can learn and are equally worthy of investment. It does not take into account that school rankings would simply confirm racist and classist stereotypes about communities and schools, and thereby make low-performing schools more vulnerable to social isolation and abandonment. Students reported experiencing the stigmatizing effect of these school rankings:

S5UBF: He went to Riverdale Elementary School. I went to Sarver Elementary and basically throughout the whole time, we were like, on the SATs [Stanford Achievement Tests] we were basically—well our test scores weren't as high as they wanted them to be and at one point we were like, in "Caution." And one year we actually did almost like pull out. And you know, you can say you went to this school. But it's like, you're—if you are like a lower standing school, it's like you really are looked down upon. But to me you're the one that really needs the—the most help.

S2UBM: [Softly] It's a stigma against you. When you go to that school it's like a black mark.

Union's lower test scores confirmed and intensified the community discourse that marked Union as an undesirable school, one populated by unmotivated students with low abilities and prone to violence. The rhetoric of accountability associated with the tests focused attention on deficits in the students, their families, and their neighborhoods. It did not, however, focus critical attention on the district policies that had created these concentrations of low-performing students in one school location. Nor did it hold anyone accountable for addressing the way the school ranking system intensified racist representations of Union High and thereby negatively impacted Union students' educational experience.

Lower Enrollment and its Effects

The negative representations of Union High, from newspaper reports to published test scores, were a social text read by Union students and that communicated messages to them about their worth, status, and possibilities. These negative representations also had specific and significant material consequences. Union's negative reputation contributed to enrollment drops. It inspired parents to seek the means to enroll their children in Northbrook and Garner rather than Union. From the first year, Northbrook and Garner had over 1,000 students. Union had just over 600 students. This prompted the district to redraw the zones a second time, moving several hundred students from the north and east feeder zones to Union's feeder zones.[8] This, however, did not equalize enrollments at the high schools nor stem the steady migration of students to Northbrook High. By 2014, Northbrook had over 1,200 students, Garner had over 900 students, and Union had just over 700 students. Northbrook High was nearly twice the size of Union High.

The splitting of the formerly unified Union High into three smaller high schools meant there would be reductions in course offerings at all three schools. However, due to the differences in the size of the three new high schools, those reductions were more severe at Union High. The migration of students to other schools was also selective. More academically ambitious students and families with the means to change residences were more likely to move.[9] This depressed academic performance reinforced Union's negative reputation, which in turn caused further declines in enrollment.

Students were watching all of this unfold with increasing pessimism. They observed parents' efforts to secure enrollment in Northbrook or Garner for their children. They attributed this to the reputation Union had for violence and the bad press it received:

S74UBF: Well, I think the parents want—that their child go to like Garner and Northbrook because they hear most of the bad things about Union and they don't hear nothing mostly about the other schools. So they think like, "Oh, Union is bad—they get to fighting every day," and they don't hear nothing about them [Northbrook and Garner], so they decide they want their students to go to Garner. Practically every day you hear about Union [voice in background, "Yeah"] in the newspaper and stuff so they think, like, "Union is a bad school. I want you to go to Garner," or "I want you to go to Northbrook."

This reputation was understood to be related to the racial identity of the school, and was inaccurate, as this student explains:

S75UBM: I have heard some people say that they're not going to send their child over there to Oakstreet or Union because Oakstreet and Union—they fight too much or they're ghetto, or something like that. And just because a majority of the kids are Black—doesn't mean basically that we're going to get into more trouble over here.

Whatever the motivations, students saw that reduced enrollments resulted in a reduction of educational opportunities at Union High. Lack of certain classes made this clear, as did the difficulty of recruiting enough students to take the AP and IB courses. Lower enrollments also meant Union had a smaller number of teachers, which meant it was often difficult to find teachers on staff who could teach all the courses that were offered at other schools. Finally, smaller enrollments also made scheduling conflicts more likely, because there were less sections of popular courses which meant less flexibility for individual student schedules. Union students tracked all of this and were acutely aware of the link between enrollment and these limitations on their educational opportunities, as this student explains:

S5UBF: Depending on your enrollment at your school, it determines how many classes you have and how many teachers you have. And that limits the students a lot. 'Cause one student is even in a bind that because she needs to get her Honors diploma—to get this diploma—the science class she needs to take takes place the same time the social studies class she needs to take. So the classes like that are in a bind, and—I feel it's because that the way they redid it [restructured], and the way, because of our enrollment we had to cut classes and take teachers.

Students observed the way limited course offerings ended up inhibiting further educational opportunities. For example, at the unified Union High there had been a robust co-op program, where students with good grades in the advanced business education classes had opportunities to get experience working in a variety of professional settings at businesses in town. Limited course offerings at the new Union High got in the way of such opportunities.

S5UBF: We cannot take the co-op—we can't drop those classes 'cause we need those and so therefore we cannot co-op because the times they have the jobs are set up when we have classes. Just like this whole first semester is just core classes. You have your—your science, you have your social studies, and English, and Math. You have all of that. You can't co-op this first semester.
S2UBM: Like, when we do get a, a rare job, like ... working for the federal government doing something with bankruptcy. And [the Union business education teacher] really tried to give that job to someone and she eventually had to give it up. And that's, you know, like the story of Union. Every time there's a really good job, we have to give it up to another school because we can't do it because it's a constraint on the schedule because we have too few teachers. So it's just a big lack of resources that just snowballs.

The snowballing, in which reputational effects led to material limitations in course offerings and faculty capacity, which led to further erosion of Union High's reputation, took many forms. The following student observed that the students at Northbrook and Garner with high grades got their names published in the newspaper. Union High students, however, did not receive this treatment.

S19UBF: I want to know who in charge of—who gets stuff in the newspaper. Every time the school section comes out. We work hard all this time. We make all As or As and Bs or good grades—you know, passing stuff, and we don't ever get in the newspaper.

S17UBF: Yup. Northbrook and Garner. They'll be having oh, like 300 names in the newspaper. As, As and Bs and all this and stuff. Look at Union—we don't even got—

S19UBF: Yeah we don't get no column. We haven't got no article.

S17UBF: When people open the newspaper—like people that's in the community. Like my grandma. People her age. Like I have grandparents and stuff like that. They look in the newspaper and they see Northbrook and Garner. My grandmamma will want to know why Union ain't in the newspaper. "Well you may have all As on your report card. Why y'all not even in the newspaper?" That's what my grandmamma want to know.

It turns out that student grades were typically reported to the paper by a faculty sponsor who volunteered for this task. Union had a smaller faculty, which made it necessary for faculty members to take on multiple roles in order to fill in the many types of sponsors the school needed. At times, some positions did not get filled or sponsorship in other activities required faculty members to triage tasks and accomplish only the most pressing ones. In this case, the grades from the other two schools were reported, while Union's grades were not. This gave the impression that high grades were not being made at Union in sufficient quantity to be listed. This contributed to Union's negative academic reputation, which contributed to suppressed enrollments, etc.

The tangle of enrollment consequences also manifested around student test scores. As already recounted, low test scores reinforced an image of Union High as a place where academic ambitions were low. They also triggered certain federal policy consequences. The NCLB policy required that districts permit parents to transfer their children out of schools not making AYP goals. Union regularly failed to make its AYP goals. As a consequence students received letters at the beginning of the school year notifying them that they were allowed to move to one of the other two high schools, both of which made AYP during the first three years of the restructuring. Each year a few students took advantage of this option, thus further reducing school enrollments. All students at Union, however, began their school year with the message that their school was failing.

Most students with whom we spoke did not accept this message at face value. They knew test scores were low, however many interpreted the letter less as a symptom of student or teacher deficiency, and more as one more way Union High was being set up to fail.

S18UBF: It was like, when I read the letter, and they was like, "You have the option of either going to Northbrook or Garner" ... I just *looked* at the letter. I'm like, "They're not sending me to—" [hits hands flat against desk]. How in the world do they imagine the attendance rate to go up if they're offering for people to go to other high schools? That's just going to try to keep Union down! That's how I saw it.

Such comments testify to the lack of trust students had in district and community leadership to create conditions conducive to their learning or, indeed, to care enough to want to do so. They saw many things that indicated to them that the district had little investment in Union High becoming a success. As one high-achieving student enrolled in AP classes asserted, the district was making questionable choices.

S17UBF: Instead of giving us the option to run away from Union, they should've been trying to fix it—because it don't make no sense if we leave. That's not going to change the problem.
S18UBF and S17UBF: [In chorus] That's not going to make it any better.
S17UBF: And it's—they sent the letter out to the wrong people. We *need* to be here!
S18UBF: They need to send some of them over here, hoping for the chance that the attendance rate'll go up ... That would've made more sense than telling us to leave here.

The students held on to the idea that Union High School as a whole needed to succeed. They believed that the district leadership should be committed to that goal as well. However, they saw little evidence of such a commitment. Instead they received written invitations to abandon Union, which is what Riverton's school district seemed to be doing.

Overall, Union students recognized that lower school enrollments were both a cause and effect of a race- and class-based stigmatization of their school. They saw the way lower enrollments resulted in reduced curriculum offerings at their school and how public media representations of their school intensified this feedback loop of degrading school reputation and enrollment suppression. On top of this, the entire social dynamic and the lack of any effective adult opposition to it constituted a social text that communicated to students that their well-being was not a priority for district leaders.

Summary and Transition

At the beginning of the school restructuring process, school leaders had assured parents that the creation of three high schools would not compromise Riverton school district's commitment to the ideal of a comprehensive high school. They articulated a goal of offering everything at the new high schools that the former Union had offered. This proved, however, to be challenging, especially at Union where enrollments were lowest. At Garner and Northbrook, where enrollments were higher, more curricular options could be kept open. There were more teachers available to sponsor extracurricular opportunities. Additionally, new educational technology provided enhanced learning opportunities at Garner and Northbrook that were lacking in the first three years at Union. And the racially diverse student body at Garner and Northbrook itself constituted a learning opportunity that was no longer available to Union students.

Union students watched this contraction of educational options. They identified the cause of the lower enrollments in the stigmatization of their school in public conversations and in the press. They recognized that this in turn caused high-achieving and economically empowered students to leave, which drove test scores lower, which further intensified the stigmatization of their school and kept enrollments low. Interviews revealed that students' interpretations played a part in the ongoing constitution of these changes. For example, the perception that the curriculum was better elsewhere led academically ambitious students to try to move to other schools. This lowered the number of students who could enroll in AP and IB courses at Union, making it less likely such courses would be offered. Lower enrollments limited the academic options as well as some very visible extracurricular programs, thus reinforcing the already limited offerings caused by the smaller size of the school. This created a self-reinforcing cycle of perceived low performance, low enrollments, and reduced investments in the school.

Students interviewed for this study were paying attention to the interlocking material and symbolic mechanisms in the machinery of resegregation that was eroding the quality of their education and affecting their lives. They consistently rejected both the explicit and implicit negative messages about their worth. However, the scope and multilayered intricacies of this relapse into building-level racial isolation was at times overwhelming. It gave the appearance that this process was inevitable and irremediable. Students could see that the net of institutionalized racism was drawing tighter around Union High and their educational possibilities.

In addition to the direct effects the resegregation process had on the curriculum made available to students, and the barely hidden curricular message that Union students were regarded as less worthy of investment than students at the other two schools, the restructuring of Riverton schools also communicated a message to students that racial justice was an unreasonable social hope. In the next chapter we examine the degree to which students internalized these corrosive messages about their worth and the possibility of social hope. We will look at how it manifested for Black and white students and how students struggled to find agency in the midst of this backslide into a racial segregation of schools.

Notes

1 This methodological debate forms along many lines, including, but not limited to, positivists vs. social constructivists, standpoint theorists vs. anti-essentialists, and behavioral realists vs. descriptive realists.

2 The term "semiotic"—the study of the operation of signs and processes of signification—is often associated exclusively with the semiology of Ferdinand de Saussure (Saussure, Bally, Sechehaye, & Riedlinger, 1986), and traditions of post-structuralist social analysis based on Saussurean linguistic semiotics (e.g. Barthes, 2006; Derrida, 1998; Foucualt, 1982; Lacan, 1998). Saussure and the post-structuralist theory he inspired focused entirely on the symbolic character of signs—the arbitrary nature of the connection between signs and the things they signified. The result was a vigorously anti-materialist form of social analysis. The exclusive association of semiotics with Saussure, however, is a historical mistake. The field of semiotics has a longer and more varied history. Most significantly, for our purposes, Charles Sanders Peirce developed a theory of semiotics a decade earlier and a continent away from Saussure. Peirce's semiotics included arbitrary symbolic forms of signification, but also included more ontologically substantive forms of sign activity, such as photographs and thermometers, both of which have a material and causal relationship to the things they signify (Rosiek & Atkinson, 2005; Rosiek, 2013; Sorrell, 2004). Our analysis uses the term "semiotic" in this Peircean sense that presumes symbolic and material forms of signification become entangled in our experience.

3 Advanced Placement courses are another internationally marketed college track curriculum that is accompanied by standardized tests that certify student achievement (see: apstudent.collegeboard.org.) Advanced Placement courses are generally more focused on content knowledge than inquiry and reflective thinking skills, and thus are often considered less demanding than the IB curriculum. "Honors" courses were a local district designation for an advanced college track curriculum that were not at the level of AP or IB courses, but were more demanding than "regular" courses. Students who assembled enough Honors courses were awarded an Honors diploma.

4 Eventually the IB program stabilized at Union High, but it never regained its former status. It continued to use combined IB/AP courses and IB and AP course offerings continued to be limited. Ten years after the restructuring of the district there still was not an IB or AP Physics course offered at Union High. The more extensive menu of AP courses offered at Northbrook is now considered by many to be the most advanced academic track available in the district.

5 We did not inquire about this after the third year.

6 This movie, directed and produced by Michael Moore, examined the pattern of gun violence perpetrated by lone white students. The movie makes a point of contrasting this to the pervasive stereotype of Black men as the iconic image of violent crime (Moore et al., 2003).

7 In 2014 Union had 87% of its students on a free and reduced lunch program. That same year Northbrook had 48% of its students enrolled in this program. Garner had 60% of its students so enrolled. These percentages had been relatively stable over the preceding decade.

8 As reported in previous chapters, the zone lines were redrawn in such a way that only Black students were rezoned to the western feeder zone. The district unconvincingly claimed that this rezoning was done in a race-blind manner and it

was coincidence and geographic necessity that resulted in all 800 transfers being Black students.

9 A school board member representing the communities of the western feeder zone reported that several Black middle class families who were long-term residents of West-Side neighborhoods sold their homes and moved north of the river in order to ensure their children's enrollment in the schools of the northern feeder zone. This, the board member lamented, deprived the western zone and western schools of much needed examples of Black family success and of the leadership they could provide. Though residential shifts were not the focus of our research, it is reasonable to believe that such decisions were made. And if this were true, it would be another layer of the compounded negative effects the restructuring of Riverton schools was having on the lives of Union High students.

Bibliography

Akinnaso, F. N., & Ajirotutu, C. S. (1982). Performance and ethnic style in job interviews. In J. J. Gumperz (Ed.), *Language and social identity* (pp. 119–144). Cambridge: Cambridge University Press.

Barthes, R. (2006). *Mythologies.* New York: Hill and Wang.

Baugh, J. (1983). *Black street speech: its history, structure, and survival.* Austin: University of Texas Press.

Bowles, S., & Gintis, H. (2002). Social capital and community governance. *The Economic Journal, 112*(483), F419–F436. http://doi.org/10.1111/1468-0297.00077

Brooks-Gunn, J., & Duncan, G. J. (1997). The effects of poverty on children. *The Future of Children, 7*(2), 55–71.

Caldas, S. J., & Bankston, C. L. (1999). Multilevel examination of student, school, and district-level effects on academic achievement. *Journal of Educational Research, 93*(2), 91–100.

Cocchiara, F. K., Bell, M. P., & Casper, W. J. (2014). Sounding "different": the role of sociolinguistic cues in evaluating job candidates. *Human Resource Management.* http://doi.org/10.1002/hrm.21675

Coleman, J. S., Campbell, E., Hobson, C., McPartland, J., Mood, A., Weinfield, F. D., & York, R. (1966). *Equality of educational opportunity.* Washington, DC: U.S. Government Printing Office.

Derrida, J. (1998). *Of grammatology* (Corrected ed.). Baltimore: Johns Hopkins University Press.

Dumas, M. J. (2014a). "Losing an arm": schooling as a site of black suffering. *Race Ethnicity and Education, 17*(1), 1–29. http://doi.org/10.1080/13613324.2013.850412

Dumas, M. J. (2014b). Contesting white accumulation: toward a materialist anti-racist analysis of school desegregation. In Bownan, K. (Ed.), *The pursuit of racial and ethnic equality in American public schools: Mendez, Brown, and beyond* (pp. 291–313). Lansing: Michigan State University Press.

Duncan, G., Brooks-Gunn, J., & Klebanov, P. K. (1994). Economic deprivation and early childhood development. *Child Development, 65*(2), 296–318.

Foucault, M. (1982). *The archaeology of knowledge.* New York: Pantheon Books.

Gurin, P., Dey, E. L., Hurtado, S., & Gurin, G. (2002). Diversity and higher education: theory and impact on educational outcomes. *Harvard Educational Review, 72*(3), 330–366.

Guryan, J. (2004). Desegregation and black dropout rates. *American Economic Review,* *94*(4), 919–943.

Herrnstein, R. J., & Murray, C. (1994). *The bell curve: intelligence and class structure in American life.* New York: Free Press.

Jacoby, R., & Glauberman, N. (Eds.). (1995). *The bell curve debate: history documents opinions.* New York: Random House.

Johnson, R. C. (2011). *Long-run impacts of school desegregation and school quality on adult attainments* (Working Paper No. 16664). NBER. Retrieved August 30, 2015 from http://www.nber.org/papers/w16664

Kainz, K., & Pan, Y. (2014). Segregated school effects on first grade reading gains: using propensity score matching to disentangle effects for African-American, Latino, and European-American students. *Early Childhood Research Quarterly, 29,* 531–537.

Lacan, J. (1998). *The four fundamental concepts of psychoanalysis.* New York: Norton.

Ladson-Billings, G. (2004). Landing on the wrong note: the price we paid for *Brown. Educational Researcher, 33*(7), 3–13.

Lareau, A. (2003). *Unequal childhoods: class, race and family life.* Berkeley: University of California Press.

Lippi-Green, R. (1997). *English with an accent: language, ideology, and discrimination in the United States.* London; New York: Routledge.

Lutz, B. F. (2011). The end of court-ordered desegregation. *American Economic Journal: Economic Policy, 3*(2), 130–168.

Mickelson, R. A., Bottia, M. C., & Lambert, R. (2013). Effects of school racial composition on K-12 mathematics outcomes: a metaregression analysis. *Review of Educational Research, 83*(1), 121–158.

Mickelson, R. A., & Nkomo, M. (2012). Integrated schooling, life course outcomes, and social cohesion in multiethnic democratic societies. *Review of Research in Education, 36*(1), 197–238.

Moore, M., Glynn, K. R., Czarnecki, J., Bishop, C., Donovan, M., Heston, C., Danitz, B., McDonough, M., Engfehr, K., & Gibbs, J. (2003). *Bowling for Columbine.* United States: MGM Home Entertainment.

No Child Left Behind (NCLB) Act of 2001, 20 U.S.C.A. § 6301 et seq. (West 2003).

Orfield, G., & Frankenberg, E. (2013). *Educational delusions? Why choice can deepen inequality and how to make schools fair.* Berkeley: University of California Press.

Orfield, G., & Frankenberg, E. (2014). Increasingly segregated and unequal schools as courts reverse policy. *Educational Administration Quarterly, 50*(5), 718–734.

Orfield, G., & Whitla, D. (2001). Diversity and legal education: student experiences in leading law schools. In Harvard Civil Rights Project (Harvard University), G. Orfield, & M. Kurlaender (Eds.), *Diversity challenged: evidence on the impact of affirmative action* (pp. 99–109). Cambridge, MA: Harvard Education.

Reardon, S. F., & Owens, A. (2014). 60 years after *Brown*: trends and consequences of school segregation. *Annual Review of Sociology, 40*(1), 199–218.

Reber, S. J. (2010). School desegregation and educational attainment for blacks. *Journal of Human Resources, 45*(4), 843–914.

Rich, M. (2012, September 19). Segregation prominent in schools, study finds. *New York Times.*

Robbins, J. F. (1988). Employers' language expectations and nonstandard dialect speakers. *English Journal, 77*(6), 22–24.

Rosenbaum, J. E., Miller, S. R., & Krei, M. S. (1996). Gatekeeping in an era of more open gates: high school counselors' views of their influence on students' college plans. *American Journal of Education, 104*(4), 257–279.

Rosiek, J., & Atkinson, B. (2005). Bridging the divides: the need for a pragmatic semiotics of teacher knowledge research. *Educational Theory, 55*(4), 421–442.

Rosiek, J. L. (2013). Pragmatism and post-qualitative futures. *International Journal of Qualitative Studies in Education, 26*(6), 692–705.

Ryan, J. E. (2010). *Five miles away, a world apart.* New York: Oxford University Press.

Saussure, F. de, Bally, C., Sechehaye, A., & Riedlinger, A. (1986). *Course in general linguistics.* LaSalle, IL: Open Court.

Sorrell, K. S. (2004). *Representative practices: Peirce, pragmatism, and feminist epistemology.* New York: Fordham University Press.

Steele, C. M., & Aronson, J. (1995). Stereotype threat and the intellectual test performance of African Americans. *Journal of Personality and Social Psychology, 69*(5), 797–811.

Strambler, M. J., & Weinstein, R. S. (2010). Psychological disengagement in elementary school among ethnic minority students. *Journal of Applied Developmental Psychology, 31*(2), 155–165.

Taylor, Y. (Ed.). (2012). *Educational diversity: the subject of difference and different subjects.* New York: Palgrave.

Terrell, S. L., & Terrell, F. (1984). Race of counselor, client sex, cultural mistrust level, and premature termination from counseling among Black clients. *Journal of Counseling Psychology, 31*(3), 371–375.

Welner, K. G. (2006). K-12 race-conscious student assignment policies: law, social science, and diversity. *Review of Educational Research, 76*(3), 349–382.

6

WHY ARE THEY DOING THIS TO US?

More Resistance than Resignation

Students in Riverton schools were immersed in a material semiotic net of racism that communicated problematic messages to them persistently, in multiple ways, on multiple registers, at school, at home, and in the community. No one thing can be isolated as the source of these effects, but instead the assemblage of demographic differences, differences in facilities, white entitlement to white spaces, differences in course offerings, media messages, teacher comments, and a backdrop of historically habituated patterns of institutional and interpersonal racism, all influenced both students' inner and outer lives. Students' encounters with/in this assemblage varied according to their different circumstances and social locations and it precipitated different subject effects in different students. However, its messages were neither random, nor incidental. Its pedagogical effect had coherence and relational consistency. The resegregation taught students—Black and white—about the inevitability of racialized hierarchy and their place within it.

This condition was not a unique feature of the racial resegregation in public schools. Schools have consistently communicated denigrating messages to Black students even during the peak of the school desegregation era. Curricular tracking ensured that classrooms remained racially segregated even after federal courts ordered building-level desegregation. The attendant material and symbolic violence of in-school segregation and the resulting stigmatization of Black students was not qualitatively different to what was happening in Riverton. All of this racial stratification of educational opportunity and the dehumanization of Black children that underwrites it is best described as continuous with what Saidya Hartman (2007) has called "the afterlife of slavery":

> Slavery . . . established a measure of man and a ranking of life and worth that has yet to be undone. If slavery persists as an issue in the political life

of black America, it is not because of an antiquarian obsession with bygone days or the burden of a too-long memory, but because black lives are still imperiled and devalued by a racial calculus and a political arithmetic that were entrenched centuries ago. This is the afterlife of slavery—skewed life chances, limited access to health and education, premature death, incarceration, and impoverishment.

(p. 6)

What makes the resegregation of public schools noteworthy within this long history of racist dehumanization is the way it marks an inflection point in a struggle against one of the most flagrant forms of institutionalized racism in our schooling systems. At such moments of inflection, institutional arrangements are less naturalized, therefore their impact on people's experience is more available for reflection and comment. The movement from a racially integrated high school in Riverton to a 100% Black school intensified the tacit racist messages that suffuse any racially stratified school system. It focused those macroaggressions like sunlight through a magnifying glass on the subset of students attending Union High and its related feeder schools. The students felt the loss of status and access to educational opportunity and strove to make sense of it.

It would be an oversimplification to say that students simply and passively internalized these denigrating messages. Our interviews did include moments where students began to describe themselves and their possibilities in the negative terms provided to them by the white-supremacist discourses enabling the resegregation. However, far more often students acknowledged these negative messages and rejected them. They named the systemic processes compromising their education, speculated about the misguided or malevolent motivations of decision makers, voiced their objections to those who would listen, and engaged in a process of counter-storytelling as a form of both advocacy and psychic self-defense. As Richard Delgado (1989) points out, this kind of resistance has a long history:

> Oppressed groups have known instinctively that stories are an essential tool to their own survival and liberation. Members of out-groups can use stories in two basic ways: first, as means of psychic self-preservation; and, second, as means of lessening their own subordination.
>
> *(p. 2436)*

The students' struggle against the corrosive messages of the resegregation process highlights a challenge to our writing practice. As scholars, we do not escape the activity of these racializing assemblages simply because we rhetorically "step back" to describe them. These assemblages include the shifting vocabularies available for writing about race and segregation. Our descriptions (and the reader's interpretation) of them are vulnerable to becoming part of the discursive processes that reproduce racialized hierarchies. For example, descriptions that focus exclusively on students as damaged victims of institutional racism risk reinforcing relational habits associated with deficit theories, theories that frame Black students in terms of what they lack as a way of rationalizing inequitable educational service.[1] Even when the intent is to draw attention to the larger structural causes of inequality and call for changes in those systemic inequities, such descriptions can reinforce oversimplified conceptions of people as passive victims of oppression, inspiring pity as opposed to effective respect and solidarity.

Eve Tuck (2009), in her essential Harvard Educational Review essay "Suspending Damage: A Letter to Communities," parses this analytic undertow that haunts much emancipatory scholarship:

> In damage-centered research, one of the major activities is to document pain or loss in an individual, community, or tribe. Though connected to deficit models—frameworks that emphasize what a particular student, family, or community is lacking to explain underachievement or failure— damage-centered research is distinct in being more socially and historically situated. It looks to historical exploitation, domination, and colonization to explain contemporary brokenness, such as poverty, poor health, and low literacy. Common sense tells us this is a good thing, but the danger in damage-centered research is that it is a pathologizing approach in which the oppression singularly defines a community.
>
> *(p. 413)*

Tuck acknowledges that the damage to people from things like settler colonialism, patriarchy, anti-Blackness, heteronormativity, etc. is real, and that research on such things has brought benefits. The danger, she warns, is that such research often "simultaneously reinforces and reinscribes a one-dimensional notion of these people as depleted, ruined, and hopeless" (p. 409). The students in Riverton, and especially at Union, were neither depleted nor could they be characterized simply as hopeless. They wrestled with hopelessness. It loomed as an implication of the scope of the material and discursive forces arrayed in the school system against their well-being. But it was not all they were. This book would do a disservice if it invited the reader to such an interpretation.

On the other hand, the suffering students experienced as a result of the resegregation of Riverton public schools was real. The material deprivation as well as the racist discourses interpolating Black students into a pathologized social status were nothing, if not hurtful. Ignoring that suffering would constitute another form of erasure, arguably as dehumanizing as identifying students exclusively with the harm done to them. In his scholarship on segregation, Michael Dumas (2014) has argued against this avoidance of the lived reality of institutionalized racism in research and policy discussions. He writes:

> Schooling is not merely a site of suffering, but I believe it is the suffering that we have been least willing or able to acknowledge or give voice to in educational scholarship, and more specifically, in educational policy analysis. To be sure, researchers have documented inequitable educational opportunities and disproportionate outcomes, and have offered incisive analyses of the relationship between educational policy and broader social and political forces.... However ... we have been less concerned with how policy is lived, and too often suffered, by those who have little hand in policy formation or implementation, and more to the point, have not been invited to weigh in on how we who research policy should assess the deep impression of policy on flesh, bone and soul.
>
> *(p. 2)*

The challenge then for our writing on this topic is to document students' struggles in a manner that does not convert it into a pathologizing spectacle, but instead invites the reader into a respectful solidarity with students who are on the receiving end of structural forms of oppression. To this end, in this chapter (and to a lesser degree throughout the book) we alternate between accounts of the hurt students experienced as a consequence of the resegregation and descriptions of students' willful resistance to the messages conveyed to them by the restructuring of the schools. Your challenge as a reader is to resist the impulse to distance yourself from the lived reality of student experiences by indulging in pity or patronizing fantasies of rescue. Instead, we encourage you to dwell where our prose will attempt to direct your attention, to the complex mixture of students' lucidity, dignity, subjection, and occasional despair as they faced the resegregation of Riverton schools. These students had a full range of human responses to their situation. They partook of a pessimism about the inevitability of racism not unlike that which characterizes much contemporary critical race theory scholarship and anti-Blackness scholarship. Like that scholarship, however, they were rarely fatalistic. Most had (and still have) a resolve to persevere and have not given up hope that something different is possible, even as old forms of social hope seemed to deteriorate around them.

Teachers Worry

Teachers worried about Union High students. As documented in preceding chapters, it would be hard to overestimate how saturated the schooling context was with signifiers of Union's lower status and pathologized views of the West Side's neighborhoods and residents. Even seemingly ordinary practices that began in the integrated school took on pernicious significance after the resegregation. For example, the Riverton school district had a TV studio that was part of its vocational education program. That studio had been used to produce a video broadcast of the morning's announcements at the unified Union High.

This practice continued after the restructuring. The Riverton Communication Network (RCN) broadcast announcements that were shown on monitors in the homerooms of all three high schools on Friday mornings. Maintaining the option for students at all three schools to participate in this broadcast was considered the fair thing to do. And the idea had been that such unified announcements would preserve some sense of connection across the three schools. The material differences between the schools, however, conspired against this intent.

E18UWF: But, whenever they watch the RCN television show—that's where we get our glimpse of what life is like at those other schools. Because there's—as you know, the segments are tailored to where the camera has a Garner segment, a Northbrook segment, and then a Union segment. I've heard the students just—they don't really say a lot but they roll their eyes, you hear the exasperation, the heavy sighs—whenever they see the other teams, the other schools' band, for example—what kind of costumes they're wearing. Or, something like that, or just watching them go down the halls in the school because the camera's right there in the classroom or in the hallway and you can sense that they can tell that it's very different. And I have heard comments like, "Look at that car, look at the building, look at the way—look at how that school looks compared to ours, how much— newer it is, how much nicer it is."

Sometimes the hidden curriculum was hidden in plain sight, indeed, was broadcasted via television for every student and teacher in the district to see and hear.

Teachers worried about the unequal quality of facilities, courses, band uniforms, educational technology, etc. provided across the three schools. They also frequently expressed concern about the holistic effect of all of these inequities on students. Teachers worried that Union students felt abandoned. As one Northbrook teacher noted:

E25NWF: This is what really concerns me. Have we forsaken a large group of our city population by making a better situation for some of the other kids? Have we forsaken some of these other kids by kind of leaving them in that situation?

Not everyone expressed such worries. A few teachers were impatient with the suggestion that being at an all-Black school was a disadvantage. As one Union High educator commented: "You don't need white people sitting next to you to learn how to read." Teachers who expressed such views did not deny something unjust was happening with the restructuring, but were concerned about the corrosive effects of dwelling on the negative aspects of the situation. The urgency with which they reframed the challenges at Union, however, constituted a tacit acknowledgement that the resegregation of the schools was potentially damaging to the students. Avert your eyes and get on with your work, was the implied recommendation to students, lest the implicit hostility becomes all you see and thus prevents you from getting the education you need and deserve.

Other teachers readily expressed global concerns about how the restructuring was influencing students' conceptions of self and society. One Garner teacher, after helping to facilitate a focus group of Black students, reflected:

E26GWF: The restructuring has shown the Union students once again that they are perceived as being second-class students. Their high school is not being built, there have been all kinds of arguing and delays about them getting, again, what is equal—what is supposed to be equal, but we all started out on the same plane. But for some reason, again they are behind. So the kids look at that. They know that. That causes some resentment all right, so, yeah, the kids notice what is going on. [Pause] Those are the kinds of things that, laying the groundwork, is how these kids feel about race relations and life in general.

This was the more prevalent view among Union High teachers. To a person, when asked "What would you do to improve schools in Riverton if you were in charge?" every teacher at Union said they would restructure again to ensure more diversity at each school. When asked why, teachers would occasionally cite the material effects of the racial and economic isolation of Union High. But they always mentioned and tended to dwell on its psychological effects. A teacher summarized this view:

E19UBM: What effect do you think it will have? If you tell a child they are stupid every day for 12 years, they will believe it—even if they are a genius. If you tell them they are bad, thugs, they will become bad. That is what this is doing! It lets students know—know they are unwanted, they are—that people don't want their kids around them. We can tell them it doesn't matter. And—don't get me wrong—we have good students, smart kids who get it. They know better. But it affects students. I hear it.

Teachers were close to students. They heard the things students talked about and could register their emotional tone. Most of these teachers had taught in the previously unified Union High, and therefore could compare and contrast student conversations before and after the restructuring. Union High teachers reported that the resegregation of Riverton schools had changed things for Union students. Even though they and the students resisted the relentless insinuations that Union was a lesser school, this transparent implication of the restructuring was a burden. For this reason the Union teachers we interviewed would have reversed the resegregation if they could have.

Student Hopelessness and Resolve

One morning in the spring of 2006, Kathy met with several West-Side students as they waited to catch their bus to Northbrook to invite them to participate in the study. Only three of the over twenty-five students there ultimately took up the invitation, which was odd since many of the students had originally expressed interest and our participation rate was generally higher. Months later, an interview with the bus driver shed some light on why they opted out. The day after inviting the students to participate in the study, one male student stood in the aisle of the bus and gave a speech stating that West-Side students were not wanted at Northbrook. He said they were being used so that they could build a school on that side of town and that eventually they would be sent back to Union. "Things will *never* change here," she reported the student saying. The bus driver stated that she was shocked at the degree of hopelessness this youth felt. She speculated that students declined to be interviewed, because they did not believe it would change things (field notes, fall 2006).

Such expressions of generalized despair were rare in our interviews. It was more common to hear resignation about the widespread low opinion of Union students and the resulting attitude of neglect accorded to their needs. The theme of abandonment also showed up in Union student comments with some frequency. The phrase "leftover" was repeatedly used to describe the way Union students felt they were regarded, as in this student's analysis of the restructuring:

S2UBM: Like, you saw predominantly the more affluent people leave the public school systems and go to private schools. And they were trying—I guess they were trying to stop that by building those two new schools and restructuring in those, you know, areas where there—there is some affluence. It was kind of a mixture of distribution of income . . . It seems like you're trying to pander to one base instead of trying to give everyone an equal education. You're going to kind of cherry pick—who gets the best of the best and the leftovers will go to Union.

Here we can see that the racial resegregation, because it was not perfect or total, led to speculation about why some Black students were at Garner and North-brook, and why others were "left" at Union. Students could see that white people had been zoned out of their school. They also saw that many more affluent Black families had been zoned for the other high schools. This led to speculation about what other considerations had driven the rezoning. It appeared to many students that there was an effort to siphon off the most talented students to Northbrook or Garner, including academic and athletic talent.

This perception was reinforced by the occasional transfer of academically ambitious students zoned for Union to the other schools and teacher comments about a "brain drain" negatively impacting course offerings. Union coaches also voiced suspicions that coaches from other schools were using Union's low Annual Yearly Progress scores—which permitted students to transfer to other schools—as an opportunity to recruit some of their better athletes to other campuses.[2] This, along with all the other indications of a low regard for Union students, conveyed the message that students who remained enrolled at Union lacked qualities that would make other school communities want them. When asked if he thought talented athletes chose to go to other schools, one younger Union student responded:

S76UBM: Nope. That ain't it. . . . White people made them leave. They going to try to—rezone the streets and stuff where all the good Black athletes stayed at and now they going to the new schools. And therefore we're— garbage people. [Laughter and nods of affirmation from other students.]

The salient point here is not whether the district actually did a house-by-house analysis of where athletically and academically talented students lived and attempted to draw zoning lines to place them at Northbrook or Garner. More significantly, such comments revealed that the resegregation communicated to some students they were unwanted not only because they were Black, but also because they were less athletically or academically talented. It communicated that their school was being neglected because the students worthy of investment had been directed elsewhere—that they personally were "leftovers" and "garbage."

Students picked up these race and class stratified representations of their schools and recirculated, even intensified, them. A Union senior recalled a meme circulating on the photo-archiving website Instagram during her first year in high school. Apparently some students at Garner began posting photos with the captions "Girls at Garner be like . . . " and "Girls at Northbrook be like . . . "

S77UBF: I remember getting on Instagram and the other high school students were posting about how different people looked at different schools. They would have pictures up saying the girls at the Northbrook school look like this—which was lighter and fair skinned and prettier. And then people at Garner looked ok, perhaps a shade darker. And the girls at Union all looked like Aunt Jemima, back in the day slavery pictures with pig tails all in their hair. These were all Black students and it was Black students posting these photos. Mostly girls, but some boys. And I thought to myself, wow, this is really how they see themselves.

Here we see the race and class stratification of the schools intersecting with hetero-patriarchal discourses, resulting in the production of racist and sexist images of Black young women at the three schools. The existence of this website was corroborated by three other students and one teacher, though the link to it could not be found. Young Black women at Garner allegedly started the website and there was soon participation from students at all three schools and the county high school as well. Although students would likely characterize the photo collection as humor, there was a clear hierarchy across the three schools on this Instagram site. Union women were represented with caricatures that signified lower status and less beauty. This lack of status and beauty was associated with the racial identity of the school as the photos used to depict Union girls were reportedly darker skinned.

Even when students saw conspiracy and racism behind the restructuring of the schools, this did not necessarily prevent the internalization of the negative representations of themselves that saturated the discursive environment. Sometimes students would name such racist motivations, but then narrate such actions as justified because Black students and Union students in particular were difficult to be around. A freshman at Union offered his view on why the board had restructured the high schools:

S78UBM: They want to see the whites do good and they want to see the Blacks do bad. They know how Black people are. They're loud. They're ghetto. They're alley. They fight. The white people don't do that. They're quiet. They're nice. And, well, they're nicer. We're mean. They know what they're doing by separating us.

Student remarks like these bring to mind the words Chief Justice of the Supreme Court Earl Warren wrote in the majority opinion of *Brown v. Board of Education*:

> To separate [Black children] from others of similar age and qualifications solely because of their race generates a feeling of inferiority as to their status in the community that may affect their hearts and minds in a way unlikely to ever be undone.

The Court's decision in that case had been based in part on Kenneth and Mamie Clark's (1950) research that demonstrated young children internalize negative messages about themselves as a consequence of living in racially segregated communities. The intervening fifty years, however, have complicated our notions of internalized racism, raising questions about the accuracy and utility of the concept.[3]

Our observations corroborate to some degree the findings that influenced the courts sixty years ago, but also support the idea that the concept of internalized racism is not nuanced enough to capture the complex effects of segregation on children's sense of self. In the above remark about "garbage people" the phrase referred to the implications of a more general policy of zoning "better" students for other high schools, not to the child's *self*-description. It also elicited laughter from his peers, signaling that the students did not take the statement literally. Still, this notion of "garbage people" is mentioned and recognized—so to some extent it was in the young man's thoughts. It is also worth noting that the comment was not explicitly disavowed by anyone present. In another focus group interview, when asked why they thought the restructuring happened, a student speculated that perhaps parents did not think their kids could get educated in classes with West-Side student because they were always acting out. This Union student added "I think maybe they are right about that," suggesting this idea had worked its way into his description of himself or his peers, though not in a totalizing manner. "*Maybe* they are right."

We can contrast these self-disparaging comments with the way a great many Union students refused the negative representations of themselves. When asked how the resegregation affected them or other Union students, the majority of students expressed an intention to do what they needed to do to succeed no matter the circumstances. As one 2014 graduate proclaimed:

S79UBM: We just take it as it is. Because there is not much that we can do about the segregation or whatever. But, it's not going to stop us from getting an education, just because it is an all-Black school. Education comes from you, your own person, your own mind. You take it how you wanna take it.

Others affirmed the harm the resegregation had caused and expressed what amounted to a grim resolve to persevere despite the unjust state of affairs. As a graduating senior wrote in an essay on the subject:

> I think it affected us a huge amount. I feel like the district created three schools and it set up Union High to fail. They didn't give us the resources we needed. And I think, for the Black people I grew up around, that really put a strain on them to learn more. It made you hungry, to learn more, to do better.

Notice that these were not denials that restructuring was a problematic policy. These student statements were resignations to the presence of institutional racism and its corrosive messages. They were refusals to be defined by those messages.

In general, we found that the boundary between students' expressed self-concept and the messages about them embedded in the resegregation was fluid. The degree to which negative messages about Union were reflected in students' own description of Union or themselves varied between students and sometimes shifted over time for the same student, even within a single interview. Most students were not temperamentally inclined to despair or to strike the pose of tragic figures. They registered many inequitable features of their schooling context and their imagination turned to the paths and possibilities that still seemed available to them. Their personal experience of the resegregation was an unstable and contested site where students were engaged in resistance work, such as counter-storytelling.

What was explicit and consistent throughout our interviews, however, was the students' eroded sense of expectation that adults in the community would find a way to provide something approaching fairness in the educational system. The only exceptions to this pattern appeared in the first year after the school restructuring, when a few students expressed the idea that a mistake had been made and that the city would not roll the clock back on desegregation. After that year student responses were characterized entirely by a background assumption that educational policy makers had acquiesced to racist influences and had left them to do the best they could amidst glaring structural inequality. Students felt "set up to fail" and experienced school in one way or another as a struggle against institutionalized neglect and hostility.

Why Are They Doing This to Us?

The sentiment of disappointment with district leadership was exemplified one winter the first year after the restructuring when a fight broke out on the court at a basketball game. It was a Northbrook High versus Union High game being held at Union High's gym. The initial confrontation was between two Black players. Two white Northbrook students quickly got involved on behalf of their teammate. Some students off the court joined in the scuffle, causing the game to halt for several minutes as order was restored. Several students in attendance were escorted from the building. The fight was reported in the Riverton newspaper and was the subject of much student discussion the next day. Who started the fight? Who was involved? Was it Union or Northbrook fans who were ejected? Several Union students with whom we spoke felt the paper made it sound like the fight happened *because* it was at Union High.

The day after the incident a teacher reported that her International Baccalaureate (IB) students were preoccupied by the topic. Students' primary concern was that just the previous year, the students involved in the fight had been friends. Students repeatedly remarked how "sad" or "stupid" it was that former friends were fighting. This teacher recounted a student conversation she heard in her class.

E26UWF: Then [—], a girl from Northbrook, blurted out "Why are they doing this to us?" It stopped the conversation. She was clearly upset. "Why are they pitting us against each other like this," she said. "Northbrook vs. Union. Garner vs. Northbrook. North vs. West Side." Another student added "Black vs. White." Then [—] said "It's like they want us to . . . fight, to hate each other," and the whole class jumped in and started talking about why the district had separated the schools and why it was better before.

The feeling that the original Union High should never have been divided was at its highest level the first two years, because more students could remember what it was like attending the unified school. However, it was not just nostalgia or a generic distaste for change that informed students' objections to the restructuring. Students from all three schools, white and Black, saw the policy as unnecessarily causing racial divisiveness. This consequence was so predictable and obvious to students that it raised doubts for them about the intentions of district leaders.

Union students experienced misgivings about adult intentions in a variety of ways, some of which have already been recounted. The publication of the Annual Yearly Progress reports on the schools required by federal No Child Left Behind (NCLB) legislation surfaced particularly pointed expressions of student mistrust of school leaders. When a school falls below its Annual Yearly Progress goals—as the new Union High has done every year of its existence—the district is required to notify students that they have the right under such circumstances to be transferred to another school. When the first-year Union students received these letters, it came as a shock to many of them. Lacking knowledge of this policy context, Union students interpreted the letters as a new district policy. Their interpretation, however, was revealing. Students saw the letters as evidence of intent to undermine Union High, to recruit away its stronger students and to further reduce enrollments.

Some students saw the letters as a moment to explicitly perform their resistance to the ill-treatment of Union High and West-Side students by rejecting the invitation. As one student defiantly declared:

S19UBF: I didn't even give it [the transfer letter] to my parents.

These students believed the transfer option presented to them under NCLB was illogical. This would not help them to resolve the problems their school faced with an enrollment that was already too small. If they left, they reasoned, the school would be worse off. A focus group of juniors in advanced classes responded similarly. They thought it would be especially damaging to Union High if they were to leave. One member of that group explained the responsibility she felt to remain at Union High:

S80UBF: We could choose pretty much what school we want to go because we didn't pass the AYP. And I know we got a letter in the mail saying—they list what we failed and what we passed and if you want to change your children's—your school—whatever—you can do so at this time. But, I mean, you don't leave something because it's failing. You should try to stay and help make it better. I mean, we're all in the advanced classes so I feel like we're the leaders of the school. Therefore if we leave the school, the school would eventually get shut down.

What is salient here is how quickly the letters were interpreted within a mindset that viewed the district officials who sent the letters with acute suspicion. Students had arrived at this mindset by watching the resegregation of Riverton schools unfold. The adamant resolve not to exercise their transfer rights was a refusal to cooperate with the institutional processes that were assaulting their school and futures.

History Classes

Nowhere was the erosion of a sense of fairness in the schooling system more clearly evident than in social studies classes where the history of race relations in the U.S., including slavery, the civil war, and civil rights era protests over school segregation, was reviewed and discussed. Having to teach these topics brought the broader implications of the school restructuring closer to the surface. Student, teacher, and school racial identity took on greater significance in the context of the new racial segregation. As a new social studies teacher assigned to Union High observed:

E27UWM: It's different teaching here. But not in the way you might think. The kids are just kids as far as I am concerned. But teaching history here is different. I have to teach about the slave trade and the middle passage—slave ships and plantations—to a room full of African-American kids. And some don't know much about it. So I have to deliver that knowledge, a white guy from [rural town]. I—[pause]—No one prepared me for that. Nothing in my teacher education program prepared me for that. The students are fine. My question was am I good enough to do this? Can I do it right for them? [Pause] I taught it last month, just before break. It wasn't my best unit, I will change some things next time. They were great the whole way. Really engaged.

It was during lessons on the civil rights era of American history that students and teachers drew the most poignant connections to Riverton school politics. Many students had relatives who had taken part in civil rights protests in the 1960s and 1970s. Some of their parents were in the first classes to desegregate Riverton's public schools. The town had been the site of famous confrontations over racial integration. A more seasoned history teacher made the connection between his curriculum and the resegregation of the schools more directly.

E3UWM: I'm always struck by the irony of teaching *Brown vs. Board of Education* in my class. You know, I am sitting there talking about an all-white Supreme Court ending segregated schools in 1954 and here we are, what, over fifty years later and I am teaching an all-Black class in a 99.5% Black school.

So, sure, I feel like I have to stop and explain that contradiction, because the text book doesn't. But then you get into the whole dynamic of trying to explain diplomatically and without offending why segregated schools are a bad thing—bad educationally.

Students, a teacher at Garner reported, were often energized by the civil rights unit prior to the restructuring. These lessons were a highpoint of the year—"It was a historical moment of triumph which many students felt personally connected with." However, the first year after the restructuring, she reported that the effect when teaching about the civil rights movement was entirely different. "Students can see that the victories of that era are being lost, right in front of them," (E2GWF). Her students were swift to conclude that the civil rights movement was a failure. One of her students wrote in an assignment:

> When the board decided to make three neighborhood high schools, they made segregated schools again. To know how hard people fought for us to be together should have led to a different decision. Doesn't anyone care that whatever accomplishments that came from *Brown* are being dissolved?

Such sentiments were not isolated to Garner High. A Union student interviewed by a local news station on the sixtieth anniversary of the *Brown v. Board of Education* court decision was asked whether she thought the *Brown* decision had affected her life. She replied, "It didn't work here, not for us, not for Riverton." When educated about the intent of the *Brown* decision and then comparing it to the restructured Riverton school system, teachers reported that students frequently expressed doubt about the possibility that racial inequality could be effectively opposed.

The history teacher at Garner attempted to challenge the growing cynicism her students expressed about the civil rights struggle. She reconfigured her unit on the civil rights movement to focus on the lives and thoughts of the young people who participated in it. She asked students to consider whether the young people at that time had reason to feel cynical about racial justice. Her students acknowledged that they did. She further asked her students what motivated them to act despite the evidence they faced that things would never change.

Rather than simply speculate, the teacher assigned students an oral history project in which they were to interview someone who was present at that time as a young person and ask why he or she did or did not participate in movement activities. The teacher invited a local civil rights movement figure to visit the class, and the class collectively practiced their interview questions and techniques with her. Many students chose to interview family members and had their permission to share their stories. The stories related to events that occurred in local places that students recognized. This intimacy made the material feel personal and powerful, the teacher reported. Students emerged from the lesson with an altered perspective on the struggle for civil rights. One of her students wrote:

> We always talk about civil rights as if it is in the past. It is something you visit in the museums or the historical sites—you feel like it is history. But now I realize civil rights has never really ended. What we heard today is a lot like what people have been talking about in Riverton the last year. *Brown* is alive—*Brown* is here.

Students were energized and wanted to do something. In another adjustment to the unit, the teacher had students write a letter to the local paper about the restructuring and a recent protest by Union students about the location of a new Union High building. Ultimately the local paper did not publish any of the letters, but her students' eagerness to engage was not diminished. The class brainstormed other actions they might take. Drawing on experiences at their own school, students came up with a plan to register students at Union High over the age of eighteen to vote. They received permission to travel to Union High during the lunch hour the following week and set up a voter registration table. They succeeded in registering seventy-seven new voters that week.

The story of this Garner history class, and reports from history teachers at Union, illustrate a few things. First, the resegregation of Riverton schools significantly altered the meaning of some of the curriculum traditionally taught in history classes. This constitutes yet another curricular effect of the resegregation. Second, the resegregation communicated specifically that the victories of the civil rights movement were not lasting and that such grassroots activism could not ultimately compete against the forces of entrenched racism. In doing so, it contributed to an erosion of students' sense of civic efficacy and social hope. Third, despite this pervasive message, students were open to countervailing messages of hope. With some help from adult instructors, students enthusiastically engaged in actions that demonstrated resistance to the racializing assemblages driving the resegregation of their schools.

A Student Walkout

The most visible gesture of student resistance to the resegregation took place during the spring semester of 2004. The restructuring of the schools had already happened. Two new schools had been built and the city was debating where to build the new Union High building. School administrators had been looking at a parcel of low lying park land that had drainage problems but considerable open space surrounding it and was located in the heart of the West-Side neighborhoods it predominantly served. Many students and parents, however, feared this location was too far away from the main thoroughfares of the city and would be forgotten and neglected. Their preferred location was the site of the old Union High. This site had the advantage of being in the center of the city and consequently very visible. The site acreage, however, was much smaller than that of the other schools.[4] This debate had delayed the building of a new Union High for a year and was threatening to delay it further. A group of Union students began looking for ways to break the stalemate concerning the construction of their new building.

These students attended several school board and city council meetings to request that the location controversy be resolved so that their school could be built. They argued that students should decide where their school was built since they were the ones who would attend it. Most of the controlling majority of the board listened, but appeared to students to ignore their input. One of the organizers described the experience:

S81UBF: [A]t first a lot of the students were just kind of—we thought that, okay, the parents would take care of this. And we was watching in the newspaper and as time went on and we saw that they were still just kind of making up their mind on how things would be done and was not listening— to the adults that were attending the meeting. Then the students started talking about it, "Well, what can be done? What do we need to do?" But before we had the actual walkout, we did attend some city council meetings and—we had told our parents how we felt about the situation and we told them what we wanted to do. So, they [referring to parents] told us how the meetings went . . . And then we went to a couple of meetings. We went to a Board of Education meeting that was open for the students to come speak. And then at one particular meeting, maybe a few weeks before the walkout occurred, there were some city councilmen that spoke out against the students coming to speak at the meetings and that really hurt our feelings because they were saying that we—basically we weren't educated enough to come up with these opinions ourselves and that they were being made— they basically told us that that's not what we believe and that's not how we feel and it was very hurtful.

Notice the reference to students' eroding expectations that adults in the community would "take care of this." This disappointment inspired action by a handful of students, who received guidance and support from their parents. When they voiced their concerns at a city council meeting, a member of the council made a public statement dismissing the students' input in a condescending fashion, reinforcing their disappointment in the political process. According to this student, that dismissal had a galvanizing effect on a larger number of students.

S81UBF: And when our classmates at school heard about that—and of course it was in the newspaper. When they read about it, they were like, "We have to do more. We have to do something because they're just not paying us any attention." And so—a lot of students [smiling as she recalls] didn't say anything to their parents that there was a rumor of a walkout.

The students, after consulting with a few adults, resolved to organize a walkout in protest of city and district leaders' failure to build a new school for Union students and in favor of building that new school at the site of the old Union High School. Students passed the word at school and over the weekend at churches and other events. As recounted at the beginning of this book, on the morning of Monday March 1, 2004, 200 Union students rose from their seats, walked out of their classrooms and into the front parking lot of the school where 100 parents and community members awaited them. This crowd marched two and a half miles to the district office carrying protest signs and chanting slogans like "What do we want? A New High School! When do we want it? Now!"

The protests received considerable local press attention. Protesting students were threatened with suspension, but no punishment was ultimately forthcoming. Later that spring, city leaders decided to build the new school on the site of the former unified Union High. Union students felt they had contributed to this outcome.

This is not a story that ends in unqualified triumph, however, one in which students learned the power of grass roots political action and had their faith in democratic process restored. The council decision did not immediately follow the protests. It came a few months later, and in that interim many students were left to feel that the protests had not been successful. Even after the final decision was made, many students viewed the protests as having had limited influence. One of the protest organizers felt racism blunted the impact of the protests and prevented the majority white city council from hearing the concerns of West-Side residents.

S82UBF: [Quietly] It's always been about a racial issue—simply because we have been overlooked, like [S5UBF] said. I mean, even though we did—get our—get what we wanted—like the school over there. It took a lot. It took a whole lot. And when we did walk to the city board it still was like they looked over us because after that, they kept on holding meetings. They kept on holding meetings. And we would all come to the meetings and it would be one person that would always have the—right. And they didn't care what everybody else said. So—I mean, it took a lot. And I think it's all about the racial—factor—of the issue.

The building of the school on their preferred site was a small victory. The schools were still racially segregated. Union High was still much smaller than the other two schools, with all of the attendant challenges. Parent booster activity remained at lower levels than the other two schools. Two years later, as the new Union High building was set to open, the school board rezoned the district again. The new map moved 800 K-12 Black students from the Northbrook and Garner zones to the Union High zone. A Union student offering a critique of this second rezoning, mentioned her pessimism about the efficacy of a second round of protests:

S83UBF: [B]ut [students in] West End and the Albina neighborhood are supposed to be coming to Union. Now, I think that Albina should stay at Garner because I feel like that they're closer to Garner. But now the whole Garner—the majority of them are Black. And the majority of West End is Black. And then the whole West Side—all of us, you might as well say, are Black. So—what is the new Union going to be? Black. And Northbrook, when they take them West End kids out and from different neighborhoods— Northbrook is going to be white and Garner is going to be predominantly white also, and the whole Union is going to be Black with a few white kids . . . then if the kids get together again like we did two years ago [referring to earlier comments about the walkout], they're going to look at it and pay no attention to it.[5]

Even though the city council eventually committed to the school location demanded by the protesters, this student did not emerge with a heightened sense of civic efficacy. She did not feel confident that city leaders' continuing resegregation of the schools could be effectively deterred.

Additionally, and somewhat perversely, the student walkout at Union High was incorporated into the pervasive discourses that framed Union High students as bad, disobedient students. It became one more signifier of their lack of commitment to learning and their lack of respect for authority in some community conversations. Letters to the editor of the local paper recommended that students participating in the protest be punished for truancy. Students were aware that this act of resistance had reinforced negative stereotypes of Union students. The following student at Garner High School commented on how the protests intensified Union High's bad reputation:

S84GBF: Basically Union—it was already being named as a bad school, but it seems like ever since those students walked out of school that day—that has been—added to the criticism that Union is a bad school. . . . They felt as if the students—they were wrong to just leave school—walking out, so— [begins to reconsider, then changes voice tone]. But I don't feel like it was wrong. I feel like they were fighting for what they believed. So—they stood up for their rights.

The protests are evidence that students did not passively accept the pathologizing messages about themselves or their school being communicated by the restructuring of Riverton schools. Nor did they universally succumb to a civic hopelessness. Students sought means to resist the isolation and the neglect of their school. This activism, however, did not signal optimism on the part of students. Students' assessments of their situation were complicated. Many of the most active students were pessimistic about the efficacy of their political actions.

The walkout remained a touchstone in student conversations about the restructuring of the school district for years to come. It functioned like a Rorschach test onto which students projected their hopes and fears for the future. For some, it was evidence of the possibility that they had some degree of agency in a system that seemed set up to work against their interests. For others it was evidence that resistance was ineffective. For many, it was both, depending on how they looked at it. It was this ambivalence that was one of the most consistent features of students' experience of the resegregation.

Summary and Transition

There was ample evidence in this study that students were resigned to the idea that racial inequality in their schools was inevitable. The constant indicators of hostility and neglect encoded in the resegregation of Riverton schools—from the racial isolation of Union High, an older school building, and biased press coverage to the lower quality athletic uniforms, reductions in curricular offerings, and letters from the district inviting students to transfer to other schools—all took their toll on student faith in the community and political processes. These macroaggressions contributed to an erosion of expectation that the community of Riverton adults was capable of providing fair and equitable education to all students. In this way the resegregation of Riverton schools taught students not to hope for racial justice.

Our interviews also provided considerable evidence that most students did not readily accept the negative messages of the resegregation as indicators of their personal worth. Perhaps because the students in this study were older than the elementary age children in Kenneth and Mamie Clark's (1950) famous doll studies, or perhaps because seventy years have seen the development of counter narratives that provide more effective means of collective psychic defense (Delgado, 1989), students did not simply internalize the hidden curricular messages of the restructuring of their public schools. More often, we found students regarded these developments as evidence of ignorance or lack of character on the part of the community and the leaders responsible for the resegregation. This externalization didn't lessen the material effects of the inequality they were experiencing, but it did alter the symbolic effects to some degree. The burden students faced was less one of lowered self-regard, and more one of coping with being immersed in an institutional context that inappropriately but relentlessly communicated hostility to their well-being.

Although pessimism about the possibility for racial equality in Riverton schools was a consistent theme in student responses, it would be neither accurate nor constructive to describe students as passive recipients of this hostility. It would not be accurate because students spoke against the resegregation among themselves. Many sought ways to resist and did so most effectively when they had the aid of teachers or parents. It would not be constructive, because portraying students simply as victims of the resegregation would invite the pathos of pity. It would risk making a spectacle of their suffering, perhaps inspiring a patronizing rescue impulse, but not a fully humanizing and politically effective response of solidarity.

Like many adults watching and participating in the national struggle for racial justice, Riverton students dwelled in a liminal space between resignation and a search for a sense of agency. Union students' refusals to exercise the transfer rights provided to them by federal NCLB legislation were simultaneously an expression of their resignation that adults managing the schools could not be trusted and a gesture of resistance to their neglect of Union High. Garner students' enthusiasm when presented with opportunities to engage in direct actions against the resegregation process was evidence of their desire for a sense of efficacy. They noted, however, that their letters to the newspaper were not published and that the seventy-seven newly registered voters did not ultimately alter the composition of the school board in the next election. Union students' participation in a protest was clear evidence of their will to push back against the district's restructuring policy. Protest organizers' sober analysis of the limited influence of that protest is evidence that they were not inclined to Pollyannaish overestimations of the effects of those protests. The Riverton students we interviewed most frequently stood at the borderland between cynicism and social hope, hearing the distressing messages of the resegregation, refusing those messages, but confronted daily with the material obduracy of the increasing racial stratification of opportunity in their schools. Our most recent interviews from 2014 suggest they are still standing there.

Notes

1 Such deficit theories include, but are not limited to, assertions that racial inequality is due to genetic deficits, linguistically caused cognitive deficits, "cultural values" deficits, learning styles deficits, literacy-poor households, ideological deception, low self-efficacy, low self-esteem, a lack of grit, etc.

2 Our study uncovered no evidence of such recruiting, which would have been illegal. More than one coach, however, mentioned concerns that this may be happening.

3 Critical theorists have highlighted the way psychology's use of the individual mind as a unit of analysis distracts from the larger structural determinants of oppression

(Gates, 2010; Horkheimer, 1982; Kelley, 1997; Shabazz, 2004). Additionally, post-structuralist and post-colonialist critiques of the unity and stability of self-concept have suggested that identity is more fragmented and fluid than the Clarks' research might suggest (Bhabha, 2004; Foucault, 1994, 1995; Gilroy, 2001; Gordon, 2006; Hall & Du Gay, 1996; Hartman, 1997; McKnight, 2010; Weheliye, 2014).

4 Union High was on a parcel of thirty-two acres, while Northbrook's was seventy and Garner's was sixty-six. The Union site did not meet the minimum acreage designated by the state for the high school. The district, however, petitioned for and was given special permission to consider this site as it had been a high school site for so many years.

5 Northbrook and Garner high schools remained majority Black after the rezoning. The percentage of white students at the schools rose, however. The social consequence was that Northbrook became even more strongly identified as a "white" school and Garner put off being identified as a primarily Black school for a few years.

Bibliography

Bhabha, H. K. (2004). *The location of culture*. London; New York: Routledge.

Clark, K. B., & Clark, M. P. (1950). Emotional factors in racial identification and preferences in Negro children. *The Journal of Negro Children*, *19*(3), 341–350.

Delgado, R. (1989). Storytelling for oppositionists and others: a plea for narrative. *Michigan Law Review*, *87*(8), 2411–2441. http://doi.org/10.2307/1289308

Dumas, M., & Anderson, G. L. (2014). Qualitative research as policy knowledge: framing policy problems and transforming education from the ground up. *Educational Policy Analysis Archives*, *22*(11).

Dumas, M. J. (2014). "Losing an arm": schooling as a site of black suffering. *Race Ethnicity and Education*, *17*(1), 1–29.

Foucault, M. (1994). *The order of things: an archaeology of the human sciences*. New York: Vintage Books.

Foucault, M. (1995). *Discipline and punish: the birth of the prison* (2nd Vintage Books ed.). New York: Vintage Books.

Gates, H. L. (2010). *Tradition and the black Atlantic: critical theory in the African diaspora*. New York: BasicCivitas.

Gilroy, P. (2001). *Against race: imagining political culture beyond the color line*. Cambridge, MA: Belknap Press of Harvard University Press.

Gordon, D. (2006). *Black identity: rhetoric, ideology, and nineteenth-century black nationalism*. Carbondale: Southern Illinois University Press.

Hall, S., & Du Gay, P. (Eds.). (1996). *Questions of cultural identity*. London; Thousand Oaks, CA: Sage.

Hartman, S. V. (1997). *Scenes of subjection: terror, slavery, and self-making in nineteenth-century America*. New York: Oxford University Press.

Hartman, S. V. (2007). *Lose your mother: a journey along the Atlantic slave route*. New York: Farrar, Straus and Giroux.

Horkheimer, M. (1982). *Critical theory: selected essays*. New York: Continuum.

Kelley, R. D. G. (1997). *Yo' mama's disfunktional! Fighting the culture wars in urban America*. Boston: Beacon Press.

McKnight, U. L. (2010). *The everyday practice of race in America: ambiguous privilege*. London; New York: Routledge.

Sexton, J. (2010). People-of-color-blindness: notes on the afterlife of slavery. *Social Text*, *28*(2 103), 31–56.

Shabazz, A. (2004). *Advancing democracy: African Americans and the struggle for access and equity in higher education in Texas*. Chapel Hill: University of North Carolina Press.

Tuck, E. (2009). Suspending damage: a letter to communities. *Harvard Educational Review*, *79*(3), 409–427.

Weheliye, A. G. (2014). *Habeas viscus: racializing assemblages, biopolitics, and black feminist theories of the human*. Durham, NC: Duke University Press.

7

CONCLUSIONS AND IMPLICATIONS

The Reality of Resegregation

Riverton school district successfully petitioned to have its desegregation order lifted in 2000. Following the national pattern, school and community leaders moved immediately and deliberately to partially resegregate the city's public schools. One of the most striking findings of this study was not just how premeditated the resegregation was, but how it was done with the full knowledge that it would negatively affect Union High students. The district's Restructuring Committee Report acknowledged that the creation of an all-Black high school was an undesirable outcome and spoke of the hope that eventually the district could attract enough white students back into the district that it would be able to racially integrate all three high schools.[1] As we saw in Chapter 2, Union High was framed as a less desirable school to attend or work at by teachers, parents, and students before the new schools even opened. The local newspaper reported that, based on the patterns of past scores at the feeder schools for the three new high schools, Union High was guaranteed to have the lowest levels of academic achievement and would be on academic probation from its first year. Its enrollment was also considerably smaller, guaranteeing it would be able to offer fewer electives and advanced courses.

How was such a policy justified? The most frequently cited rationale for the restructuring of Riverton schools revealed the complexity of the discourses enabling the new segregation in U.S. public schools. Whereas defenses of racial segregation in the middle of the twentieth century were most often grounded in a rhetoric that affirmed racism and a sense of entitlement to white-only spaces, the rhetoric used to support the resegregation of Riverton schools was not so direct. The district was not seeking to create white-only schools. Instead, it sought to create schools with *a higher proportion* of white students. This was rationalized as a means of avoiding levels of Black enrollment at a single integrated high school that would trigger the secession of a wealthy majority white neighborhood from the school district or accelerate white flight to county and private schools. Referred to as "the tipping point argument," this threat was used to justify the racial resegregation of Riverton schools, ironically, *as a defense of the ideal of racial integration.*

The creation of an all-Black high school was described by many adults, including parents, teachers, administrators and board members, as a way to prevent the racism of unspecified others from causing the complete racial segregation of Riverton public schools. Better to partially resegregate in a managed way, than have that happen, was the frequently expressed view. The tipping point argument permitted people to support the restructuring and secure any perceived benefits that came with it, while maintaining the claim that they, in principle, opposed racial segregation in schools. The responsibility for the resegregation was projected onto the prejudices of others.

The tipping point argument was, of course, a profoundly flawed analysis. First, it failed to examine or challenge the idea that white parents were entitled to schools with a minimum percentage of white attendance. There is no documented educational benefit to white students for attending a school with a slightly higher percentage of white students. The only benefit accruing to families enrolled in such schools is a sense of ethnocentric comfort and perhaps social capital accrued by attending a school regarded as higher status in the local community. On the other hand, there is extensive documentation that racial segregation of schools has detrimental effects on non-white students in racially isolated schools (Mickelson & Nkomo, 2012; Orfield & Frankenberg, 2014; Reardon & Owens, 2014; Reber, 2010)

This brings us to the second, and arguably more profound, flaw in the tipping point argument. It essentially ignored the experiences of the students assigned to the all-Black high school as a significant consideration. Framed in this way, the preservation of two racially integrated high schools could be touted by school board members as a district achievement. The school superintendent was given an award for the leadership provided during the restructuring process, which cited a commitment to promoting educational equity as one of the reasons for the award. These claims of achievement, however, were never accompanied by an acknowledgment of the cost of that achievement—the creation of a racially and economically isolated high school in the district. The district website, for example, listed racial integration as one of the virtues of Garner High and Northbrook High, but it did not describe Union High as a racially segregated school. This silence was an implicit indication that district officials knew that the consequences of the restructuring for Union High students did not reflect well on the school system.

If the school district avoided explicitly commenting on the consequences of the restructuring for Union High, its policies and practices implicitly signaled that Union High was less of a priority and that less was expected of Union

High students. From the clearly intentional creation of an all-Black school in a region and nation with a history of institutional anti-Black racism, initially locating the school in inferior facilities, and assigning used equipment and uniforms, to explicit efforts in the district to deny the International Baccalaureate (IB) program to Union High, drawing the zones in a way that guaranteed Union High would have low average test scores and therefore be on state-wide academic probation from its first year, and being zoned for lower enrollments which meant less electives, advanced curriculum, and extracurricular activities could be offered to students, the district marked Union High as the lesser of the three new high schools.

These signifiers of lower status and lower expectations were taken up, circulated, and amplified in community discourse. Students, teachers, and parents commented on the differential features of the schools as if they were natural consequences of the character of the students in the schools. Union was not only a school with nearly 100% Black student enrollment. It became in the popular imagination a school associated with higher levels of violence—despite the levels of disciplinary infraction and violence being higher at the other schools. The district discouraged West-Side students from enrolling in IB courses because they believed the program would not thrive there, then low enrollments in those courses were taken as a sign that Union students did not want to be in such advanced courses.

The social consequences of the restructuring were neither simply material nor symbolic, but were a complex semiotic interweaving of the two. Fewer advanced courses at Union High was in part a consequence of lower enrollments, but it was often interpreted as a consequence of a lack of academic ability and/or interest in learning among Union students and families. This reputation for lack of student interest in higher level courses contributed to some academically ambitious students leaving Union and lower enrollments generally, which intensified the material conditions that constrained course offerings in the first place.

Being placed in an older facility while the other two high schools received new campus facilities had material consequences in the form of less new technology, poorer athletic facilities with compromised access to those facilities, and the general maintenance problems that come with older buildings. It also had symbolic consequences, as it communicated to Union students that the district placed less value on their education. The symbolism of being in an older facility was compounded by the building students were placed in being the site of the all-Black high school in the era before the federal desegregation order. Students, teachers, and parents commented on the way this signaled that the district was moving backwards to a time of racially segregated schools.

As previous chapters have documented, students read this social text of the resegregation of Riverton schools. Many features of the resegregation appeared to them to be a "set up" in which structural inequalities were interpreted in the community dialogue as the consequence of student and community pathology. Union was the "bad school" and Union students were the "bad Black kids." Students recognized that although racism had always been present in Riverton schools, the racist pathologization of an entire school community did not happen when the high school was integrated and thus was not racially identifiable. The restructuring had made Union students more vulnerable to this kind of symbolic violence.

Student experience and thought were not just caught in this material and symbolic semiotic net of racism, they were a constitutive part of it. Students took up some of these messages and recirculated them, referring to their own school as "Ghetto West" or transferring to other schools to escape the restricted curricular options and pathologization. Or they objected to the negative representations of their school, generated counter-stories that pathologized district personnel and racist parents for their role in the resegregation, but in the process still repeated the offending representations. Even when students overtly resisted the marginalization of Union High, as when they organized a walkout in protest over their lack of a new school building, their resistance was interpreted by some as a further sign that they were bad and unruly students.

Students at Union High labored under the awareness that the new design of their school system encoded at best a continued racist disregard for their well-being and at worst an intensified hostility toward them and their community. Students watched as their school became a screen onto which parents, teachers, and the press projected their fear of Black people. They recognized how their gestures of resistance either had limited effect, or were incorporated into the discourses that pathologized their school. In this way, the resegregation of Riverton public schools functioned like a multilayered hidden curriculum. As recounted in Chapter 6, in some cases this hidden curriculum had effects similar to those documented by Kenneth and Mamie Clark in their doll experiments over a half century ago. Students internalized the negative accounts of themselves or their community. Some transferred to other schools. Others said they didn't blame white parents for taking their children elsewhere. Still others referred to their own school as "ghetto" and themselves as "leftovers" and "garbage." More often students interviewed for this study resisted internalizing the negative messages of this hidden curriculum by objecting to the denigrating implications of the school restructuring policy. Their practice of vernacular critique, however, did not insulate them entirely from the negative symbolic effects of the resegregation. Whether resisting the hidden curriculum conveyed by the resegregation or not, its messages permeated the school ethos, and could not help but influence student choices, aspirations, and sense of social possibility.

Implications for Teacher and Administrator Education

A few policy implications emerge from this research. The first we will mention is the most immediate and least structural. It concerns teacher education and might be described as the triage work we need to do while we get on with the larger effort to address institutionalized racism. If the racial resegregation of our public schools is functioning like a curriculum that teaches hostile messages to students, and if the resegregation of schools shows no sign of abating anytime soon, then we are going to be subjecting children to this harmful messaging for the foreseeable future. Additionally, even in schools that are not segregated at the building level, there is the consistent fact of classroom-based segregation in U.S. public schools. Racialized tracking, we can safely assume, inflicts some of the same macroaggressions on students as does building level racial segregation. It communicates similar denigrating messages.

Teachers need to be prepared to identify the hidden curriculum of racial segregation, interrupt its demeaning messages, and offer students counter-stories that provide some defense against the deficit imaginary it projects onto them, their families, and their communities. Teachers need to be prepared to materially mitigate the pernicious effects of racial segregation where they can. Where they cannot alter its material effects, teachers need to make efforts to deflect the symbolic violence of resegregation by validating student objections and publicly critiquing the institutionalized inequities students face. The same is true of the education of counselors and school administrators.

This will require more than multicultural education classes that take a holiday and heroes approach to examining diversity in schools or that offers discreet teaching strategies as a way of closing the achievement gap. It will require teachers and administrators to be educated about the political history of schooling institutions and to be taught to see their professional responsibility as not simply to implement state and federal policy, but also to protect students from the often brutal excesses of such policy. Where these two responsibilities fundamentally conflict, the needs of children must take precedence. Educators will need to be prepared to enact a politics and pedagogy of refusal, which would include naming the material and psychic assault on students and organizing with other educators to refuse the authority of racist state agencies to determine the curriculum of resegregation, so that students are not left alone to struggle with its corrosive messages. Teachers, counselors, and administrators must talk back against the barrage of negative messaging resegregation inflicts on students. Nothing less is ethically acceptable.

Since resegregation policies are often developed and enacted by local school boards with the support of state and federal levels of governance, teachers, counselors, and administrators will need to be provided with professional protections for validating critiques of district policies or making such critiques themselves. This cuts against the grain of policy trends in recent decades that have seen a steady erosion of professional autonomy for teachers and administrators. State- and federal-level policy makers have sought to create an audit culture in schools focused on testing students and micromanaging the behavior of teachers and administrators as a way of holding teachers and schools accountable for achieving measurable learning outcomes. Such top-down approaches to school management and improvement presume the good intentions of local, state, and federal policy makers and that they are competent to prescribe practices that will care for all students fairly and equally. The last four decades of policy around issues of racial segregation in schools demonstrates unequivocally that this is not a warranted assumption.

Recent history has shown that local, state, and federal educational leaders cannot be counted on to recognize the narrowness of their top-down reform efforts. In the short term, teachers and building-level administrators are the professionals best positioned to recognize and respond constructively to the hidden curriculum of segregation. Teachers, counselors, and principals may not be able to change the demographic patterns in our schools. They can, however, be taught about the return of racial segregation in public education and taught not to leave students on their own to decipher the implications of such racial stratification. In order to provide such educational service, educators need to be reasonably insulated from charges of insubordination for acknowledging the obvious inequalities being imposed by school boards, state government, and federal education policy. This study therefore lends support to calls from others to restore reasonable checks and balances in educational practice by returning to a balance of federal, state, local, and teacher influence on decisions about curriculum and instructional practice (Ravitch, 2011; Rosiek & Clandinin, 2016; Sahlberg, 2015; Zhao, 2014).

Providing teachers and administrators with this sort of critical education and reasonable professional protections is not a solution to the problem of resegregation. It is a moral necessity required by the problem. If we are going to send children into racially segregated schools, then we need to send educators into those schools who recognize the need to help them with the negative messages communicated by racial segregation in their schools. We need educators who can stand in solidarity with these students and their families in the struggle to survive and learn in a structurally inequitable and semiotically abusive education system.

Implications for School Demographics Policy

The second implication of the Riverton study concerns state, federal, and local policy about school demographics. Having just acknowledged the difficulty of implementing policies that address the macrostructural racial stratification of educational opportunity in our schools, this study implies that such policies are nonetheless needed. The racial resegregation of schools functions like a curriculum, communicating implicit negative messages to students about their social status, perceived worth, and about the possibility for racial justice in our society, and this adds to the list of well-documented detrimental effects of racial segregation in schools (Guryan, 2004; Kainz & Pan, 2014; Lutz, 2011; Mickelson,

Bottia, & Lambert, 2013; Mickelson & Nkomo, 2012; Orfield & Frankenberg, 2014; Reardon & Owens, 2014; Reber, 2010). If a school board member or legislator introduced a proposal to mandate a curriculum that taught students that they were less educable and more violent because of their racial or ethnic identity, that they were social detritus whose education mattered less than other students in the district, that racial justice in our nation is an unreasonable expectation, and that students of color should resign themselves to second class status, the proposal would be received with outrage and the proposer would be subject to public and professional censure. This, however, is exactly what students at Riverton were learning from the resegregation of their schools. The restructuring policy implemented at Riverton was not just a zoning policy. It was not just about buildings. It was also—intentionally or not—a curricular policy.

But what form should such an intervention take? On the one hand, this study lends support to arguments that have already been made by many others that we need to renew our commitment to the racial desegregation of public schools. Although this study examined one school, it is reasonable to believe that similar dynamics are playing out in districts all across the country. Everywhere schools have had desegregation orders lifted, they have moved back in the direction of greater racial segregation (Reardon, Grewal, Kalogrides, & Greenberg, 2012; Reardon & Owens, 2014; Reardon & Yun, 2003; Rumberger & Palardy, 2005). In schools where the enrollment is majority students of color, school funding declines (Spatig-Amerikaner, 2012) and student performance often declines (Kainz & Pan, 2014; Logan, Minca, & Adar, 2012). These patterns, combined with pervasive racist discourses, lead to a decline in a racially isolated school's reputation and status (Baum-Snow & Lutz, 2011; Woldoff, 2011). This study documents the way these broader reputational dynamics inflict symbolic violence on the individual students attending racially isolated schools by functioning as a corrosive hidden curriculum. Lacking any effective means to alter the social conditions that economically isolate and discursively pathologize non-white racially isolated schools, schools that are still under desegregation orders should remain so, lest the hidden curriculum of resegregation be inflicted on other students. For school districts that are already racially segregated, either due to the lifting of a desegregation order or because one was never imposed, this study suggests that educators and policy makers should be concerned not only about the measurable effects of school demographics on test scores and drop-out rates. They should also be concerned about what the demographic arrangements teach students.

On the other hand, we could just as easily, and with equal empirical justification, argue that we lack any effective means to achieve a robust and genuinely inclusive racial integration of public schools. The first desegregation movement was neither sustained, nor did it reach beyond the building level, or very far beyond schools in the southeastern United States. The force of federal desegregation orders have been blunted and then rolled back since the early 1980s. White parents and property owners have consistently demonstrated their unwillingness to tolerate proximity to Black majority spaces. Our schools have yet to show an ability to adequately care for Black hearts and minds in white majority spaces.[2] Racial integration of schools gives Black students access to the increased resources that follow white bodies in our schooling system, but it has never closed the achievement gap as measured by indexes such as standardized test scores and drop-out rates.

Additionally, the corrosive curricular messages documented in this book are not uniquely the consequence of racial resegregation in schools. Resegregation simply intensifies racial macroaggressions that have been a part of public schooling processes before and during the desegregation movement. Well before the *Brown v. Board of Education* decision, for example, W.E.B. Du Bois (1935) argued against seeking racial integration of schools. He could see a consensus in favor of desegregation emerging among Black leaders and a growing feeling that acceptance of segregated schools was being framed as giving up on racial equality (p. 330). He objected on the grounds that the white majority could not be trusted to adequately care for Black children:

> I am no fool; and I know that race prejudice in the United States today is such that most Negroes cannot receive proper education in white institutions. If the public schools of Atlanta, Nashville, New Orleans and Jacksonville were thrown open to all races tomorrow, the education that colored children would get in them would be worse than pitiable. It would not be education. And in the same way, there are many public school systems in the North where Negroes are admitted and tolerated, but they are not educated; they are crucified.
>
> *(pp. 328–329)*

It is a catastrophic national shame that in 2015 institutionalized racism, pervasive microaggressions and macroaggressions, and persistent achievement gaps make Du Bois' words still relevant.

These kind of considerations are at the core of much critical race theory (CRT) and anti-Blackness theory pessimism about desegregation policies (Bell, 1980, 1992; Dumas, 2014b; Ladson-Billings, 2004) that presume simply placing Black children in schools where white children attend will be an unqualified benefit to Black children. Given this justifiable pessimism, our policy discourse needs to acknowledge that skepticism about school desegregation is warranted and that occasional calls from within Black communities for an emphasis on equity of funding and curricular self-determination as an alternative to ineffective desegregation are imminently reasonable. All of our apparent policy options seem compromised. We face conditions in which it is hard to imagine white majorities either supporting genuine and thorough desegregation of educational opportunity or sharing resources and status equitably within racially segregated schools. We need to acknowledge that, despite the significant and hard-won political achievements of the civil rights era school desegregation movement, the cultural formation of whiteness has never released its grasp on our schooling system.

So what should we do? If forced to choose, at this moment, in this book, we would advocate for a commitment to a new and more robust desegregation of schools. By this we mean a desegregation that finds a way to go beyond simply including Black bodies in seats next to white bodies, accompanied by a neglect of their needs and the political disempowerment of Black parents and citizens in the educational decision making. Instead, we need a form of desegregation that includes, minimally, changes in curriculum that addresses Black history and literature—for all students. We need a reconsideration of teacher hiring policies and a significant revision of pre-service and in-service teacher education curriculum that would bring teachers into schools who understand the kind of institutional violence that has been inflicted on students of color and understand their professional responsibility includes working to eliminate such violence. Additionally, it would require structural changes that ensure substantive involvement by Black community members in educational decision making. Perhaps this would include revised school governance structures in which representatives of underserved populations have veto power over school policy initiatives. In Riverton, school enrollments were 70% Black but the school board was consistently 70% white, a consequence of a profoundly flawed at-large voting system. Votes on the board were often split along racial lines. Black school board members did not support the restructuring of the schools nor would they have supported delayed construction of the Union school site. Where Black or Brown constituencies are less than the majority in a district, then extra-democratic governance processes may be needed in the effort to check intractable racial stratification of opportunity. Perhaps community panels need to be established, the responsibility of which is to advocate for the needs of traditionally underserved groups of students, and which could be given veto power over school policy. There will, of course, be problems and limitations with any proposed revisions of school governance procedures. Creative alternatives, however, are called for, because simple forms of representational democracy have not sufficed to address racially stratified opportunities to learn in our schooling systems.

For now, we favor a commitment to some kind of renewal of desegregation—as opposed to advocating for a new version of "separate but equal" schooling—for three reasons:

1. Material resources matter. They may matter most. The immediate risk of intensified material school inequity seems greater if we acquiesce to the racial resegregation of schools. Placing Black students in schools with white

students has proven to be the most reliable way so far to reduce the educational resource gap.

2. Positionality matters. White authors recommending acquiescence to white racism by advocating for equitably funded but still racially segregated schooling feels too much like abandoning anti-racist struggle. It would constitute an abdication of the work that needs to be done by white persons within our own communities. It is utterly reasonable for parents of Black children—for all of us—to be skeptical of this intention to "do better" in integrated public schools. Therefore, efforts within Black communities to assert educational self-determination, including separatist approaches to education, as a response to current conditions warrant our considered support. Ultimately, we aspire to a futurity that supports both efforts at robust racial desegregation in schools and equitably funded efforts at Black self-determination of curricular and educational practices.[3] In the meantime, it is neither reasonable nor acceptable for white majorities to cease from the effort to create institutions that are more effectively and vigorously inclusive.

3. Confronting the cultural formation of whiteness matters. Our argument is premised on the idea that whiteness and white entitlement to white majority spaces is a living predatory force that respects no boundaries. We don't believe this cultural force will respect any racial détente that communities might seek to establish—such as a promise of racially segregated but equally funded schools. Endemic racism will keep funding and other forms of support unequal. We believe that whiteness—the cultural formation that has relentlessly produced racial stratification of wealth, well-being, and freedom since before the days of slavery all the way up to this very moment—must be destroyed as a precondition of any genuine form of equality, however far-fetched that aspiration may seem.

Class versus Race Segregation

A third implication concerns a debate within the school resegregation literature about whether it is class isolation or racial isolation that is actually the most significant determinant of the negative consequences of school racial segregation. Justified pessimism about the possibility of renewing a policy commitment to desegregation has led some scholars to look closely at whether it might actually be class segregation that is the cause of most negative outcomes (Reardon, Grewal, Kalogrides, & Greenburg, 2012; Reardon & Owens, 2014). If it were true that class differences explained more of the negative impacts of racial segregation than the racial identity of students, this would suggest that policies focused on class equity and integration might be a more politically viable means of achieving both racial and class equality in schools.

It is important to note that this is a different form of pessimism than that espoused by critical race theorists (Bell, 1992; Delgado & Stefancic, 2012;

Ladson-Billings, 2005) discussed in the previous section. Critical race theory scholars often espouse a pessimism about the possibility of racism ever being eliminated as part of an argument against thinking of policies intended to deal with racial inequality as *temporary,* as if they can be repealed when our communities have outgrown racism. Court-ordered school desegregation and affirmative policies are examples of this. Both were framed as temporary expedients. Instead, CRT scholars argue that we should presume racism is a permanent feature of society and consider such policies as ongoing remedies to social problems that will be with us indefinitely. The pessimism referred to in this section, however, is simply a pessimism about the practical possibility of being able to pass and implement desegregation policy. The implication, as a result, is that policy should minimize the racial justice implications of school zoning policies and use other means—such as class justice as a proxy for racial justice—to advance the cause of racial equality in schools. This is the opposite of the CRT position that pervasive racism needs to be acknowledged and made an explicit feature of jurisprudence and school policy making.

Most scholars who examine the topic acknowledge that racial segregation in U.S. public schools is overdetermined by both racial and economic factors (Dumas, 2014a; Leonardo, 2009; Orfield & Frankenberg, 2014; Wells, 2009). Many, however, are skeptical about the implication that it might be possible for policy makers to effectively address racial inequality in schools while avoiding directly addressing the racism motivating racial segregation in schools. Race and socioeconomic status are too tightly correlated for this to work, it is argued. Avoiding addressing one inevitably undermines the effectiveness of addressing the other. In their paper "E Pluribus ... Separation: Deepening Double Segregation for More Students" Gary Orfield, John Kucsera, and Genevieve Siegel-Hawley (2012) observe:

> The history of our society links opportunity to race in ways that produce self-perpetuating inequalities—even without any intentional discrimination by educational and political leaders. If we were a nation where most Black children were educated like the Obama children, and most white children were living in the kind of isolated poverty that is seen in some white communities in Appalachia, for example, then it would be a tremendous educational advantage for white children to go to Black schools. But that is neither the way our society was organized historically, nor the way it is organized today.
>
> *(p. xv)*

The Riverton study corroborates the assertion that our schools face a *double segregation.* Riverton school zones increased both race and class segregation, with the West-Side zone simultaneously having higher percentages of Black students and low-income students. Our study also supports skepticism about the prospect of addressing racial resegregation in public schools by advocating primarily for income- and economics-based equity policy. Our research suggests that even if certain measurable class and race effects of resegregation in Riverton could be statistically disaggregated, and if economic factors could be shown to have a higher correlation with many of the measurable negative outcomes of attending racially segregated schools, the symbolic content of school segregation in Riverton remained primarily racial. Riverton community leaders did not create a school that was 100% low income. They created a school that was 100% Black. Community members did not worry about the percentage of low-income students at their school reaching a tipping point. They spoke exclusively of a racial tipping point. Students at Union High spoke primarily about racial isolation. When they mentioned the income stigmatization of the West-Side neighborhoods, it was almost always in conjunction with the racial demography of those neighborhoods and school zones. When students reflected on their situation, they saw racist animus driving the resegregation of Riverton public schools far more frequently than they saw aversion to associating with students from low-income households.

These observations add an additional layer to Orfield, Kucsera, and Siegel-Hawley's (2012) argument. Even if school funding was equal across the three high schools, and even if income level integration could be equalized while schools remained racially segregated, the Riverton study suggests that the symbolic force of racist ideologies would remain and continue to negatively affect students. The problem is not only that race and class happen to be demographically entangled presently, so that we would not be able to practically achieve the above rearrangement. The problem also lies with the obduracy of racist discourses in our communities. Even when Union High had the only district IB curriculum, the Advanced Placement (AP) classes at Northbrook gained the reputation of being the highest academic track in town. Even when Union High had lower rates and less severe cases of disciplinary referrals, Union High nonetheless had the reputation for being the most violent of the three high schools. The creation of all-Black schools will always incur the kind of hidden curricular assault we documented in Riverton, as long as racism remains an organizing feature of our individual and collective lives. Absent other discursive interventions, we would expect it to do this, even if economic parity for racially isolated schools is provided—a condition that Orfield, Kucsera, and Siegel-Hawley (2012) as well as a host of other scholars point out is not likely to happen anytime soon (e.g. Bell, 1980, 1992; Du Bois, 1999; Dumas, 2014b; Ladson-Billings, 2004).

Performative Implication

The fourth and final implication of our study concerns what is arguably most urgently needed in our national conversation about resegregation. "Implication," however, is probably not the right word. "Goal" is better. "Performative goal" is better still. The performative goal of this book is not simply to provide an accurate description of the social and psychic consequences of school resegregation and to syllogistically trace out practice and policy implications from that description. Descriptions of student suffering turn too easily into spectacles, spectacles that inspire pity. Pity distances us from others, makes them tragic figures whose suffering is lamentable but inevitable. This emotional distance is increased the more the human experience of inequality is turned into an object—ethnographic or statistical—to be dispassionately observed and recorded. Such forms of representation engage in an often unacknowledged trade-off, providing clarity in rendering the object of study, but producing an ethically unengaged spectator-subject in the researcher and the consumer of the research.

Our goal instead has been to craft an empirically *and* affectively compelling portrait of Union students as complex human beings, in the midst of forces beyond their control and at times beyond their ken, but which they recognize in part and struggle against. This condition could, if we are honest, describe any of us as we shuffle through this mortal coil. The goal has not been to position you, the reader, as a simple spectator of this struggle, but to invite you into a respectful empathic relation with Riverton students, a connection that can inspire a political solidarity and motivate action.

There are precedents for research that seek such ends. Sarah Lawrence-Lightfoot, author of the famous text *The Good High School* (1983), developed a methodology she later called "portraiture" whose purpose is to "capture the richness, complexity, and dimensionality of human experience in social and cultural context, conveying the perspectives of the people who are negotiating those experiences" (Lawrence-Lightfoot & Davis, 1997, p. 3). Elliot Eisner and Tom Barone, founding contributors of what has become known as the field of arts-based social research, invested their careers developing frameworks for and examples of scholarship that make "empathic participation possible because they create forms that are evocative and compelling" (Barone & Eisner, 2012, p. 3). Critical race theorists such as Richard Delgado (1989) have called for storytelling in legal scholarship that "shatter complacency," "quicken and engage conscience," and build "a common culture of shared understanding, and deeper, more vital, ethics" (pp. 2414–2415). Many other scholars have made the case for scholarship that moves us to appreciate the full range of human consequences of social policy and practices including, but not limited to, Derrick Bell, Nel Noddings, Sylvia Winston, Clifford Geertz, Norman Denzin, Mike Rose, Amy Stuart Wells, and Michael Dumas. The warrant for such descriptions of social processes lies only partially in their faithful representation of real events. Their warrant lies also in their capacity to move us individually and collectively to break the habits of thought and feeling that trap us in an abusive present, and so make possible an ameliorated future.

The Riverton study represents real events, real comments made by students, teachers, and others, and real patterns within those events and comments. Our presentation of those realities is intended to cognitively and affectively disturb complacency in public and policy discourse about racial resegregation in our schools, to interrupt gross oversimplifications that attribute educational achievement gaps exclusively to the characteristics of students and families, and to make readers uncomfortable with the disjunctions between our educational practices and our expressed ideals.

Of what use is such scholarship to policy makers who already have access to large database research that rigorously documents the ill effects of racial resegregation in public schools? With some social issues where there is a broad consensus on what should be done,[4] scholarship that seeks to evoke empathic connection as a means of motivating change in personal values and community priorities may be unnecessary. In such cases all that may be needed is a clear parsing of empirical data that reveals the most effective means of achieving agreed-upon objectives. However for some social issues, where a consensus of values cannot be counted on, more is required of scholarship. In these cases large database studies are necessary, but are not sufficient to inform and clarify debate. What is needed additionally is scholarship that presents a full range of a policy's human consequences in a manner that inspires empathy and motivates solidarity. Affective identification alone cannot leverage policy change, but it can destabilize comfortable mindsets, the ease of which is purchased through the erasure of the lives and experiences of others. It can enflame outrage where previously only the dull ache of disappointment had previously been. It may not do this for everyone, but it may do it for enough so that new avenues of political action become possible and new educational futurities become viable.

This kind of research is especially needed where race relations in this country are concerned. There may remain a superficial consensus that racial segregation in schools is generally undesirable. But the empirical data show that when communities are considering their own schools, they increasingly choose segregation. We can profess a lack of bias, but as the research on implicit bias has shown, racial bias can operate in our thoughts and actions anyway (Girvan, 2015; Greenwald & Krieger, 2006). It is not an accident that we currently have a social movement in this country organized around the simple slogan, "Black lives matter." Why does it seem necessary to so many people to assert this obviously valid claim with such urgency? While almost everyone participating in the public political sphere would claim that they believe "Black lives do matter," our policy, policing, and governing practices do not reflect such values. Where issues of racial segregation in schools are concerned, as a national community we have not yet resolved that Black students' lives matter. The story of the resegregation of Riverton schools presented in these pages constitutes an effort to rhetorically enable a respectful empathic connection with the lives of youth living and learning in increasingly racially isolated schools for those who lack such a connection. For those with a connection, it represents an effort to reinforce, inform, and intensify those relations. Recognizing, feeling, and becoming increasingly entangled in the moral significance of these students' experiences, we believe, is the necessary precursor to any effective collective political engagement with the social and political scourge of racial segregation in our schools.

The validity of this performative aspect of the stories told in this book ultimately lies, not only in the qualities of the text itself, but in how it is relationally taken up by readers and what it inspires us to do. In this way, this text is incomplete by design and is continued in readers' interpretations of it and the social text of the actions it informs.[5]

Summary and Closure

The brief moment in which the ideal of racial desegregation held sway in U.S. schools should not be romanticized. U.S. schools never achieved complete building-level racial integration in its schools and there was never a significant national effort to address classroom-level racial segregation within racially integrated schools (Dumas, 2014a). Racial integration of public schools eliminated a whole sector of middle-class teaching jobs in African-American communities (Fultz, 2004; Haney, 1978; Hudson & Holmes, 1994; Ladson-Billings, 2004). It put the hearts and minds of Black children in the care of an overwhelmingly white teaching profession still in the thrall of explicit and implicit racism and which lacked familiarity with these new students' lives (Dumas, 2014b; Ladson-Billings, 2004; Orfield & Frankenberg, 2014; Walker, 1996). The hidden curriculum of racism in public schools did not begin with resegregation. Resegregation simply intensifies an already existing feature of our institutions and culture. Given all of this, any reasonable effort at addressing increasing racial segregation in public schools cannot consist of a mere return to past desegregation policy. It will require a transformation and improvement of those policies and accompanying educational practices. And that, in turn, will require the more profound work of changing our values and ways of being with each other. Nothing less will be adequate.

Having acknowledged these considerable limitations, it is equally important to acknowledge that the desegregation of U.S. public schools remains one of the most successful educational equity-promoting policies of the last half century. Desegregated schools provided students of color greater access to better funded classrooms and schools, exposure to more challenging curriculum, and broadened social experiences (Orfield, Kucsera, & Siegel-Hawley, 2012; Orfield & Frankenberg, 2014). Desegregation of schools has had a positive influence on key measurable educational outcomes for students of color, such as higher test scores, lower drop-out rates, higher rates of college attendance, and higher long-term earnings (Borman & Dowling, 2010; Knaus, 2007; Mickelson, Bottia, &

Lambert, R., 2013; Orfield, 1983; Wells, 1995). It also changed a generation's experience of racial difference (Mickelson & Nkomo, 2012; Wells, 1995, 2009; Wells, Holme, Revilla, & Atanda, 2004). Desegregation of public schools—however imperfectly enacted—was successful at promoting racial equality in a variety of ways. It is not surprising, therefore, that it became an important symbol of a national commitment to the ideal of racial egalitarianism.

That symbol is in the process of being torn down, not unlike a national monument being pulled from its foundations and broken into pieces by hostile parties. Legal and policy commitments to desegregated public schools have been deliberately and systematically dismantled over the last forty years. As a result, public schools across the nation have become more racially segregated (Orfield, Kucsera, & Siegel-Hawley, 2012; Orfield & Frankenberg, 2014). By some indexes, our schools are now more racially segregated than they were in 1968 when the desegregation movement began in earnest. This resegregation is having a variety of well-documented negative effects on the lives of students. Essentially the measurable positive effects of civil rights era school desegregation are being reversed.

Resegregation is also having less easily measurable effects. This book has documented the way the creation of a nearly all-Black high school where there was not one before marked that school in a variety of negative ways even before the school was built and students had been assigned to attend there. Once students enrolled at Union, they found themselves facing an intricate tangle of mutually reinforcing material and symbolic effects of the resegregation of their school. The students in Riverton schools, and we may assume students in similar situations all over the nation, are watching all of this happen. More importantly, perhaps, they are watching us acquiesce to the return of this social evil. They interpret our actions and inactions and learn things from them, whether we intended for them to do so or not. They learn that some students are less valued, considered less worthy of investment, are assumed to be more violent, and are assumed to be less educable. They learn that these designations are largely resistant to their efforts to refute them. They learn that fairness and racial justice in schools are an unreasonable expectation and that civil rights era advances in racial equality and justice were historical aberrations. This is what the hidden curriculum of resegregation communicates to students. By any reasonable standard, we should not be teaching such things to our children.

Notes

1 This hope was never realized. Although the restructuring attracted a small percentage of white private school students back into the district, white flight to private and county schools resumed shortly thereafter. By 2015 Northbrook had 70% Black enrollment, Garner had 80% Black enrollment, and Union remained nearly 100% Black.

2 This statement, of course, could include other non-Black demographic groups that have shown aversion to enrolling their children in Black majority schools as well as aversions shown to Latino majority schools and spaces.

3 The either/or logic of policy discourse aimed at identifying the one best—most efficient, most just, most effective, most comprehensive, most anything—policy solution to the challenge of racial stratification of educational opportunity is a feature of epistemologically foundationalist conceptions of social change. Here we can see the merits of the agential realist conception of inquiry outlined in the Preface to this book. Agential realism rejects the idea that there is one real version of a phenomenon like racial segregation in schools awaiting our accurate representation of it. Instead, reality is a relational entanglement established in part by the way we engage a phenomena and in part by the way the world—in this case institutionalized racism/whiteness/anti-Blackness—engages us. Multiple onto-epistemic entanglements with racial segregation in schools are possible and can be contradictory whilst also being equally real. Regarded in this way, the idea of anti-racist educators advocating for robust desegregation of schools in certain moments and from certain positionalities and equitably funded self-determination of educational options from within communities of color in other moments does not constitute a fundamental contradiction. Instead it represents a desirable epistemic and relational flexibility that will be necessary for responding to the ontologically protean phenomenon of whiteness.

4 Or what CRT scholars like Derrick Bell (1980, 1992) have called "interest convergence."

5 This resembles, but is not identical to, what Patti Lather calls "catalytic validity" (Lather, 1991, p. 68).

Bibliography

Barone, T., & Eisner, E. W. (2012). *Arts based research*. Los Angeles: SAGE.

Baum-Snow, N., & Lutz, B. F. (2011). School desegregation, school choice, and changes in residential location patterns by race. *American Economic Review, 101*(7), 3019–3046.

Bell, D. (Ed.). (1980). *Shades of* Brown*: new perspectives on school desegregation*. New York: Teachers College Press, Columbia University.

Bell, D. A. (1992). *Faces at the bottom of the well: the permanence of racism*. New York: Basic Books.

Borman, G., & Dowling, M. (2010). Schools and inequality: a multilevel analysis of Coleman's equality of educational opportunity data. *Teachers College Record, 112*(5), 1201–1246.

Delgado, R. (1989). Storytelling for oppositionists and others: a plea for narrative. *Michigan Law Review, 87*(8), 2411–2441. http://doi.org/10.2307/1289308

Delgado, R., & Stefancic, J. (2012). *Critical race theory: an introduction* (2nd ed.). New York: New York University Press.

Du Bois, W. E. B. (1935). Does the negro need separate education? *Journal of Negro Education, 4,* 328–335.

Du Bois, W. E. B. (1999). The souls of white folk. In *Darkwater: voices from within the veil* (pp. 55–75). Mineola, NY: Dover Publications.

Dumas, M. (2014a). Contesting white accumulation: toward a materialist antiracist analysis of school desegregation. In Bownan, K. (Ed.), *The pursuit of racial and ethnic equality in American public schools: Mendez, Brown, and beyond* (pp. 291–313). Lansing: Michigan State University Press.

Dumas, M. J. (2014b). "Losing an arm": schooling as a site of black suffering. *Race Ethnicity and Education, 17*(1), 1–29. http://doi.org/10.1080/13613324.2013.850412

Fultz, M. (2004). The displacement of Black educators post-*Brown*: an overview and analysis. *History of Education Quarterly, 44*(1), 11–45.

Girvan, E. J. (2015). On using the psychological science of implicit bias to advance antidiscrimination law, *George Mason University Civil Rights Law Journal, 26*, ___ (in press).

Greenwald, A. G., & Krieger, L. H. (2006). Implicit bias: scientific foundations. *California Law Review, 94*(4), 945. http://doi.org/10.2307/20439056

Guryan, J. (2004). Desegregation and black dropout rates. *American Economic Review, 94*(4), 919–943.

Haney, J. E. (1978). The effects of the *Brown* decision on black educators. *Journal of Negro Education*, 88–95.

Hudson, M. J., & Holmes, B. J. (1994). Missing teachers, impaired communities: the unanticipated consequences of *Brown v. Board of Education* on the African American teaching force at the precollegiate level. *Journal of Negro Education*, 388–393.

Kainz, K., & Pan, Y. (2014). Segregated school effects on first grade reading gains: Using propensity score matching to disentangle effects for African-American, Latino, and European-American students. *Early Childhood Research Quarterly, 29*, 531–537.

Knaus, C. (2007). Still segregated, still unequal: analyzing the impact of No Child Left Behind on African-American students. In The National Urban League (Ed.), *The state of black America: portrait of the black male*. Silver Spring, MD: Beckham Publications Group.

Ladson-Billings, G. (2004). Landing on the wrong note: the price we paid for *Brown*. *Educational Researcher*, 3–13.

Ladson-Billings, G. (2005). The evolving role of critical race theory in educational scholarship. *Race Ethnicity and Education, 8*(1), 115–119.

Lather, P. (1991). *Getting smart: feminist research and pedagogy with/in the postmodern*. New York: Routledge.

Lawrence-Lightfoot, S. L. (1983). *The good high school: portraits of character and culture*. New York: Basic Books.

Lawrence-Lightfoot, S., & Davis, J. H. (1997). *The art and science of portraiture*. San Francisco: Jossey-Bass.

Leonardo, Z. (2009). *Race, whiteness, and education*. New York: Routledge.

Logan, J. R., Minca, E., & Adar, S. (2012). The geography of inequality: why separate means unequal in American public schools. *Sociology of Education, 85*(3), 287–301. http://doi.org/10.1177/0038040711431588

Lutz, B. F. (2011). The end of court-ordered desegregation. *American Economic Journal: Economic Policy, 3*(2), 130–168.

Mickelson, R. A., Bottia, M. C., & Lambert, R. (2013). Effects of school racial composition on K-12 mathematics outcomes: a metaregression analysis. *Review of Educational Research, 83*(1), 121–158.

Mickelson, R. A., & Nkomo, M. (2012). Integrated schooling, life course outcomes, and social cohesion in multiethnic democratic societies. *Review of Research in Education, 36*(1), 197–238.

Orfield, G. (1983). *Public school desegregation in the United States, 1968–1980*. Washington D.C.: Joint Center of Political Studies.

Orfield, G., & Frankenberg, E. (2014). Increasingly segregated and unequal schools as courts reverse policy. *Educational Administration Quarterly, 50*(5), 718–734.

Orfield, G., Kucsera, J., & Siegel-Hawley, G. (2012). *E pluribus . . . separation: deepening double segregation for more students.* UCLA: The Civil Rights Project/Proyecto Derechos Civiles. Retrieved from http://escholarship.org/uc/item/8g58m2v9

Patterson, J. T. (2002). *Brown v. Board of Education: a civil rights milestone and its troubled legacy.* Oxford: Oxford University Press.

Ravitch, D. (2011). *The death and life of the great American school system: how testing and choice are undermining education* (Rev. and expanded ed.). New York: Basic Books.

Reardon, S. F., Grewal, E., Kalogrides, D., & Greenburg, E. (2012). *Brown* fades: the end of court ordered school desegregation and the resegregation of American public schools. *Journal of Policy Analysis and Management, 31*(4).

Reardon, S. F., & Owens, A. (2014). 60 years after *Brown*: trends and consequences of school segregation. *Annual Review of Sociology, 40*, 199–218.

Reardon, S. F., & Yun, J. T. (2003). Integrating neighborhoods, segregating schools: the retreat from school desegregation in the South, 1990–2000. *North Carolina Law Review, 81*(4), 1563–1596.

Reber, S. J. (2010). School desegregation and educational attainment for blacks. *Journal of Human Resources, 45*(4), 843–914.

Rosiek, J., & Clandinin J. (2016). Teachers as curriculum makers. In D. Wyse, L. Haywood, & J. Pandya (Eds.), *The Sage Handbook of Curriculum, Pedagogy, and Assessment.* Thousand Oaks: Sage Publishing.

Rumberger, R. W., & Palardy, G. J. (2005). Test scores, dropout rates, and transfer rates as alternative indicators of high school performance. *American Educational Research Journal, 42*(1), 3–42. http://doi.org/10.3102/00028312042001003

Sahlberg, P. (2015). *Finnish lessons 2.0: what can the world learn from educational change in Finland?* (2nd ed.). New York: Teachers College, Columbia University.

Sexton, J. (2010). People-of-color-blindness: notes on the afterlife of slavery. *Social Text, 28*(2 103), 31–56.

Spatig-Amerikaner, A. (2012). *Unequal education: federal loophole enables lower spending on students of color.* Washington, DC.: Center for American Progress. Retrieved from https://www.americanprogress.org/wp-content/uploads/2012/08/UnequalEduation.pdf

Walker, V. S. (1996). *Their highest potential: an African American school community in the segregated South.* Chapel Hill: University of North Carolina Press.

Wells, A. S. (1995). Reexamining social science research on school desegregation: long-versus short-term effects. *Teachers College Record, 96*(4), 691–704.

Wells, A. S. (Ed.). (2009). *Both sides now: the story of school desegregation's graduates.* Berkeley, CA: University of California Press.

Wells, A. S., Holme, J. J., Revilla, A. T., & Atanda, A. K. (2004). *How desegregation changed us: the effects of racially mixed schools on students and society.* Paper presented at the Annual Meeting of the American Educational Research Association, San Diego, CA.

Woldoff, R. (2011). *White flight/black flight: the dynamics of racial change in an American neighborhood.* Ithaca, NY: Cornell University Press.

Zhao, Y. (2014). *Who's afraid of the big bad dragon? Why China has the best (and worst) education system in the world.* San Francisco: Jossey-Bass & Pfeiffer.

EPILOGUE

This book has been an extended gesture of listening to students in segregated schools and taking their experiences seriously, not as a source of unmediated truth, but as morally significant realities in themselves. It therefore seems appropriate to close this book with comments from some of these students. At the end of our interviews we often invited students to speak directly to our readers about the restructuring of their schools. Here are their closing words on the subject.

I: Riverton is not unique. Similar things are happening in districts all across the country. If you had an opportunity to speak to a national audience about these issues, what would you say to them?

S27UBF: I think this pattern will continue until somebody actually gets up and stands up to it. I know that a few people may have stood up to it. But it takes more than one to get it done. And until a lot more people stand up and say "Hey, this is what we want. This is not fair," it won't change on down the line and this is what we will have.

S85UBM: It's still going on. It's always been going on. You got people who still believe in slavery. They want to control you, get you to do what they want you to do. It ain't slavery because they don't beat us no more. It's the same thing, though they have found ways to get around it, so it don't get so rowdy and so ugly. It ain't gonna change.

S86UBM: No matter where you at, no matter what your background, no matter what situation you are in or are forced to be in, you gotta make the best out of it. Because at the end of the day it is still your life. No matter what, you gotta still grind it out. You can say what you wanna say. They are gonna change it or not.

S84UBF: We need to push to have more integrated schools, because it ain't gonna feel right growing up not knowing how to talk to people. Then they're just gonna push you back even further and it's gonna feel like you can't do nothing at all. You gonna be right back to where you started. It already feels like that.

S17UBF: We should be past this.

S87UBM: Personally, I feel like this is an injustice, the way this is set up. The way we were brought here [Union High] to fail. And now it is becoming a reality. I think five or ten years more down the line it's going to be horrible. Seriously, it's going to be horrible.

S82UBF: I would simply ask, what is the purpose of segregating schools? What is it going to solve, really? Is it that they feel that as though African-Americans being more violent, that their kids are going to get picked on? But we're not, no more than anyone else. I don't get the point of segregation. Every school should be desegregated. All kids can live in one community, work together, communicate, have fun, play, enjoy one another's company. There is no purpose to having a segregated school.

S5UBF: It's enough. It is time to really grow up as a nation and focus on the problem that is at hand. That is the challenge for the next generation. We need to have education in a way that everybody succeeds—Black, white, Latino, Asian, any race.

S3UBM: For the benefit of your children, for the benefit of your friends and their children, it's going to have to come to a point where we agree on something. Through segregation, you are not going to learn anything about other people, you are not going learn how to deal with people, so you can go out and be successful in life. If you are only dealing with Black people or you are only dealing with white people, you are going to have to come together at some point and realize we are going to have to co-exist.

S88GWF: We can do better than this. It seems so wrong. It is wrong. And when you think about it, we have to live with this separation, like, forever. Because you never get to do high school again. But I don't know what to do about it. There should be something we can do. What was so bad about all being in the same school?

S20UBF: I guess I would ask why? Why separate us like this? Do people just think we are just going away? I mean white people. Where do you think we are going? We are not going anywhere. We will always be here. We will *always* be here. You need to deal.

S89UBF: I don't know. [Pause] I don't know what I would say.

INDEX

CPSIA information can be obtained
at www.ICGtesting.com
Printed in the USA
FFHW01n2025210918
48496531-52356FF